Feeling Like a State

Global and Insurgent Legalities
A series edited by Eve Darian-Smith and Jonathan Goldberg-Hiller

DAVINA COOPER

Feeling Like a State

Desire, Denial, and the Recasting of Authority

Duke University Press   Durham and London   2019

© 2019 Duke University Press. All rights reserved
Printed and bound by CPI Group (UK) Ltd, Croydon, CR0 4YY
Designed by Courtney Leigh Baker
Typeset in Whitman and Univers LT Std.
by Westchester Publishing Services

Library of Congress Cataloging-in-Publication Data
Names: Cooper, Davina, [date] author.
Title: Feeling like a state : desire, denial, and the recasting of authority /
Davina Cooper.
Description: Durham : Duke University Press, 2019. | Series: Global
and insurgent legalities | Includes bibliographical references and
index.
Identifiers: LCCN 2018057042 (print)
LCCN 2019010607 (ebook)
ISBN 9781478005575 (ebook)
ISBN 9781478004134 (hardcover : alk. paper)
ISBN 9781478004745 (pbk. : alk. paper)
Subjects: LCSH: State, The. | Progressivism (United States politics) |
Conservatism—United States. | Right and left (Political science) |
Social action—United States. | Political participation—Social
aspects—United States.
Classification: LCC JC11 (ebook) | LCC JC11 .c65 2019 (print) |
DDC 320.1—dc23
LC record available at https://lccn.loc.gov/2018057042

COVER ART: *Fantasia.* © Image DJ/Alamy Stock Photo.

FOR JANET AND JOHN

CONTENTS

There are many people whose advice, feedback, and encouragement contributed to the writing and publication of this book. I am grateful to Jon Goldberg-Hiller and Eve Darian Smith for including the book in their new series and for giving me feedback on earlier drafts. I thank Courtney Berger for her incisive editorial advice, Sandra Korn for her assistance in preparing the manuscript, Susan Deeks and Christopher Catanese for their editorial work, and the three anonymous readers who reviewed earlier versions of the book for Duke University Press.

I was lucky to have excellent research assistance at different times from Deana Lewis, Amy Marsella, Jessica Smith, and Isabelle Stone. Flora Renz also provided tremendous help with some of the book's research, subsequently becoming a colleague and research partner (on another project) during its writing.

When it came to getting feedback on chapters or asking for advice, I turned to colleagues and friends in different jurisdictions. I am grateful to those who read chapters, helped me when I was stuck, and answered emails with suggestions. In some cases, a tangential remark or curious thought, often at the end of a meal, prodded me to think harder about parts of my argument and methodology. I thank Mohammad Afshary, Jon Binnie, Doris Buss, Marianne Constable, Michael Cooper, Mariano Croce, Eleanor Curran, Margaret Davies, Chiara de Cesari, Nikita Dhawan, Judy Fudge, Conor Gearty, Avery Gordon, Emily Grabham, Helen Graham, Bonnie Honig, Rosemary Hunter, Suhraiya Jivraj, Sarah Keenan, Tom Kemp,

Ruth Kinna, Vivi Lachs, Sarah Lamble, Ruth Levitas, Maleiha Malik, James Martel, Daniel Monk, Sasha Roseneil, Miriam Smith, Antu Sorainen, Mariana Valverde, Robert Wintemute, and Margot Young.

I am grateful to the Dickson Poon School of Law, King's College London, for supporting the final stages of this book. I began this project in 2013 while working at Kent Law School. This book would not have happened without their research support, including through sabbatical leaves, research assistance, and a collegial and stimulating working environment. Almost a year before its completion, the manuscript was discussed at a Kent book workshop. Suggestions, encouragement, and criticism from colleagues who read and commented on chapters—namely, from John Ackerman, Kate Bedford, Emily Grabham, Emily Haslam, Sara Kendall, Rose Sydney Parfitt, and Connal Parsley—provided wonderful "grit" in working through the final stages of the manuscript.

Janet Newman and John Clarke have, for many years, encouraged and inspired my thinking around states, governance, and progressive institutional politics. I am indebted to them for doing so, and for responding to my oblique, random-seeming queries, with brilliance and humor. This book is dedicated to them.

Finally, my thanks go to Didi Herman. What can I say? A reader of countless drafts, talking over the book's ideas as they moved from inchoate thoughts to written text, and helping me in countless ways to write (and to finish), she provides far more of the reason than perhaps she realizes for the hopefulness expressed here.

Parts of chapter 4 were published in earlier form as "Possessive Attachments: Identity Beliefs, Equality Law and the Politics of State Play," *Theory, Culture, and Society* 35 (2) (2018): 115–35.

INTRODUCTION. **Reimagining the State**

In 2016, Country Mill Farms applied for a license to sell its produce at East Lansing Farmer's Market in Michigan for the following year.[1] Selling produce there was something the farm had done since 2010. However, on this occasion its license application was turned down. In 2014, the farm had rejected two women's request to have their wedding ceremony in the farm's orchard because of the owner's religious beliefs. In response, one of the women had posted a Facebook message "discouraging people from patronizing Country Mill."[2] Shortly afterward, the farm's owner also posted a statement on Facebook affirming his commitment to the belief that "marriage is a sacramental union between one man and one woman."[3] His action brought the farm into conflict with the City of East Lansing.

On 7 March 2017, the city wrote to the farm refusing its application to sell produce at the market. The letter stated, "It was brought to our attention that The Country Mill's general business practices do not comply with East Lansing's Civil Rights ordinances and public policy against discrimination as set forth in Chapter 22 of the City Code and outlined in the 2017 Market Vendor Guidelines."[4]

Much can be gleaned from a legal episode such as this, with its juxtaposition of religious and secular discourse. As "deeply held beliefs" get pitted against city codes and legal ordinances, liberal state authority confronts the conservative Christian views of a family business. In this book, I am interested in such episodes in terms of what we can learn about the state. Conservative Christians have been very ready to denounce liberal state authorities as oppressive and overreaching, improperly intervening in people's personal and religious lives to promote a pro-gay agenda. However, I want to explore these episodes to think about something else. Can we take up conflicts such as this one, in which selling at a farmer's market becomes the price for refusing two women an orchard wedding, to support thinking in transformative progressive ways about what the state could come to mean and be?

"The state" is a controversial term in political imaginaries of socially transformed, more just ways of living. Much recent work on thinking about better worlds, and how to accomplish them, treats scaled-up political and institutional structures as part of the problem. This is particularly apparent in anarchist writing, but not only there. Feminist, Marxist, antiracist, and other left-leaning politically motivated scholarship also imagines change in ways that regularly pit progressive forces *against* state power and authority. This is unsurprising since nation-states, particularly in the global North, emerge as prime movers when it comes to social injustice and harm, from colonialism and environmental depredation to propping up transnational corporations and imprisoning poor and stigmatized populations. But can states be otherwise; importantly, do we need to *think* the possibility of states being otherwise to imagine, and support the realization of, new forms of governing? Thinking states otherwise tends to refer to states *as we currently know them* behaving in new ways, including through wholesale practical reform. But there is another register for thinking states otherwise: it involves *conceptually reimagining what it means to be a state*. This second register lies at the heart of this book.

I want to use the language of statehood to think *toward* public political governance formations as responsible, activist, and caring; governing in ways that are horizontal, engaged, playful and sensory.[5] And since states, and the political conditions of state thinking, vary considerably between geopolitical polities, this book focuses on a set of (neo)liberal common law polities in the global North.[6] Liberals sometimes adopt an idealized approach toward those formations *currently understood as state formations* (or at least some of them), identifying in their essence possibilities for democratic renewal. From a more radical perspective, however, reimagining what states might *do* also requires reimagining what states *are*.[7] This ontological dimension is particularly important when it comes to questions of responsibility and power. While these are often reduced to their exercise, also important for the account of states in this book is the presence of power and responsibility as potential—in other words, as dimensions of what it is to be a state that can be "held" as well as done. But if it makes sense to hold on to the state as an entity, what kind of entity is it? To the extent the state demonstrates the conceptual flux and plurality associated with many concepts, what ways of thinking about the state might prove helpful for a transformative social justice politics (recognizing that this will of course vary by time and place)? For instance, is it useful to think about the state as "embodied"—appreciating that this does not have to take a human form?[8] Is the state better imagined as a terrain or field through which diverse networked relations are forged? Can we usefully think of states as diversely scaled and overlapping, drawing their authority from different, even contrasting, sources? And should we approach states as acting deliberately, and with intention; or instead treat what they do as merely the systemic effects of particular rationalities, interests and logics?

When it comes to the state, resources for thinking in progressive hopeful ways, by which I mean in ways oriented to greater social equality in power, resources, and freedoms within, beyond, and between social spaces; to living more collaboratively and less competitively; and to supporting ecological welfare among people, other animals, and varied vegetative life and landscapes, come from a number of places. One is utopian writing, including fiction.[9] Ruth Levitas (2000: 28) describes "utopia's strongest function" as being "its capacity to inspire the pursuit of a world transformed." While developing desire for another way of living can be enhanced by novels depicting wonderfully perfect places, much contemporary utopian fiction has changed tack, producing places that are complex, evolving, and conflict-ridden.[10] Here, utopian fiction provides resources for the imagination in thinking about the challenges that less hierarchical forms of governing confront. With their flaws and histories of the future, they speak to progressive utopian concerns with what is possible rather than with what is merely daydreamed (Levitas 2000: 28). A different resource for thinking the state in more progressive ways comes from "real-life" experiments in governing.[11] In his Real Utopias Project, Erik Olin Wright (2010) advocates working the tension between imagining a better world and engaging with what is practical and, indeed, *practiced*.[12] From this perspective, radical local government, democratic participatory ventures, and other actualized counterinstitutions offer material grounds from which not only to organize governing differently but also—despite the antistate tenor of some of this work—to *rethink* what government or states (could) mean and entail, challenging the assumption that states must be oppressive, territorial, self-interested, and national.[13] Utopian fiction and experiments in governing are important stimulants to the left imagination, but the approach of this book involves something else. It takes up a "real" contemporary experience rather than an imagined place or future. Yet the aim is not to extend the experience or realize its ambitions. Instead, and rather queerly, the book draws on a contemporary legal drama involving conservative religious activism to explore the lines of thinking it offers for reorienting the concept of the state leftward toward a progressive transformative politics.[14]

Conservative Christians' withdrawal of goods, services, or membership from gay subjects and activities on religious grounds,[15] and public bodies' ensuing withdrawal of contracts, employment, grants, and subsidies from withholding conservative Christians, has generated extensive legal action and attention. In this book, I explore both in pursuit of three objectives. The first is to reimagine what it could mean to be a state. Adopting an approach that treats the concept of the state as inevitably plural and contested—Are for-profit providers of public goods part of the state? What about organized religion or the institution of the family?—I want to think about different imagined and material "cuts" (Barad 2003: 816). By this I mean different ways of framing, combining, and separating the elements that assemble, and that are assembled, as state elements to support a progressive account. Clearly, there is no single way to do this. As the book unfolds, I explore a conception of the state organized around the assumption of responsibility, where responsibility is public, collective, and reflexive—as it stretches beyond particular preexisting obligations. Responsibility can manifest itself in authoritarian as well as democratic ways, as right-wing as well as left-wing. This book approaches responsibility in terms of the pursuit of social justice, care, and democratic forms of embeddedness. But rather than focus on the policies or reforms that would allow states to operate in this way, I am interested in the contribution that *reconceptualizing* the state around notions of responsibility might make. If we orient ourselves in this way to what states could come to mean, what qualities and dimensions, including those currently glimpsed (or at least glimpsable), become important? Of course, this might include qualities identified as integral to *hegemonic* accounts of the (neo)liberal state. But this book focuses on other elements—ones that help to compose current state practices but are yet largely ignored as too marginal to warrant much attention. Being oriented to these elements, which also requires *reading for* these elements, plural forms of statehood, dissident elements in the state's makeup, and practices of sensory governing emerge; so, too, does play. This is not simply the cruel strategic play that politicians and nation-states undertake, but also state play that is creative, open-ended, pleasurable, and sometimes artful and wily. Play is an interesting, in many ways counterintuitive, register for thinking about state activity. One question this book poses is whether it would be good for practices of governing to be more playful and, as important, what transformations would be required for such play to be conducted willingly, equally, and free from the pressures of core unmet needs?

The second aim of the book is to explore the politics of withdrawal: of subjects pulling out and pulling things out. Withdrawal is an important, if contentious, technique of political activism. It is also an important, if contentious, means of governing. Carried out for different reasons, the withdrawal centered in this book is rationalized by the drive to avoid endorsing or legitimating the political "other," an "other" that is sometimes gay, sometimes conservative Christian, and sometimes the liberal state. Failing to pull out, protagonists argue, risks leaving a personal residue within rejected activities and people while becoming tainted by their touch in turn. Pulling out is often approached as an exercise of sovereign authority and force, powerfully and painfully withdrawing. This imaginary is present here, but what is also expressed is a quite different politics of governing that involves circuits or chains of "reciprocating" and interacting withdrawals (as the farmer's market episode at the start of this chapter illustrates). Thus, despite the at times polarizing discourse of two forces confronting each other (conservative Christians against secular state bodies; conservative Christians against gay-equality advocates), relations are more muddied and complex. Withdrawal is also not simply a severance or departure but a way of retying bodies together, including through the intense sensory experience its enacting can precipitate (chapter 3).

Finally, reimagining the state through a legal drama brought about by conservative Christian withdrawal provides an opportunity to explore a queer, utopian conceptual method for developing transformative progressive thinking.[16] This method parallels other postcritical approaches in pursuing a reading that is generative and hopeful rather than negative and dystopic. Thus, the book does not focus critical energy on conservative Christianity or the (neo)liberal state, despite my sharp disagreements with both. Critical work on right-wing Christian forces and (neo)liberal states has been extensively and powerfully carried out, and my discussion seeks neither to replicate nor to negate this work. I do not want to repair conservative Christianity or the capitalist state—to uncover and celebrate nice, positive stuff in either. Rather, I am interested in the unexpected traction this legal drama offers for thinking about the state in some different ways, taking up Rita Felski's (2015: 12) suggestion that we consider what a text "unfurls, calls forth, makes possible." Applied to conservative religious activism, this is a method that aims to expand the conceptual resources available for progressive thinking—something that should not have to rely exclusively on left-wing practices, radical initiatives, and imagined utopias. But it is also a method that raises challenges and difficulties: how exactly do we work with a legal drama, such as this, to develop left conceptual thinking on the state? In this sense, the book is an experiment: to examine where this method might take us. What conceptual pathways are opened up, and how might these conceptual pathways—in which the state is reimagined—come to be practically forged and enacted?

Withdrawal: A Third Moment in Conservative Christian Antigay Politics

Conservative Christian antigay withdrawal came to prominence in the 1990s and continued to swell across the common law jurisdictions of the United States, Canada, and Britain and, to a lesser degree, Australia, New Zealand, and South Africa.[17] By the second decade of the twenty-first century, the flow of news stories had become something of a gush as story after story described conservative Christians' duels with secular state (and other public) authorities over their entitlement to be exempt from human rights and equality laws outlawing discrimination on sexuality grounds. The *Ladele* case, in which a London marriage registrar refused to perform (same-sex) civil partnerships on religious grounds, is one of the best-known British examples.[18] However, the "conscientious objection" dramas in which service providers (police officers, doctors, social workers, teachers, therapists, librarians, and adjudicators) refused to fulfill gay-equality obligations because of their religious beliefs are not alone. They sit alongside a range of other withdrawal scenarios. Explored more fully in chapter 1, they include small businesses, such as printers, wedding-cake makers, and venue owners refusing to make their goods and services available to gay (or gay-positive) customers; Christian organizations excluding or dismissing (out) gay members and staff; and public bodies run or dominated by conservative Christian agendas, such as school boards or City Councils, withholding gay-positive resources.

Yet this legal drama, as I have said, not only involved withholding Christians. Alongside their many instances of refusal were those of public bodies who withdrew goods from conservative Christians, reacting to prior religious acts of omission (and sometimes commission). They included regulatory bodies denying accreditation to Christian colleges (or withholding access to professions, such as the bar); cities' and school districts' withdrawal of transportation, accommodation, and other subsidies from youth groups, such as the Boy Scouts of America, for taking a public antigay stance; universities withdrawing recognition from conservative Christian student societies whose membership criteria discriminated on grounds of sexuality; local authorities withdrawing adoption contracts from Catholic organizations for refusing to work with gay prospective parents; and the demotion and sacking of public sector staff who refused to work in a nondiscriminatory manner.

Withdrawal is part of a complex and much longer history of Christian approaches to homosexuality, and of a conservative Christian agenda that also takes in antifeminist, anti-trans,[19] racist, deregulatory, and anti-immigrant politics.[20] It constitutes a third moment within contemporary (neo)liberal state-Christian-gay politics, where opposing decriminalization constitutes one moment and resisting gay civil rights constitutes another.[21] This third moment emerged as gay equality passed from being a social-movement aspiration and much fought-over civil right to a signature policy of liberal governments as national leaders and representatives used gay rights to represent the kind of state they were. When the Conservative Party leader David Cameron resigned as prime minister of Britain in July 2016, he described the introduction of gay marriage as one of the "greatest achievements" of his term.[22] Yet affirming gay equality was never just about the "we." Presented as a core feature of liberal statehood, it quickly acquired an external aspect (indeed, its outward-facing application helped confirm its domestic status) as states took gay rights up as a litmus test of others' civilized values. For migrants, in some cases, and nation-states, in others, demonstrating a willingness to accept or introduce gay equality came to symbolize transnationally "shared" norms of liberal tolerance, human rights, and cosmopolitan ethics.[23] As such, it also functioned as one section of a gateway to accessing sought-after international resources and goods, including political membership. East European countries confronted the dilemmas of a growing gay rights momentum, as decriminalization and antidiscrimination provisions became accession criteria for joining the European Union.[24] Carl Stychin (2003) describes how such provisions constituted a political staging post in normalizing homosexuality but also, in turn, in normalizing countries such as Romania.[25] Yet as states used gay rights to demonstrate their liberalness, conservative opponents expressed their opposition to liberalism through a mirroring antigay stance.[26] In Romania, the archbishop declared, "We want to join Europe, not Sodom" (see Stychin 2003: 122).[27]

Identifying and mobilizing as the gay rights other—and so also using gay rights as an identity-confirming device—did not just involve cross-border relations.[28] In different countries, conservative Christians took up the stance of an embattled domestic minority to demand the right *not* to participate in advancing gay equality and to suffer no loss of public and professional benefits as a consequence.[29] The self-depiction of religious people being forced to withdraw from commercial and governmental transactions to pursue religiously upright lives reveals a very different political juncture to that witnessed in struggles by the Christian right against decriminalization and civil rights. In the battle over decriminalization, it was gay activists and supporters who were compelled to demonstrate that gay lives would not be harmful to others—an argument for keeping gay sex private and closeted so that a (presumptively heterosexual) public would not take offense. Civil and human rights protections and antidiscrimination laws, while also contingent on reassuring that there would be no "straight" harm, depended on demonstrating that gay people had a right to lead fruitful, meaningful lives as gay, a right that state protection would help secure (see also Herman 1997). But in this third (neo)liberal moment, with human rights protections and antidiscrimination laws for both sexual and religious identities in place, the focus shifted. Instead of the spotlight being on a gay minority, it moved to the rights and freedom of *dissenters* and what they were also due. Conservative Christians argued that the struggle over equality and rights was not about defeating others' (undeserving but nevertheless legally institutionalized) identity rights but about protecting their own (see also Lewis 2017; McIvor 2018). Their right to "be," and to be Christian, was in jeopardy, thanks to public bodies' refusing to recognize their religious entitlement to live according to deeply held beliefs—to inhabit and dwell within a Christian normative universe rather than be forced to leave it in order to work, trade, and access public goods.

In contrast to other moments in which Christian opposition focused on the harms homosexuality caused—corrupted children, damaged families, and disease[30]—in this drama, conservative Christians focused on the harms caused to them by compelled activity and by the state. Insisting that gays would not be affected by their "conscientious" withdrawal (since alternative willing providers were readily available), conservative Christians claimed that the state and other liberal public bodies were hurting and damaging them by forcing them to act against their beliefs.[31] Discussing Lillian Ladele, the London registrar who refused to perform same-sex partnership ceremonies, the Australian academic Patrick Parkinson (2011: 290) remarked, "Ms. Ladele didn't seek for her views on same-sex civil partnerships to become the law of the country but that her personal and conscientious objections be respected." Here, instead of focusing directly on gay beliefs and activities, as happened during other moments, conservative Christian dissenters focused on what *they* themselves believed in and wished to do, where compelled compliance with sexual-equality rights would severely undermine their capacity to pursue authentic and committed lives. Yet in doing so, they were also able to create a discursive space for religious antigay beliefs regarding sin. This was not done ostensibly to delegitimate gay rights (or to argue the state should treat gay sexuality as less valid) but to legitimate *their own right* not to participate.

It would be wrong, however, to read conservative Christians' demands for legal accommodation as driven simply by a desire to be left alone. There has been extensive discussion on the place of religion within contemporary (neo)liberal public spheres. Writers debate the public legitimacy and utility of explicitly religious arguments and rationales; how and whether states should recognize religion as a (stable) source of values or as a fit basis for public service provision;[32] and how to balance dominant, minority, and nonreligious belief structures in institutional arrangements,[33] as well as in a nation's ongoing story (or stories). These discussions have taken different forms across the jurisdictions of this book, being inflected by national religious cultures, histories, demographics, and, specifically in Britain, the enduring established status of the Church of England, with its official fusion of church and state (see, e.g., Commission on Religion and Belief in British Public Life 2015).[34] They are also discussions that have taken shape within different religious communities, including Christian ones, at times with great ferocity between (and among) more liberal and conservative wings.[35] Since the status of Christianity in political and policy discourse has been extensively addressed, I do not want to spend longer on it here. What is important for our purposes is the claim that legal accommodation was not simply about conservative Christians' opposition to gay rights but part of a more ambitious Christian project. It is striking that the litigation discussed in this book, precipitated by the religiously motivated withdrawal of gay-positive goods and services, almost entirely involved Christians and Christian organizations rather than conservative Muslims, Jews, and Hindus, for example. This discrepancy can be explained in terms of access to resources, strategic priorities, and the complexion of faith-based litigating organizations (including, specifically, the presence of several very active conservative Christian litigation organizations).[36] But it also reflects two other social factors: first, many Christians' sense of lost entitlement as they watched (and depicted themselves watching) their hegemonic status slip away; and second, their ambition to advance public Christianity, using litigation in the struggle to do so.

In the rest of this chapter, I explore in more detail how a Christian project of maintenance, resistance, and advancement can contribute to reimagining the state as a salient concept for a transformative progressive politics. At first glance, it seems rather odd to imagine that a legal drama over conservative religious activism—a drama that foregrounds withdrawal rather than provision; that reveals state power in its disciplinary and extractive (some would add, punitive) form; and that is framed, at least here, by the litigation that ensued—can provide fruitful ground from which to reimagine, leftward, what it could mean to be a state.[37] I want therefore to focus on three core dimensions of this legal drama: the expression of dissenting religious beliefs, withdrawal, and litigation.

Minority Dissenting Beliefs

Conservative Christian action provides an interesting site from which to think about the political work of dissenting beliefs. From a left perspective, resistance and dissent are typically approached in a positive, empathetic, even celebratory manner, predicated on the assumption that the dissent in question involves left-wing opposition or refusal. But when dissent comes from right-wing forces, interpellating themselves as vulnerable minorities, what does this mean for progressive political thought? While some radical academics favor all dissent for its attachment to minority status, and for keeping hegemonic projects precarious, others want to secure progressive hegemonic state projects. But how, in the process, should objectors be treated? Here we are talking not about objectors waving placards or marching in public civic spaces, but about objectors who dissent by refusing to comply with, or otherwise disputing, the terms and reach of already-in-operation equality law. Should objectors be compelled to comply; should wiggle room be made available through legal accommodation as "conscientious objectors";[38] or should other means be found for dissent to be performed in less adversarial registers, such as through state-based forms of play (see chapter 4)? These kinds of normative and policy questions surface regularly in debates about agonistic democracy. I want to approach them from a different angle: how should we treat minority dissidence in conceptualizing what it is and means to be a state?

There is a tendency for both supporters and opponents of conservative Christian dissenters to treat them as the *recipients* of state action, separate from the state even as states act on them (and sometimes in partnership with them). But when and why are they separate? Does it have to do with their status, inasmuch as they are users and clients of state provision or publics affected by the state's regulatory reach? Is it because their expressed beliefs are minor, dissident, or improper? This would suggest that religious people may form a state part—for instance, as employees—but in the process their beliefs and illegitimate actions are stripped from what they bring to composing the state. The place of *minor* elements in the conceptualization of the state is a recurring theme of this book. Routinely, what is deemed to make up the state is limited to hegemonic and durable systems, values, and forces. But if we want to explore what statehood could mean when constituted according to more democratic forms, including as a responsive part of heterogeneous everyday life, we may want a *conception* of the state that not only incorporates dissident, minority, even fleeting values, forces, and actors, but that recognizes them as already incorporated. We may also want a conception of the state that is not restricted to the *provision* of regulation, control, and of goods and services but that also encompasses their receipt and usage (see chapter 2). Withdrawal by conservative Christians foregrounds the value of such a move by drawing attention to the shifting, often ambiguous distinctions drawn between providers and users of state goods—Where, for instance, do foster carers sit?—while highlighting some of the minor political rationalities carried into state processes by both. As with many issues in this book, the question of how and where to place minor rationalities and beliefs has both normative and interpretive dimensions: what kinds of beliefs *should* be (and become) part of the state's composition, and how should we understand and think about those beliefs *already identified as present*? What makes something "part of" a state rather than "within" it? And does it matter? What is at stake in how we address this question?

Conservative Christian legal activism draws attention to the marriage registrars, teachers, firefighters, foster parents, and others who occupy state positions and roles yet refuse to affirm gay equality. It also helps us to think about state form and reach in the overlap and clash of entities that claim to "feel like a state." Conservative Christianity signals a sovereignty that seems far from progressive with its religious hierarchy and authorities—deific and human. Nevertheless, despite (perhaps even because of) its authoritarian key, conservative Christianity—like other countersovereign religious structures—poses a powerful challenge to state-assumed monopolies on organized political sovereignty. Certainly, the history of state-church relations, in the jurisdictions of this book, is an entwined one, as secular (lite) states in countries such as Britain emerged from histories of religious political power in ways that, over time, mirrored, deposed, resisted, delimited, and revised Christian body politics. Yet as this book explores, the litigation that withdrawal has generated, and the claims made during its course, reveal how contested political and legal authority remain. This book does not focus on Christian conceptions of sovereignty in any detail. However, it takes up their challenge to a state sovereign monopoly as an entry point for thinking about other governance forms. To the extent these forms are overlapping and competing, they suggest a version of "strong state pluralism" particularly when governance forms do not recognize each other as animate or existing, let alone as having legitimacy (see chapter 3). But while conservative Christian withdrawal stimulates thinking about contested authority within (neo)liberal polities, the legal and political rhetoric surrounding attempts to withdraw from gay-equality entitlements simultaneously invokes visions of monolithic and monstrous states overstretching their proper mandate and role. I explore these depictions of an overreaching state in chapter 2. Certainly, they can be read as deliberately exaggerated. Nevertheless, from the perspective of reimagining the state they are helpful in thinking about how state boundaries and limits should be (and are) conceptualized. Is there a space beyond the state—the conventional terrain coded as civil society—or should we treat the state as reaching everywhere and everything? Conservative Christians present the extensive state as a form of liberal fascism, but there are other ways to think about a more pervasive state presence that do not assume all social relations are entirely or fully captured by it.

Thinking through Withdrawal

The second primary dimension of this book, withdrawal, foregrounds a wide spectrum of different norms and rationalities. When undertaken by states, withdrawal can mean the removal of welfare and other goods from those deemed undeserving. As such, it produces (but also reveals) the precarity of those whom states abandon or permit to be legally subjected to abandonment by others (see chapter 1). Yet withdrawal can also be a part of social activist, trade union, Indigenous, and nationalist politics. In the form of strikes and boycotts, withdrawal aims to exert economic or political pressure or to symbolize opposition to another's actions along with a refusal to be implicated.[39] Withdrawal can act as a denial of state sovereignty and legitimacy, such as when Indigenous or minoritized nations withdraw recognition from colonial powers, asserting their right to autonomy or countersovereignty instead.[40] It can also assert national attachments against a transnational regional structure, witnessed in the movement of withdrawal to have shadowed this book's writing, namely of the UK's planned departure from the European Union. The withdrawal discussed in this book, however, cannot be easily compartmentalized because it involves varying rationalities on the part of (neo)liberal states, conservative Christians, and others as independence, autonomy, legitimacy, punishment, and reattachment provide important justifications within this mix.

Withdrawal is an important composite political concept. But it has received limited academic attention as an overarching term. Discussion tends to focus on one or another of its strands and rationalities. As a mechanism for governing and for politics, withdrawal contributes to the institutional and political (re)allocation of respect and allegiance; (re)directs resources, opportunities, and recognition; and expresses public rejection of certain values while affirming others. As an episode of disruption or challenge, it also provides a productive analytical frame. Different scholars have described how breaks, ruptures, exceptions, and refusals refract social life in generative ways, creating understandings that can get missed when life goes on as always. Withdrawal illuminates relations, resources, and practices obscured by the repetitions of ordinary government. I want to briefly signal three that are central to reimagining the state: responsibility, the quotidian, and sensation.

Questions of responsibility arise in relation to the distribution and consequences of withdrawal. As I discuss in chapter 1, political and legal discourse often distinguishes between the rights of religious organizations to withdraw membership from those, such as "out" gays, deemed to be embodying a message inconsistent with the values of the organization, and the obligation placed on state bodies *not* to discriminate. In this way, conservative Christians argue for their own right to withdraw, while at the same time demanding unconditional provision from the state—that its goods, including employment opportunities, should not be withdrawn from them simply because they withdraw from others. This distinction speaks to a perception of state responsibility as being significantly different from that of social movements or religious or charitable organizations. Conservative Christians characterize their movements and organizations as legitimately able to set conditions for accessing their resources. However, they don't feel the same about the state—or, at least, the conditions states impose, conservative Christians argue, should not curtail religious freedom. This argument has not been adopted in full by the courts, although the law varies between jurisdictions. For our purposes, what is important is the anchoring of this argument of distinction in claims about the state's proper reach, powers, membership, and responsibilities. Critics argue that these distinctive features cause the state's withdrawal of contracts, resources, and benefits to look very different from withdrawal by religious and community organizations, even when the withdrawal concerns an analogous benefit, such as employment. The distinction between the state and civil society is one that liberals and many conservatives accept. However, if reimagining the state unsettles it, one question is: in what direction? Treating state bodies as akin to community organizations may suggest that states should also have the freedom to differentiate between lawful identities on normative grounds and so be able to provide jobs, resources, and services to some but not to others. Alternatively, community organizations may be properly treated more like responsible state organizations and so prohibited from applying "private" values. One problem with both proposals is that they rely on *existing* conceptions of the state or community in constructing one as the paradigmatic norm. If we reimagine what it means to be a state, both state and wider society get reconstituted in the process. This has implications for how we think about responsibility and what it means to act like a state.

The second facet that withdrawal highlights is the *everyday* character of governmental resources: the jobs, membership, leisure activities, festive spaces, schoolbooks, accreditation, and recognition that public bodies provide. Governing here is not some abstract activity operating on a lofty plane but centrally concerned with the substance and availability of those everyday goods on which people rely. In the legal drama of this book, the goods in question come from many sources. It is not simply that one (elite, powerful) body offers and so has power to withdraw goods from another. Both provision and withdrawal are far more dispersed and dynamic. What different bodies withdraw may diverge, but even seemingly power-poor actors—frontline workers and sole traders, for instance—can withdraw sought-after goods, including their bodies, its labor, and the symbols of community approval.

Tracing withdrawal, particularly as it moves through circuits of bodies pulling out and pulling back, draws attention, thirdly, to the rich texture of governing. At one level, withdrawal foregrounds the formal mechanisms and systems through which a prior (or anticipated) contact takes shape: from market purchases to accreditation systems, policy agreements, and contracts. But at another level, it foregrounds the sensory character of governance, as pulling out—refusing to provide a service or benefit—generates friction and so, in effect, contact (see chapter 5). Writing on state touch or contact focuses largely on its coercive and dominating qualities (see, e.g.,

Woodward and Bruzzone 2015; Zengin 2016). But if we are interested in reimagining what it could mean to be a state in ways that give the state a conceptual relevance for transformative progressive politics, the capacity for other kinds of state touch to be possible is hugely important.[41] Certainly, instances exist of seemingly kinder, gentler forms of touch in relation to particular public services. These forms have not been exempt from criticism. At the same time, they provide a jumping off point for thinking about other forms of sensory government. Reimagining what it could mean to be a state, as this book does, unsettles prevailing left assumptions about what state touch *necessarily* entails. It asks, What would be required for state touch to be replenishing, stimulating, and satisfying, or to be teasing, playful, and lighthearted? Chapter 5 explores these questions by bringing the concept of the erotic to bear on this drama of withdrawal. In relation to the state, the erotic-as-sex is usually deemed a pernicious form of political power. But are there other, horizontal, pleasurable, consensual ways to approach erotic governance, attuned to governance's vital, desiring, sensual qualities? And what can a legal drama about conservative Christian withdrawal contribute to this discussion?

Litigation and Legal Narratives

Finally, this book is about litigation. Within gay, queer, and other sexual movements, intense debate has occurred for some decades over the political place and value of litigation in contrast to other, seemingly less individualized, reactive, and commodified ways of pursuing social change.[42] This debate has been immensely fruitful in developing a nuanced, more equivocal, account of rights. This book deals with similar kinds of legal conflict, but I do not approach the cases as instances of the legalization or juridification of politics. My aim is not to evaluate the effects of litigation—the difference that tallying wins and losses might make; how litigation influences social movement politics; or whether the courts are the wrong place for this kind of political controversy.[43] I am not reading court decisions to understand their underlying legal rules, principles, and values; to analyze their rhetorical techniques; to appreciate how the courts think about the terms of the dispute; or to identify better jurisprudential ways to resolve them. This work has been extensively and effectively done. Rather, I am interested in legal narratives (and the discursive utterances that surround such narratives)[44] for the representational and organizational work they do in telling a particular, *authoritative* story of events, depicting a social drama that, in the process, they also actualize and shape.[45] Court documents, from briefs to judgments, produce a story that is far from transparent and unmediated. As feminist, queer, antiracist, and other legal scholars have long argued, legal documents presuppose, reinforce, and generate particular ways of understanding the world. Their juridical form and underpinning legal principles order events and evidence in ways that, purposefully (and otherwise), edit and frame the views of litigants, witnesses, and other participants. In a politicized drama such as this one, litigants' and witnesses' words also arrive carefully sculpted—not least by litigating organizations engaged in manufacturing "stock narratives" of loss and hardship.[46] Their words cannot be read as expressing, in any straightforward way, the authentic or autonomous beliefs, understandings, and feelings of those to whom they are assigned.

Still, the legal narratives cast by this drama are productive for reimagining the state even as they foreground certain relations and practices rather than others. (Indeed, it is because they so clearly represent the world through and from a particular institutional place, as Patricia Ewick and Susan Silbey (1995) discuss, that legal narratives shed light on the situated character of other, less obviously institutionalized knowledge claims about the state.) First, they are sites of political multiplicity. This is most clearly evident in the utterances and texts preceding and surrounding legal decisions,[47] but even judgments weave different voices together, incorporating divergent, often clashing, narratives as they constitute a particular preferred reading of the conflict. The polyglossia of court documents as spaces in which counternarratives and counterdiscourses coexist with hegemonic ones is well known. For my purposes, the value of legal texts here comes particularly from the stories judges tell.[48] These are stories of victimization, discrimination, and hurt; of intention and motivation; of the legal constraints actions confront; and of investments, risk, and loss. They are also stories about values; about what it means to practice equality, fairness, and justice; and about the legitimacy (or illegitimacy) of discipline, order, and hierarchy when the alignment of right and left with hegemonic and subversive perspectives—of which is which—remains far from settled and clear. In this drama, judicial stories, and the stories told around these stories, are fundamentally stories of the power, scope, and responsibilities of governing. As such, they offer a detailed reconstruction of institutional practice and the intricacies of organizational interactions in conditions where secular liberal governance projects confront challenging religious assertions of sovereignty.

Litigation over withdrawal provides the primary archive for this book—a varied, sometimes jumbled collection of materials that helps with the task of reimagining what it could mean to be a state. The texts I assemble and draw on are a mix of judicial findings (and declarations); legislators' assertions; and organizations', litigants', and activists' predictions, claims, and fears. Not unlike the free-running discussed in chapter 4, these varied texts provide a terrain that I work with and repurpose, moving among different segments and strands of this legal drama's landscape to develop an account of the state, oriented to what it *could* mean and be. I have spent some time tracing how a legal drama over conservative Christian refusal can support progressive reimaginings of what it could mean to be a state, recognizing that this legal drama may seem a queer or strange ground from which (and with which) to engage in transformative state thinking. Yet so far my discussion has presupposed that states are worth transforming, materially and imaginatively. I therefore want to turn finally to this question: why should progressive actors hold on to the state in thinking about transformative politics, and how might it be done?

Why Hold On to the State?

Left critiques of the state are legion and take a variety of forms. There are those who reject the state, conceptually, as an unhelpful and mystifying abstraction that reifies (and overstates) concentrations of political power. Addressing feminist state scholarship, Judith Allen (1990: 22) describes the abstract category of the state as "too aggregative, too unitary and too unspecific to be of much use." Philip Abrams (1988: 77) also famously objected to the concept of the state on the grounds that it reified a "legitimating illusion." Abrams (1988: 79) argued that, to avoid *believing* in the state, it was important to recognize "two distinct objects": "the state system and the state-idea." Abrams (1988: 77) writes, "The postulate of the state serves to my mind not only to protect us from the perception of our own ideological captivity but more immediately to obscure an otherwise perceptible feature of institutionalised political power, the state system, in capitalist societies."

The charge that the concept of the state is excessively general, idealized, and grandiose, and that it masks key relations of power is an important one. (It also parallels contemporary critiques of other, quite different concepts, including gender.) A different critique focuses less on the state as an abstraction of form and more on its value as a governance concept. According to this critique, the state has become (or is becoming) an anachronism, its prominence (and dominance) as concept and object evaporating in the face of other growing forms and techniques of contemporary rule and identification. While the nation-state once had importance, coherence, and meaning as a political formation, the globalization of neoliberal markets and the growth in non-state forms of governance have whittled its status and significance away so that it is no longer an exceptional source of power or rule (see, e.g., Shearing and Wood 2003; Strange 1996). Economic and political power resides with international geopolitical forces and transnational corporations. These now determine, in large part, the goods, services, and regulatory structures that states once controlled, while identifications and attachments work at scales above and below the nation or involve other social affiliations, such as gender, sexuality, religion, or ethnicity.[49] In the contemporary world, the nation-state is in rapid decline, at best a minor support to other, more powerful entities.

The third main critique of the state, and the one that is most relevant to this book, is an activist and normative one, emerging from anarchist and other radical forces and commentators opposed to the notion that states can ever support the relocation of power and resources. For left critics, the state is a key source of domination (for some, *the* key source of domination) within national societies. It is a symbol of order and discipline (see, e.g., Newman 2001) and a primary mechanism for reproducing not only dominant economic relations but also racialized, gendered, sexual, and geopolitical ones.[50] States do not just oppress through physical coercion and violence. This may represent state domination in its most excessive or spectacular register, but states also rule through other means. For many radicals, even seemingly progressive state initiatives stultify transformative grassroots politics as states colonize social justice projects, dominate public rationalities, promote conformist moralities, and domesticate progressive identities and desires (see chapter 4). Bonnie Honig (2009: 136–37; emphasis added) remarks, "In seeking the best legislative and juridical practices, we must be mindful of how *such endeavors press us* to make our cases and envision ourselves and our political futures in terms quite different from those we might otherwise imagine and seek to vouchsafe." Honig does not reject institutional and state politics; her concern here is with their cultural power. For others, however, radical change is impossible within or through the state; there is no helpful "dictatorship of the proletariat" en route to the state's "withering away" (a point I return to at the end of the book). For anarchists and their fellow travelers, because the power and authority of the state comes, at least in part, from its acceptance and naturalization in routine everyday engagements, communities need to withdraw recognition, resituating transformative energy and attention within non-state social worlds, particularly the commons (see Kinna 2019; see also chapter 5). The radical geographers Jenny Pickerill and Paul Chatterton (2006: 736, 731) argue for the value of autonomous "networked and connected spaces" within "broader transnational networks, where extra-local connections are vital social building blocks" as "part of a [politically enacted non-state] vocabulary of urgency, hope and inspiration."

These three primary critiques of the state—conceptual, analytical, and political—have proved hugely significant. They have also generated considerable debate as other activists and writers argue for the state's continuing significance. The conceptual critique generated the rejoinder that, while the abstract state may be a fiction, as an idea held and deployed by officials, politicians, community activists, academics, and others, it produced important effects—"state effects" in the consequential and adjectival rather than illusory (magical) sense. Colin Hay (2014: 463) suggested that the state might be approached "as if it is real," given "the *analytical* utility of the concept" in order to avoid the irresolvable discussion, attendant on its abstract character, of determining whether or not it in fact is.[51] Analytically, the claim of anachronism has generated a swathe of counterargument, anchored in the notion that the state—and specifically, the nation-state—remains an important site of attachment, concern, and interest,[52] while its vertical order provides a key form for domestic governance and international extraterritorial agency.[53] The importance of the state as an organizing source of regulatory control has been explored in relation to the state-based management and constitution of economically precarious subjects, including through detention, conditional welfare payments, and the use of "orders" to manage nonnormative behavior (e.g., Crawford 2006). Others focus on the (neo)liberal state's ongoing economic role; transnational corporations may exercise considerable power, but this power is facilitated by state action. In other words, internationally powerful states remain crucial for the reproduction of capitalist economic relations; manage a range of transnational processes; and actively shape international policy regimes as governments project the interests of domestic capital abroad.[54] States, Bob Jessop (2010, 2016) suggests, may *interiorize* capitalist interests and be subject to their speed (in ways that also privilege some state parts over others),[55] but they are not passive terrains or containers of action; nor can their authority and presence be assessed by their visible influence alone, given states' indirect abilities to structure the power and capacity of others.

Finally, the critique of the state as a legitimate site of transformative politics is challenged by those activists and writers who believe that democratic states, as sites of public provision, resource redistribution, and regulation, remain important for progressive, social justice politics.[56] This argument has both a descriptive and a normative dimension. While left-wing state retrievers recognize the validity and necessity of critiquing economic colonizing projects, along with the racism, security agendas, and "prison-industrial complexes" of neoliberal states in the global North, they also approach such states in terms of their histories and possibilities for progressive developments. If states condense social relations, they also condense the unevenness and struggles around these relations.[57] State formations may support the interests of powerful classes, including through the assertion of favorable sociopolitical rationalities and processes,[58] but (neo)liberal states do not operate simply and exclusively as agents of hegemonic forces and projects—thanks to those gains pressed on institutional processes from "below," and thanks to the (neo) liberal state's investment (if an uneven one) in social stability. Progressive initiatives in (neo)liberal states may be overshadowed by other, more powerful agendas and projects, but if the state is an evolving historical formation, with neoliberalism far from permanent, absolute, or unitary, progressive state practices and projects can (and do) emerge and develop also.[59]

Janet Newman and John Clarke (2014: 154, 164) point to the potential for a more progressive version of the British state to provide "a bulwark against the market's destructive powers," promote "the public good," and advance "sustainable futures." Such a state does not have to monopolize progressive politics, extinguishing the oxygen of non-state initiatives. Rather, the "dialogic state" they describe can develop and facilitate *public* action beyond the state over matters of shared concern, providing resources for social experimentation and innovation. In their short, hopeful discussion, Newman and Clarke (2014) are keen not to romanticize states. They recognize that states in the global North can also destroy publicness; that they support capitalism and function as intrusive apparatuses of security and surveillance. Nevertheless, they argue, the state should not be abandoned. It constitutes a political and organizational formation (and idea) essential to mobilize *and renew* if major transformative changes are to occur.

The state, then, might be retrieved as a useful conceptual frame— approached "as if" it is real. It might, analytically, offer a meaningful place-holder for the national political apparatuses that support capitalist markets, sustain social control, and stage affective attachments. More hopefully, the state might promise a bulwark for people against the pernicious effects of these processes. However, there are other critical reasons for holding on to the concept of the state. One, paradoxically, is to avoid the state's over-reification. Treating the state, *but not other social formations*, as irretrievable implies that the state has an essence, that it is a thing with boundaries and an exterior such that we can know when we are dealing with the state and when we are not. Left state critics recognize that states may be tangled up with other bodies and forces, but they tend to treat the state as an entity with a clearly defined outside, and it is there in this outside where real transformative politics are expected to occur. In this book, I want to avoid exceptionalizing the state; to refrain from treating the nation-state as a formation elevated above social life; to explore similarities between states and other governing formations; and to address their interconnec-tions and relationships in conditions where less is conceptually and po-litically at stake—where being defined as state or non-state does not make *all* the difference (even if there are some particular uses we might want specifically of the state). Avoiding a state/non-state binary also avoids the counterromanticization of civil society evident in the work of some anar-chists. For instance, the geographer Simon Springer (2012: 1617) writes: "Anarchist geographies of co-operation are to be born from outside the ex-isting *order*, from sites that the state has failed to enclose, and from the infinite possibilities that statist logics ignore, repel, plunder, and deny." Yet, as critics and commentators on contemporary anarchism point out, exclusions, hierarchy, and authoritarianism are not just characteristics of the state. They also occur within non-state forms, including small-scale, self-regulating communities or peer-based forms of mutualism (see, e.g., Benkler 2013). The challenge is not simply to shift scales from the national to the local or to replace impersonal institutional structures and systems with highly personal, constantly deliberating modes of decision making and practice, but to find new ways of combining and imagining them.

This book takes as its starting point a radical democratic willingness to treat the state as having value. It recognizes that this value is a contextually specific one, subject to the social and historical conditions which make the state conceptually available for progressive thinking. It also recognizes this value *may be just a transitional value*. But within the conditions of progressive politics in the global North, this book is anchored by a refusal to relinquish (or abandon) the state, including as a politically *imagined* formation. It is a refusal to allow elite forces and coercive forms of authoritarian capitalist practice to appropriate what state-based public governance might mean. This refusal does not deny the oppressive ways in which currently identified state formations act. However, in contrast to accounts that focus on materially reforming the state, oriented to what can be done *with* state power in service of an altogether different political agenda or regime—a "left art of government," in the Foucauldian terms James Ferguson (2011: 63) takes up—this book instead focuses conceptually on what it is and means to be a state, treating the "the state" *as an orienting rather than a defining concept.* By this I mean that I am less interested in "pinning" the state down than in taking it up as a way to orient our discussion of public governance toward questions of form, scale, and ethos. As a result, my discussion does not pursue new institutional designs. It does not address practical state projects and the changes in ownership, taxation, planning, environmental policies, international agendas, and welfare provision that they might demand, as vital as these are. It does not address how best to deploy the institutional power of existing political machinery. Rather, it addresses the more conceptual, and in some ways anterior, question of how to think about the state.

Quentin Skinner (1989) has very usefully traced historical changes and developments in the postmedieval application and constitution of the state concept in Western Europe. His account demonstrates how certain state conceptions achieved dominance—namely, those that treated the state as a realm of governing separate from the people (and in some instances, as a distinct persona separate from government). His account also reveals the decline and defeat of other more democratic conceptions. Today, conceptions of the state among contemporary theorists are various as writers draw the boundaries, connections, apparatuses, and practices that statehood entails in radically different ways. The extent of this variation poses questions (rarely directly addressed) about what statehood *could* (and *should*) *come to mean*. Working from a legal drama over conservative Christian withdrawal, I explore lines of thought for the state's reimagining, lines that entail making new imaginary cuts and joins in the political-institutional landscape *to reframe and regather what is taken to be a state.* As the book progresses,

I move toward a conception of the state organized around the shape and condition of public governance. But my aim is not to sally out to defend the language and terms of statehood so much as to *provisionally* take them up to repurpose them.

Reimagining the state in this book involves four primary moves: foregrounding the heterogeneous composition of state formations; pluralizing state imaginations; exploring play as a register of governing; and resituating desire and the erotic within state action. Underpinning these moves is an intuition that reimagining states as heterogeneous, plural, socially embedded, and quotidian *may* support democratic participation and public "ownership" of the state rather than the reverse (of states possessing people) and that pleasurable, playful, and sensual governing may be valuable in its own right, as well as supporting—and, as I discuss, *necessitating*—the development of different kinds of states. These moves suggest a conception of the state that diverges from the more established thought paths of many liberals and radicals. But what, fundamentally, can such a conception do? Aside from all of the ways in which future-directed projects fail,[60] the lines of state thinking I have suggested can seem thoroughly risky. Appealing, perhaps, in some future utopia—yet as a way of rereading and reorienting the contemporary (neo)liberal state, they may seem to naively underestimate the organized reality and force of the state's current form. Heterogeneity, plurality, play, and pleasure may also seem to drastically underestimate the need for "serious" state power to advance and secure progressive "ends."

Max Haiven and Alex Khasnabish (2014: 3) describe the "radical imagination" as "the ability to imagine the world, life and social institutions not as they are but as they might otherwise be. . . . [T]he radical imagination is not just about dreaming of different futures. It's about bringing those possible futures 'back' *to work on* the present, to inspire action and new forms of solidarity today." Conceptual prefiguration is one aspect of this return in which practices are undertaken "as if" meanings were otherwise (Cooper 2017).[61] In this book I pursue a slightly different conceptual practice based on *reorienting* a critical conception of the state so that it is not saturated by the oppressive experiences of statehood to date. This is not in any way to dismiss critical accounts or to suggest that the approach adopted here takes place at a distance from them. However, if the state can be productively conceptualized in multiple ways, being explored and shaped through different paradigms and usages,[62] what this book offers is a *postnormative* account. Thus, it does not invoke ideals of the perfect state or suggest criteria for evaluation, strategies for transition, or modes of reform and improvement, important as these all are.[63] Instead, it aims to complement work that pursues these lines by focusing on the development of provisional and situated conceptual threads that draw on social glimpses and ideas in the present to turn toward something else.

Locating this "something" in the future as that which is "not yet" is not unproblematic. Nor do I want to suggest that transformative projects should face only in this direction. Progressive conceptions of the state can work across many temporalities, as work on historic utopias and critical uses of nostalgia demonstrate. At the same time, Hirokazu Miyazaki's (2004) invocation of hope as a prospectively oriented epistemological method is suggestive for approaching concepts in anticipatory ways. Here, transformative accounts may require recognition of the inchoate character of new conceptual lines in which hope is also "an embrace of the limits of knowledge" (Miyazaki 2016: 10). Gilles Deleuze and Félix Guattari (1994) suggest the process of inventing concepts experiments with what is emerging and under way, speaking to people's desires for new ways of being and living (see also Patton 2010: chap. 2). Their focus, however, is philosophical concepts. My interest, in contrast, is in exploring the life of everyday concepts—those more widely and heterogeneously held, concepts not marked by any single person's name or signature.[64] Anticipatory conceptual lines are not "academic gifts" bequeathed to an unknown future. Emerging in multiple places through multiple forms of practice by people in all kinds of roles, they are undertakings of the present,[65] shaped by and in turn shaping what differently placed actors do, desire, plan, aim for, and oppose.[66] What, then, does this mean for the state? We can explore how conceptions of the state shape what actors do, as Nick Gill (2010) evocatively explores in his discussion of different refugee organizations' engagements with the state. But how can non-elite actors in (neo)liberal polities put their desires and ambitions about what states could be (and become) into practice? This is the subject of my final chapter, which explores state play with revisions as a way to develop and try out new state and institutional imaginaries.

Chapter Outline

In closing, I want to briefly trace the arc of discussion through the chapters that follow. Chapter 1 explores in more detail the different kinds of withdrawal—by both conservative Christian and liberal state bodies—that have emerged in this legal drama. Working both from and away from the notion that withdrawal means abandonment, the chapter focuses on the subjects, authority, and political imaginaries generated by litigated withdrawal to provide a ground for thinking about embodiment, power, governing, attachment, and discharge in the rest of the book. Chapters 2 and 3 turn to the question of state form. Chapter 2 asks how we might more expansively reimagine the makeup of the state in developing an account of state heterogeneity and embedding. It explores how the legal drama over conservative Christian withdrawal helps challenge the standard state account, supporting instead an account of state composition that makes room for the fleeting and dissident. Focusing on acts of dissent within state formations reveals one way that wider social life permeates states, but to develop a broader understanding of the embedded state, the chapter also explores the wider terrain in which states inhere and asks, following a democratic logic, how this wider terrain, in turn, might inhere in the state. Such a relationship of constitution can take different forms. If conservative Christians' animus is partly driven by a perception that their part in the makeup of the state is a passive one, merely intended to extend the state's reach, what does a more active relationship to state authority involve? Chapter 3 continues this exploration, drawing on the legal drama of this book to consider the relationship between the nation-state and other state forms. Central to this chapter is the question of state plurality in terms of what counts as a state; how states evolve and change; and how states are known. Challenging nation-states' claims to an objectively defined form and exclusive state status, the chapter explores other state forms and knowledges, including through touch, to advance a radically plural conception of the state.

Chapters 4 and 5 take up the book's legal drama to explore the state from a different angle. Instead of focusing principally on what it could mean to be a state, the discussion turns to the question of state ethos, to those ways of behaving that can be considered state ways. Chapter 4 tackles this question in relation to play. Its starting point is the way antidiscrimination and human rights law have consolidated religious and identity beliefs into a form of property that state law will protect and recognize. Since this works to depoliticize beliefs, the chapter asks whether state-engaged play can contribute to unsettling and repoliticizing this proprietary relationship. It pursues this question through three play forms: state-engineered role playing in which conservative Christian and gay-equality advocates attempt to leave their clashing beliefs behind to consider other perspectives; as state experimentation, where taking up and advancing beliefs in gay equality constitute a form of "nationalization"; and as "free-running," where gay activists challenge refusals by City Councils to provide Gay Pride proclamations, using provincial state commitments to gay equality in order to do so. Through exploring how states play in this legal drama, the chapter asks whether play is something states should do and examines the conditions required to play more justly. Chapter 5 turns to the question of the erotic state. Paralleling the previous chapter, the discussion is oriented to the question of whether public governing might benefit from being attuned to the erotic. However, this question is approached, in postnormative terms, through an erotic reading of the state invoked by the legal drama of this book. This reading examines withdrawal, attachment, and governing in terms of their desires and sensations, attending to questions of friction, discharge, waste, and the sensory pleasures of collaboratively creating public goods. While chapters 2 and 3 address how to combine two different understandings of state form—namely, as the shape and condition of public governing and as gathered formations—chapters 4 and 5 take up this dual account to explore the relations and tensions that might constitute progressive state practice when approached as quotidian, activist, and caring.

More generally, across these four chapters I focus on the task of reimagining what it could mean to be a state, tracing lines of thinking through heterogeneity, plurality, play, and the erotic. Yet while reimagining is important, the *manifestation* of new state forms is at least equally so. As practical enactments with political authority, newly imagined states are extremely hard to realize, particularly by grassroots actors. In the final chapter, I consider one modality for doing so. Role-play-with-revisions provides a way of simulating tribunals, constitutions, currencies, universities, adjudicators and statehood in a progressive, transformative key. Taking up lines of argument developed in earlier chapters, I explore what these forms of role playing bring to thinking about the democratic everyday state and to the relationship between state care and activism. Finally, the chapter explores what state play, when retrieved and spun into different networks of political action, can do.

ONE. Legal Dramas of Refusal

Hello Vanessa,
Sorry if our last response was a confusing one. Yes, you are correct in saying we do not photograph same-sex weddings, but again, thanks for checking out our site!

Have a great day,
ELAINE

In the early twenty-first century, conservative Christian opposition to gay politics in the (neo)liberal North acquired a new form. With equality and human rights laws extending to embrace sexual orientation, Christian bodies changed tack. With gays unwilling to turn away from their desires, conservative Christians felt compelled to turn away from them, demanding legal recognition of their right to do so. In this way, gay people became the sex act from which conservative Christians sought to lawfully abstain.

Yet to characterize this conservative Christian move as one of withdrawal does not mean that religious individuals or organizations had previously been supportive. In some cases, lesbians and gays collectively lost something they had previously acquired—such as when the new mayor of a Canadian city refused to issue the annual Gay Pride proclamation granted by his predecessor (see chapter 4). In other cases, withdrawal involved the loss of expectations and provision that a normative sexuality would have gained or retained. The employee of a Christian organization who came out and lost her job, or the gay couple who were asked whether their venue booking was for a same-sex partnership ceremony and then found the booking canceled, faced the withdrawal of an opportunity or resource *that would have stayed available* had they not been marked as gay.[1] In these cases of employment or commercial agreement, an individual lost what she or he had previously been granted or promised. But withdrawal also occurred in cases where nothing had been secured, as in *Vanessa Willock v. Elane Photography*. There, withdrawal operated as a retraction or deduction in relation to a norm—what would be given *except* to those identified as gay. Withdrawal, in this sense, was not just about the loss that followed subjects' falling short of a heterosexual norm. Central to its operation were equality and human rights laws requiring nondiscrimination in relation to sexual orientation. These laws were not always held at the "highest" state level, but for withdrawal to be meaningful as something more than a subtraction from the norm (what would have been), to function as a *retraction of the norm* (what should have been), gay equality needed to constitute a strong animating norm within the polity. Otherwise, refusal was simply the banal and unexceptional form of differentiation that conservative Christians declared it to be (no different from morally singling out pedophiles, adulterers, or bigamists),[2] even as the unrelenting stress placed on gay equality, alongside abortion and gender transitioning, constituted these wrongs as theo-politically exceptional.

The legal drama of this book, however, does not just concern conservative Christian withdrawal. Scholarship on refusal and resistance often centers on actions *against* the state (see, e.g., Weiss 2014). But here, state bodies also turned away,[3] withdrawing jobs, promotions, contracts, opportunities, resources, and even words,[4] from withholding Christians. In contrast to many accounts in which one set of bodies simply withdraws from another, or where withdrawal constitutes a single, discrete act in which something once offered becomes lost, in this legal drama withdrawal proved far more dynamic and serial.[5] We might describe it as an economy of withdrawal, involving different bodies as the American case of *Rumsfeld v. Forum for Academic and Institutional Rights* illustrates.[6] In that case, a group of law schools (unsuccessfully) challenged the withholding of federal funds resulting from their collective decision to deny "best access" to military recruiters on campus because of the recruiters' employment discrimination on sexuality grounds. In this drama, then, we have the military's withdrawal of employment opportunities from openly gay men and lesbians, causing law schools to withdraw recruitment privileges, leading to the federal state's withdrawal of funds. Episodes such as this, and the political imaginaries and practices they invoke, constitute the empirical heart of this book. In this chapter, I trace their drama. Reimagining the state through a drama of withdrawal foregrounds the subjects, conflicting authorities, competing normative worlds, and fusion and separation of bodies and things, with all the feelings and textures this engages. These themes provide the basis for discussing the state in the chapters that follow.

Thinking about Withdrawal

Although infrequently discussed in general overarching terms, withdrawal is a pervasive technique within world politics. Sometimes it takes shape as a self-healing or self-maintenance measure, as when radical separatist groups withdraw from a shared polity or when conservative religious groupings withdraw from a state-regulated secular world to establish their own, communal governmental structures, with courts, schools, care facilities, accommodation, and employment. Withdrawal can also be an assertion of sovereignty,[7] or something demanded of others, including by nations in conditions of colonization withholding legitimacy from the dominant state. Audra Simpson (2014) traces this in her account of Kahnawá:ke Mohawks' refusal to recognize the territorial authority and borders of the Canadian state, despite considerable personal inconvenience and cost.[8] In other contexts, withdrawal takes place to avoid sustaining and being implicated in undesired practices or as a way to penalize people and bodies for behaving undesirably. A punitive rationality is often tied to governmental action in conditions in which states withdraw benefits—from welfare payments to physical protection, housing, and even the right to inhabit particular spaces—to express their opprobrium or incentivize "better" behavior. Likewise, employees, companies, and consumers use withdrawal to pressure others to act, as in boycotts or strikes, where money, labor, participation, and recognition are withheld to compel companies, nation-states, and nongovernmental organizations (NGOs) to introduce new policies, practices, and allegiances.

Withdrawal takes away goods and benefits. It also takes away the specific activities, uses, and relations those goods bear within the networks of action in which they exist. Yet withdrawal is also more than simply *loss*. Drawing back and acts of refusal bring other practices and meanings into play.[9] Withdrawal, like refusal, is typically interpreted as a cutting of relations as the move to take the UK out of the European Union exemplifies (see also Mauss 1967; McGranahan 2016: 335); however, dramas of withdrawal should not be juxtaposed with dramas of connection. Just as law is involved and present in the so-called state of exception, and just as conservative Christians' denial of gay-positive recognition involves its endless sexual citation, so chains of withdrawal engender contact. We can find contact in the conflictual relations that develop through withdrawal, supported by the mediating figures and spaces that withdrawal often involves; in the reconfigured relations with those withdrawn from that take shape postwithdrawal (generating, in turn, the anxiety that separation may not prove possible); and in the new or consolidated associations that form as withdrawal from one set of bodies produces contact or closer contact with others (see chapter 5). Withdrawal is a curiously productive focus for thinking about political contact. But if this legal drama is to stimulate our thinking about how states touch and feel, and how different forms of contact compose them, how might it do so? In this chapter, I want to trace some of the relations and rationalities to emerge and be expressed in this drama, to ask: What is taking shape in those instances in which conservative Christians claim the right to make an exception, to treat specific others differently from the norm, and to have their own departure from new norms accommodated?[10]

One useful starting point is the academic work that draws on Giorgio Agamben's (1998, 2005) and Carl Schmitt's ([1934] 2005) work on sovereignty and the "exception" to think about everyday (neo)liberal political life (see, e.g., Farías and Flores 2017; Gray and Porter 2015; Neilson 2014; Sarat and Clarke 2008). In the legal drama of this book, declaring an exception to the law (or the right to lift or cross its demands) takes shape in ways that are partial, contested, and certainly outside state claims to emergency. In such conditions, where rights and freedoms appear to collide, Bonnie Honig's (2009: xvii) phrase "everyday emergencies of maintenance" is helpful. Conservative Christian claims, in particular, are replete with talk of sovereignty, urgency, crisis, and the need to act in the name of religious freedom. They are also replete with expressed anxieties about banishment, exclusion, and discrimination in response to their own need to withdraw (see chapter 2). In such conditions, work on quotidian crises and dramas of sovereignty—on exceptions rather than *the* exception—illuminate key stakes and discourses in this conflict.

One central theme is the contested and plural character of political authority, hailed by different subjects even as it also hails them. Hosna Shewly explores the implications of competing forms of sovereignty, focusing on the harms that result when multiple authorities withdraw. Drawing on Agamben, she addresses the abandonment of people trapped between two states (India and Bangladesh), where they are "geographically located in one country but politically and legally [belong] to another" (Shewly 2013: 23). In Shewly's example, people are not transported to camps or extraterritorial prisons but abandoned in their own land. Their territorially remote home nation fails to provide most basic rights; the host nation, which surrounds them politically, intrudes only to further its own interests, disregarding urgently needed local rights and services. Shewly's account reveals experiences of powerlessness that seem far more acute than those evidenced in the legal drama of this book. Nevertheless, her focus on the withdrawal of political responsibility as a result of competing sovereign authorities is instructive for thinking about the relationship between exclusion, sovereignty, and plurality. In the legal drama over conservative Christian withdrawal, the problem is not so much the *absence* of legal authority as its multiplicity in conditions in which conservative Christians subordinate state-enacted rights to religious norms. Many democratic theorists adopt a celebratory attitude toward rights, driven by their desire to extend its project and vision. But the encounter between *conflicting* rights projects, including the right *not* to be subjected to others' rights (as conservative Christians demand), highlights how rights cannot be simply and harmoniously extended in conditions where gains for some become read (or felt) as losses for others.

Religious and secular political bodies confront a changing sociolegal and cultural landscape of obligations, freedoms, and entitlements; within this landscape, withdrawal provides an important political and governmental technique. In the main section of this chapter, I focus on three of its dimensions: the subjectivities that withdrawal expresses and constitutes; its authorities and authorizations; and its scope and reach. Agamben's influence has led many authors to trace these dimensions in terms of bare life (or *homo sacer*), the sovereign declaration of emergency, and the state of exception, respectively. In this legal drama, these dimensions acquire a rather different shape. So subjectivities are variously represented (and constituted) as immoral, abject, desertable, governing, and playing; questions of authority and authorization foreground diverse sovereign projects as different authorities justify, confront, and perform refusal. Meanwhile, the scope and reach of withdrawal brings to the fore divergent notions of the normative world and its bodies (as whole, divided, and sticky). But before discussing these dimensions further, I want to map the five primary forms of refusal to have taken place in this legal drama.

Mapping Withdrawal

1. *Conscientious objection.* The first and probably best-known set of cases concern state officials and other public sector agents demanding the right to be an exception. Christian marriage registrars, doctors, firefighters, police officials, and others here refused to carry out particular work responsibilities, where gay clients were involved, on grounds of their religious conscience, that "ethical regulator . . . [which] require[s] the individual to privilege these imperatives above other social obligations" (Weiss 2014: 6). Facing their own religious communities but speaking in ways that rippled through other publics, conservative Christians claimed that their conscience required them to refrain from acting when doing otherwise would constitute an endorsement of gay sexuality or same-sex relationships (see chapters 2 and 5).[11] These refusals did not go down well with many state employers. Demotions, dismissals, suspensions, and, in some cases, compulsory diversity training followed, leading conservative Christians, in turn, to challenge their employers' actions in court. Litigated cases include family panel adjudicators who refused to participate in adoption decisions where gay people were being considered as parents;[12] marriage and civil partnership registrars who declined to conduct ceremonial or "marriage" formalities for gay couples;[13] and firefighters who refused to accompany or participate in Gay Pride events (see Baskerville 2011: 97–98).[14] But withdrawal did not just involve pulling back from contact with gay individuals, couples, or groups.[15] It also included unwillingness to create gay-positive environments on the part of schoolteachers and librarians; refusals by foster parents to raise children in their care with positive attitudes toward gay sexuality;[16] and even a refusal by public sector workers to attend gay-positive training sessions.[17] One news story tells of a federal government

official who refused to watch a video on LGBT diversity, or to sign a document saying he had watched it, on the grounds that affirmative contact with such a video would itself "certify sin."[18]

2. *Political representation.* The political refusal to reconfigure the boundaries of the "normal" constitutes a second strand of this legal drama as (elected) public bodies declined to provide gay equality with support or political backing. In one set of cases, Canadian cities in British Columbia and Ontario withheld mayoral proclamations supporting Gay Pride in contexts in which proclamations for other causes and events were routinely given (see chapter 4). In *Kelowna v. O'Byrne*, the mayor was prepared to proclaim "a lesbian and gay day" but refused to add the word "pride."[19] In *Hudler v. City of London*, the mayor declared she would "never grant this proclamation" since, as an evangelical Christian, turning her "back on God . . . would lose [her] authority as mayor."[20] In other cases, resisting gay equality measures came from school boards and districts. In the Canadian case, *Chamberlain v. Surrey School District No. 36*, an elected school board refused a teacher's request to be allowed to use books depicting lesbian and gay families (see chapter 3).[21] In *A. W. et al. v. Davis School District*, a children's book depicting lesbian parents was removed from school shelves and placed behind the library counter (available only with parental permission).[22] In *Parents, Families, and Friends of Lesbians and Gays, Inc. v. Camdenton R-III School District*, a public school district in Missouri used Internet filtering software to prevent students from accessing LGBT-positive websites.[23]

3. *Commercial refusal.* While the first two clusters of cases involved public sector services, a claimed right to discriminate commercially arose in a number of cases in which gay and lesbian customers sought to purchase venue space use, speech acts, and other goods and services. Here, typically small (family) businesses, sole traders, and the trading arms of religious organizations demanded the right to make an exception and say "no" despite the presence of human rights and equality protections on sexual orientation grounds.[24] Instances of refusal included guesthouses that would not let anyone other than married heterosexual couples share a room;[25] owners of cake making, calligraphy, and printing companies, alongside venues for rent, who refused to provide their services for gay weddings or commitment ceremonies;[26] and printing firms that would not take on work that they claimed promoted Gay Pride or gay rights.[27] In contrast to the conscientious objection cases, which typically involved Christian workers bringing employment cases against public bodies, challenging the

sanctions imposed on them for refusing to "do their jobs," here cases were brought by gay advocates, allies, and those who identified as gay or in same-sex relationships on being denied a service. Thus, the cases demonstrate how an exception to a general norm of service availability can be asserted in the course of a transaction or after agreement has been reached as the decision to withdraw follows and disrupts a prior decision to provide.[28] Numerous court judgments describe gay couples, happy in the knowledge that they have found a venue for their wedding or postcommitment ceremony party, then discovering that the owners, on learning of their sexuality (or gender), have changed their mind. Repeatedly, legal narratives describe that moment in which gay people or couples are told, often cursorily by phone and with no further assistance offered, that the service or accommodation they have booked or requested is no longer available, as in the Canadian guesthouse case of *Eadie and Thomas v. Riverbend Bed and Breakfast and Others (No. 2)*:

> Mr. Molnar recalled that he phoned Mr. Eadie and said "Hello, this is Les Molnar, my wife just took a reservation for a Shaun." He then asked "Is this Brian." The reply he received was "No, this is Shaun." He . . . then ask[ed] Mr. Eadie if they were a gay couple. The reply was "yes."
>
> Mr. Molnar testified that he then said "Shaun, I am sorry, I don't think it is going to work." . . . He recalled that Mr. Eadie was surprised, said "wow" very loud and hung up the phone. Mr. Molnar was surprised by that, and then realized that Mr. Eadie was angry. . . .
>
> [He] made no further attempt to speak with Mr. Eadie. He recalls saying to Mrs. Molnar that perhaps he should call Mr. Eadie back, invite him over for breakfast and to talk, but that she said that he sounded angry and they should not aggravate him anymore.[29]

4. *Withdrawal of community.* In the commercial cases just discussed, litigants chose particular traders for what they were selling, not for their beliefs. I therefore want to distinguish withdrawal of secular commercial services from a fourth cluster of cases. Here, organizations asserted their right to make an exception—withdrawing membership, recognition, employment, or equal participation—from committed participants for reasons of organizational or community integrity. In such cases, gay-identified participants in Christian organizations (who were unable or unwilling to promise celibacy) or those who breached church rules on sexuality found

their membership, officiating licenses, or jobs withdrawn.[30] In one high-profile U.S. case, a Boy Scouts of America (BSA) leader was forced to quit on the grounds that, as an openly gay leader, he sent a message incompatible with BSA values, which required members "to be morally straight and clean in word and deed."[31]

Loss of membership for breaching an explicit or tacit organizational rule reveals the sanctions organizations have brought to bear on those deemed to have misbehaved yet seek to remain in place. In cases in which the gay organizational member is *framed* as unacceptably "gay" prior to their banishment (or exodus), court judgments describe a kind of haunting (see also Gordon 1997). Although forced to leave, they have not yet gone; they remain, hanging on, in the face of escalating hostility and relentless persecution. Legal narratives emphasize the duration of this process, telling of people whose membership status has become indistinct as the seeming certainty of the expulsion to come gives their presence a translucent quality.[32] But it is not only the gay member whose body is depicted as insubstantial and at risk. A striking feature of these cases is the organizational imaginary that defendants present. As one care organization remarked, responding to litigation brought by a worker who was forced out of her job after coming out, "When we ask people to come and join the ministry of Christian Horizons, it's not just that they could do a job *but that they become part of the body*."[33] In many of these cases, workers and volunteers want to remain part of this Christian body. Thus, the litigation is about more than mere membership or employment.[34] In these cases, those expelled face the loss of a "Christian home" and sometimes something even more corporeal, witnessed in the proprioceptive disorientation expelled litigants describe thanks to their excision and elimination from religious social flesh.[35]

5. *Liberal state withdrawal.* Finally, we come to cases dealing not with conservative Christian withdrawal but with the *countervailing* withdrawal of liberal state and other public bodies opposed to discriminatory treatment on sexual orientation grounds. In these cases, it is the state's refusal to make an exception, conservative Christians argue, that produces them as an exception, as they become excluded from the polity. In the U.S. case that opened this book, a Michigan farmer was excluded from selling produce at a farmer's market as a result of his refusal to allow same-sex marriages on his farm.[36] This case demonstrates the oblique relationship that can form between the goods that public bodies withdraw (e.g., a market license) and the prior withdrawal (e.g., a wedding venue space) that they oppose. In

marking their displeasure, state and public bodies attend to the diversity of powers and tools at their disposal—performing the "activist" state with its energetic keenness to take up new forms of responsibility by harnessing unexpected governmental measures, including withdrawal.[37] As a result of refusing to treat gay (potential) participants equally, organizations—from Catholic adoption agencies to university student clubs[38]—lost state contracts, tax benefits, access, meeting venues, subsidized facilities, and formal recognition.[39] In the United States, litigation on the loss of public benefits arose following the Supreme Court decision in *Boy Scouts of America v. Dale* (the case mentioned earlier). In response to the Boy Scouts' public identification as an explicitly heterosexual-promoting organization, public authorities across the country cut or limited ties with the Scouting movement, withdrawing charitable fundraising opportunities, subsidized or rent-free venues, and school-based support and transportation facilities.[40]

The withdrawal of benefits from organizations sits alongside a second cluster of cases involving liberal state bodies. Here, subordinate (rather than independent) others were disciplined and penalized as public bodies marked the edges of the acceptable, responding to prior acts of *commission* rather than omission. In these episodes, which mainly revolved around employment disputes, individuals faced sanctions as a result of expressing antigay sentiment.[41] In some respects, these cases coincide with the conscientious objection disputes mentioned earlier. However, here state withdrawal did not follow a Christian employee's *refusal* to do parts of their job but instead arose from "inappropriate" activities and remarks made at work or, in some cases, outside of it.[42] These included negative views about gay sexuality being sent to a gay website through the email system of a public employer,[43] being posted on Facebook,[44] shared with colleagues,[45] and, in a case involving a teacher, shared with school students.[46] In one British incident, an employee of Lambeth Borough Council, in London, distributed Bible segments to colleagues during a prayer meeting (permitted by his municipal employer), describing the punishment for gay sex.[47]

In the chapters that follow, I return to these cases to explore how the exclusion, discrimination, and withholding they narrate might stimulate and support a progressive reimagining of what it could mean to be a state. Here, though, I want to explore the subjects, authorities, normative worlds, and justifications that this legal drama of withdrawal engaged and invoked. At the heart of my account is the constant shifting of positions, power, authority, and borders that took place. Withdrawal not only structured the movement of benefits and losses, it also bore the relentlessly calculative relationship between what should have been, what could have been, and what in fact was.

Subjects of Withdrawal

I want to start at the start—with the claim that antigay withdrawal, and especially its legal sanctioning, would generate suffering. In one case, where a Canadian city refused to issue an LGBT Pride Day proclamation, a witness testified that "living in Terrace was like being in prison."[48] In another case, in which a Christian college required students and staff to sign a Community Covenant promising, among other things, not to have sex outside heterosexual marriage, expert testimony detailed the consequences of being outed as gay: how the threat and "shame of expulsion" generated an increased "likelihood of suffering stress, anxiety, depression, and [could] even lead to suicidal ideation, attempts, and death."[49] The subjectivity forged when others were allowed to withdraw or "opt out" of provision was depicted as vulnerable and exposed. If Christians (and others) could legally refuse to provide jobs, membership, services, and goods to sexual minorities for reasons of religious belief, a secure gay life became uncertain, particularly in conservative religious localities, and particularly in conditions in which the state's offloading of services onto NGOs and companies threatened to extend the scope and impact of religious decision making (see also chapter 2).

In his account of conservative popular sovereignties, Chad Kautzer (2015) describes how states can facilitate white male rule when they refrain from creating or enforcing incompatible legal regimes—in other words, when they withdraw from acting.[50] Kautzer's (2015: 175) focus is the under-regulated presence of guns in spaces where "freedom is identified with the right of self-defense and the right of self-defense is identified with possession of a firearm." Gay-equality advocates expressed similar fears about states leaving people subject to local forms of social power. Douglas NeJaime and Reva Siegel (2015: 2574) write, "Refusals have the capacity to construct separate, localized legal orders in which same-sex couples face an unpredictable marketplace . . . and continue to encounter stigma and rejection." In the cases described above, the exclusions resulting from expressions of conservative Christian sovereignty were repeatedly cited. In *Heintz v. Christian Horizons*, the court declared: "The effect of the discriminatory policy was to say to her, because of who you are, you are no longer welcome . . . to make her a pariah within the organization. . . . [It] was a fundamental affront to Ms. Heintz's dignity and respect. . . . She felt hurt that the organization that she had worked for, and was so dedicated to, had abandoned her."[51] In another case, in which a gay young man failed to be appointed as a Church of England youth officer (despite his extracted promise to remain celibate), the court remarked: "The Claimant was, as he said in evidence, so upset by the end of the conversation that he felt and was physically sick on the way home. He did feel personal rejection. He also felt a great sense of injustice and unfairness because of the reluctance of the Bishop to embrace the assurances that he had given to him."[52]

Legal narratives tell of accusations, confrontations, and lengthy, intrusive interrogations of the person "suspected" of being gay, and of the person who, on coming out as gay or lesbian, has failed voluntarily to withdraw. In *Heintz*, Ms. Heintz detailed how "staff and co-workers . . . thought she was 'scum and dirt' and did not treat her like a human being."[53] Yet for the most part, the subjects of these legal dramas are not permanently or completely abandoned or stripped of social and legal support. Indeed, conservative Christian advocates repeatedly claimed, and relied on the claim, that their withdrawal would not harm gay people since they could access sought-after services from another provider.[54] Conservative Christians did not argue here for gays to be abandoned by everyone—the *homines sacri* in relation to whom *all* are sovereigns (Agamben 1998). Rather, they argued, Christians (and other religious actors) should be treated as the exception—in the sense of being allowed to *apply* an exception to gays that others could not (or should not) make.[55] From the queer left, too, claims to abjection as a result of conservative Christian withdrawal were also challenged; here on the grounds that they seemed to relate to the benefits of conventional middle-class life. Critical queer studies has been sharply hostile to the idea that gay men and lesbians, living normative lives in the global North—and litigating because they have been turned down by a guesthouse or wedding bakery—experience a level of exclusion or vulnerability emerging from the loss of protection and social goods that in any way approaches "bare life."[56]

This queer critique is important. At the same time, aside from difficulties in calculation, the loss subtending this legal drama involved more than the conventional privatized benefits of wedding services or guesthouse bookings, since it also included losses of public benefits, such as employment, healthcare, youth services provision, and community recognition.

The question of loss also begs the question: loss to whom? At the heart of my discussion, in the chapters that follow, is the constant reframing and contestation of status position as the identification of who were the wounded or abject subjects was repeatedly challenged and relocated.[57] Gay people were not the only ones claiming abandonment.[58] With their lives given to Jesus rather than styled by nonprocreative sexual desires, conservative Christians also claimed to have been stigmatized, degraded, and marginalized. Liberal state and public bodies were coercing them into accepting "alternative patterns of living and of family life," as God, Jesus, and practices of discipleship became banished from the public realm (see Christian Institute 2009; Strhan 2015).[59] After the Johns' foster parent application stalled because the couple would not promise to provide a gay-positive environment for children in their care, Eunice Johns remarked, "We feel excluded and that there is no place for us in society."[60] Likewise, Christian commentator Daniel Boucher (2010: 24) wrote, "There is . . . a form of discrimination more demeaning than having one's identity violated negatively, and that is . . . by being actively required to do something in contradiction of one's identity/beliefs." If productive ties with liberal state and other public bodies depend on being able to accord lesbian and gay subjects and sexualities equal treatment, those who claim an inability to do so become legally excludable from public jobs, contracts, subsidies, and licenses (see chapter 2).[61]

I have focused so far on the subjectivities wrought by (and around) abandonment and vulnerability because of their prominence in the litigation and in the surrounding social drama—of which this litigation proved an important animating part. Unsurprisingly, the psychological, symbolic, and material effects of exclusion for particular social constituencies were central to the legal and political claims expressed. In relation to the state, the precarity that withdrawal generates foregrounds the power of provision, and so what is at stake in its loss. It also highlights a negative, calculative relationship to responsibility, for at the heart of the withdrawal discussed here is the refusal to support one set of lives in one set of circumstances, thanks, it is claimed, to incompatible responsibilities owed to others (see chapter 2). A school, for instance, cannot sustain the teaching career of a teacher who makes antigay remarks where this undermines their pedagogic and welfare responsibilities to students. But disavowal and vulnerability are not the only subject positions this legal drama expressed and produced—discursively or materially. Others, such as sovereign, law

follower, decision maker, and player, animate the chapters that follow—
particularly that of player. Litigants and their support-providing organizations can be read as players in this legal drama, but this is not my focus
in thinking about play. Rather, I want to consider how withdrawal itself
expresses and helps to create players. These players contribute glimpses,
not always intentionally, of a reimagined state through their utterances and
practices as dissenting, risk-taking, creative political figures. In chapter 4,
I consider the gay activists who "free-ran" local city governments, moving among officials, committees, politicians, and full council meetings to
persuade mayors to issue pride proclamations. But there is another sense
in which participants in this legal drama functioned as players, and that is
in how acts of withdrawal, especially by conservative Christians, prefiguratively inhabited the world *as if* it were otherwise.[62] Strategies of campaigning exert pressure on other bodies to change their policies; prefiguration,
by contrast, involves living in the present as if it resembled the future that
is sought.[63] In this drama, conservative Christian withdrawal expressed and
enacted a world in which people provided goods, services, and belonging
only to desired members, service users, and customers, and only in support
of desired ways of living. Conservative Christians attempted to live as if
this world was already in place (even as they undertook acts of withdrawal
knowing that it was not). However, their efforts to do so were thwarted,
with fines, loss of employment, and even jail sentences. The capacity of
conservative Christians' acts of withdrawal to have the performative effects
they ostensibly sought was impeded and limited. In this sense, they were
players, imitating a world of action and choices they could not fully realize
(see chapter 6).

Competing Authorities and Inalienable Bodies

Yet there is a provisional quality to characterizing conservative Christians
as players in this latter sense, for political and legal outcomes could have
been, *and may still come to be*, otherwise. But I want to wind back here from
the effects of the conflict to consider the corporeal relations and ravages of
authority that were expressed in the struggle between different sovereign
claims. Protagonists brought both state and God to bear on the question of
whether conservative Christians could be exempt from gay-equality norms,
allowing conservative Christians, in turn, to exercise an exception. And as
expressed through appointed and self-appointed spokespeople, the views

of state and God often seemed to diverge. But while God and the state were invoked as authorities, they were not the only ones to act authoritatively. Importantly for this book, political and governmental authority was assumed, taken up, and cultivated by a wide range of bodies through routine as well as one-off actions. One repeated source of authority involved employers and property owners declaring their right to determine, within legal limits, when an exception must or could be made. Another involved employees asserting a residual authority over the routes and tasks undertaken by their laboring bodies.

Dramas of withdrawal can, in this way, play an important role in forging power's complex arrangements and in shaping which bodies get to determine how withdrawal will unfold. In the case of religious norms, conservative Christian claims to authority oscillated between posing a competing and superior legal order that would allow—indeed, *require*—state law to be breached or suspended, and providing a ground or provision for legitimate accommodation *within* state legal regimes. In his written submission to the European Court of Human Rights on behalf of Gary McFarlane, who was dismissed for refusing to provide psychosexual counseling to lesbian couples, the former Anglican Archbishop Lord Carey declared, "Religious rights are clearly primary rights; religion directs every aspect of an individual's life. It is a comprehensive code of conduct . . . between man and God."[64] Yet while Carey's statement gave voice to a dual system in which religious rights were superior, his claim (like others in this conflict) got made in the course of litigation within secular state courts. And it was here, in these courts, that conservative Christians argued for legal accommodation, for secular law to respect religious law's primacy as a social (or, at least, personal) fact that individuals had (or gave themselves) no choice but to obey. In the Canadian *Riverbend* case, the owners of the guesthouse justified their withdrawal of the two men's booking in terms of their lack of choice. Their lives were accountable to God, and their home was a gift to be used for his ministry. God expected them to exert a level of control over what happened in their home, and allowing gay couples to share a room would cause him offense and shame.[65] Similar claims were made when an American cake maker withheld his services for a gay wedding: "Phillips is a devout Christian. He has explained that his 'main goal in life is to be obedient to' Jesus Christ and Christ's 'teachings.'"[66] Gray and Porter (2015: 385) describe necessity as "a moral concept to release a particular case from the application of the law." For litigating conservative Christians, necessity was a discourse of release that would not suspend the law but generate accommodation within it for those claiming they could not do otherwise.[67]

Yet conservative Christian depictions of necessity were countered by the courts. English courts proved particularly notable in denying not only recognition to a system of dual authority but also in refusing to give Christianity in particular, and religion in general, "special treatment" in antidiscrimination law. In the case of the Christian therapist, McFarlane, who would not counsel same-sex couples, Lord Justice Laws remarked, "The conferment of any legal protection or preference upon a particular substantive moral position on the ground only that it is espoused by the adherents of a particular faith . . . is deeply unprincipled."[68] In the marriage registrar case *Ladele v. London Borough of Islington*, Mr. Justice Elias confirmed that public bodies can require employees to act in accordance with lawful policies; to do otherwise would allow religious belief to act as "a solvent dissolving all inconsistent legal obligations owed to the employer. [G]iven . . . the fact that beliefs may cover a vast range of subjective opinions, the consequences would be extraordinary."[69] English legal doctrine here treated conservative Christians *as if* they had a choice; they could choose *not* to withdraw and so provide an equal service. To the extent they experienced such a choice as impossible, their remaining option was to withdraw from their post (or trade).[70]

While the refusal to defer to the "traditions" and "rich" culture of Christian norms may seem progressive in some respects,[71] English judges in these cases also produced an account of property, contract, and government anchored in the *sovereignty and ownership of the employer*. Property held by the employer made the necessity of withdrawing irrelevant since it was not workers but their employer who acted when labor was undertaken. And since workers did not own their labor once they were employed by someone else, they could not (properly) withhold it. In the Canadian case *Chiang v. Vancouver Board of Education and Others*, in which a school librarian refused to comply with her school's gay-positive initiatives, the court stated, "Ms. Chiang was insubordinate. . . . It is not discriminatory for an employer to require an employee to comply with the lawful directions of management, nor to warn them of the possible consequences of refusing to do so."[72] Employees cannot pick and choose which parts of a job they are prepared to fulfill. In taking a job, the worker has "rented" out their labor; ownership of it, at least temporarily, lies with the employer. It is they who have stamped the employee's work, adding their "imprimatur" so the work becomes theirs (see also chapter 4).[73] What proved striking, then, about conservative Christians' acts of withdrawal was their refusal to accept this situation. Conservative Christians spoke about *following* God's laws, but their actions demonstrated their own, assumed authority in the interpretive and calculated decisions they made to withdraw—decisions that tacitly asserted the inalienability, or only partial alienability, of their labor within secular workplaces. Others might reduce them to a resource (contributing nothing of themselves to what was done), but conservative Christians emphasized the self that remained part of, and responsible for, this labor. Their social subjectivity could not be severed from what they did. As Carole Pateman (2002: 33) remarked, a "worker cannot send along capacities or services *by themselves* to an employer" (emphasis added).[74] But conservative Christian litigants did not stop there. Depicting their bodies as accompanying and not severable from their labor also meant they needed to exercise care and caution in what their bodies did and what they left behind. Since both bore their signature, conservative Christians had a need and a right to exercise control over what their bodies made and where they went.

The Scope and Justification of Withdrawal

I return to this trail of bodily remains shortly, since it also highlights a further set of disagreements over the scope and reach of legitimate withdrawal. Legal disputes about withdrawal have involved a lot of redefinition and line drawing: is a guesthouse commercial or domestic space? Is a wedding cake for a gay couple a gay wedding cake or simply a cake? In the process, divergent notions of social life collide as imaginaries of orderly, bounded, side-by-side difference confront imaginaries of normative wholes, on the one hand, and imaginaries of porous, seeping, intermingling difference, on the other. These imaginaries were certainly shaped by legal doctrine and the parameters of legal argument. However, to reduce their rationalization to mere legal sophistry would be to miss their wider conceptual significance, including for thinking about the state. My argument does not depend on these social rationalities being authentic to (or, indeed, as originating with) those who expressed them. Rather, I am interested in the fundamental questions of governmental shape and form they gesture to and stimulate. In later chapters, I explore these rationalities in relation to the state. Here I want to explore how withdrawal animated contrasting normative imaginaries of the social, beginning with a vision of normative walls, structuring and confining where withdrawal could legitimately occur.

In the legal drama of conservative Christian opposition to gay equality, the challenge of drawing distinctions was engaged in avidly by activists, lawyers, courts, politicians, and academics. Normative distinctions between acceptable and unacceptable withdrawal typically involved one of three concerns: What was the basis for withdrawal? What was withdrawn? And where did withdrawal occur? The first was the subject of extensive discussion, especially in the U.S. context, as legal players and commentators argued over the difference (and capacity to distinguish) between identity (or status-based) discrimination and practice-based forms of discrimination, which were seen as more legitimate, at least at first glance.[75] Earlier versions of this legal debate focused on the split between gay being and gay doing, where gay doing took the form of coming out and having sex (see, e.g., Eaton 1995; Stychin 1996). Subsequently, marriage and marriage-equality speech acts became the things from which conservative Christians demanded the right to refrain.[76] Routinely in court, conservative Christian traders proclaimed their willingness—and, indeed, their history—in providing goods for gay customers but felt obliged to draw a limit when it came to provisions defined as supporting and endorsing unacceptable activities, such as same-sex marriage or engaging in "compelled speech."[77] One Minnesota couple, the Larsens, sought to make videos for clients "promoting their view of marriage."[78] The Larsens explained that they would "'gladly work with all people' regardless of sexual orientation or religious belief, but they decline[d] requests for their creative services unless 'they [could] use their story-telling talents and editorial control to convey only messages they [were] comfortable conveying given their religious beliefs.'"[79] In other words, the Larsens would refuse to "promote any conception of marriage other than as a lifelong institution between one man and one woman."[80] In another case, a printing business in Kentucky was asked to create customized T-shirts for a pride festival.[81] The outfitter, a Christian, is quoted as saying, "It's not that we have a sign on the front door that says, 'No Gays Allowed.' . . . We'll work with anybody. But if there's a specific message that conflicts with my convictions, then I can't promote that."[82] Like the inalienable labor just discussed, the notion of compelled speech assumes that speech retains a relationship to the authoring body even when speech has been produced for another. In other words, against the assumption that "compelled speech" cannot be meaningfully "owned" by those forced to produce it, since its very description as "compelled" suggests no authorial agency has been vested in it by its creator, conservative

Christians depicted proleptic speech (what would have been expressed had they not refused) as remaining uncomfortably theirs, in the process unsettling the nexus between speech and its purchaser. Unable to fully own what they have purchased, since it still "belongs" constitutively—if not as a commodity (Cooper 2014: chap. 6)—to the speech's compelled creator, the buyer becomes re-envisioned and displaced. With the purchase no longer erasing all preexisting ties of production, the purchaser comes to resemble a discursive foster parent, carrying speech (on T-shirts, cakes, and so on) produced *and indelibly marked* by someone else.[83]

Intersecting these distinctions based on the character of the provided good and its different ties to those creating and consuming it is a further set, concerned with the location or siting of withdrawal. Here, the distribution of public and private comes into play, with its legal assumption of greater tolerance for intolerance if it can be defined as legitimately private. One striking feature of this legal drama (and of other legal dramas to do with discrimination) is the legal alignment of the marketplace with the public domain rather than with the private life to which liberal sociopolitical discourse typically ties it. Emphasizing the necessary and legitimate constraints placed on *sellers* who seek to discriminate on sexuality grounds (despite legal norms supporting religious freedom), the courts in these sexuality cases to date have largely reaffirmed the *public* marketplace, as being clearly delineated and apart from the private domain of the home or the religious domain of community membership and worship.[84] In domestic contexts, private sovereignty may hold sway such that householders can decide, for instance, whom to admit. However, as the court stated in *Riverbend*, "While the business was operated by individuals with sincere religious beliefs respecting same-sex couples, and out of . . . their personal residence, it was still a commercial activity."[85] Entering the secular marketplace (and the marketplace largely appears in this drama as presumptively secular), providers hold themselves out as treating all (prospective) customers fairly. They cannot take certain goods provisionally out of circulation by making them unavailable for customers with legally protected characteristics. Indeed, several judges commented disapprovingly about organizations that deliberately downplayed their religious and antigay beliefs to gain a "competitive advantage in the market."[86] Having done so, litigants could not subsequently assert their religious sensibilities to legally justify their refusal to provide gay-positive services.

Yet against the liberal spatio-functional norms of division and compartmentalization that litigants faced, and often found themselves obliged to adopt (or adapt), was a quite different set of imaginaries.[87] In the United States, conservative Christians opposed the publicly secular character of the marketplace by arguing that companies were entitled to express religious and moral agendas.[88] Drawing on Ronald Colombo's concept of "religiously expressive corporations," Rex Ahdar (2016: 4) describes such companies as "eschew[ing] a rigid dualism between the sacred and the secular spheres in favor of a holistic view of life. . . . [F]aith and work are integrated and one's faith is expressed through one's work" (see also Rivers 2007). This position was advanced in several of the legal challenges discussed here. In one, *Brush and Nib Studio v. City of Phoenix*, an American calligrapher and card-making partnership challenged a Phoenix law prohibiting discrimination on the grounds it would have to "create art" that "celebrat[ed] same-sex wedding ceremonies" in the same way that it celebrated "opposite-sex" ones.[89] According to their complaint, the applicants could not "separate their religious duties, religious identity, or religious beliefs into work and non-work, secular and sacred, private and public. . . . [They] must live *authentic, holistic Christian lives.*"[90]

The claim that being Christian is not a Sunday outfit that can be put on and taken off resonates with all-inclusive approaches to religiosity.[91] While a refusal to delimit the reach of Christianity is a well-known aspect of conservative and evangelical forms, what proved striking in this legal drama was the way an expansive, limitless imaginary informed discussion and claims relating to very different kinds of bodies: from the broad social body to particular human and organizational forms. In the case of Christian organizations, "wholeness" advocates argued that organizations should be legally respected as forms of *private* government or communal authority, structured through internal "social contracts." Self-governance for conservative Christian organizations—indeed, their very survival as self-determining distinct entities—depended on the right to their own rules (or laws) and the right to exclude those who broke them.[92] The care organization Christian Horizons argued that if it could not ensure that all members and employees "adhere[d] to the core faith beliefs, then the organization [would] lose its unique character and . . . die."[93] Gay litigants might claim that their sexual self was a private part not given over to the religious organization to which they belonged, or as impinging on it.

However, from the perspective of conservative Christian organizations, gay sexual identities and acts (such as taking a boyfriend to a school prom) brought something undesired and infectious into the organizational body, muddying its integrity and mission.[94]

The question of bodies, and how to think about them, as I explore later, is important for considering the state—not just how the state treats other bodies, individual or organizational, but its own embodied depiction (see chapters 2–5). What emerges in this legal drama is a self-depiction of organized bodies—organized Christian bodies but not just these—as hierarchical and whole. At the same time, these are bodies obliged to fight to prevent others from entering or themselves from seeping, leaving a trail of where they have been, and what they, in turn, have been in(to). The depiction of bodily relations here is complex. In one sense, refusal and retraction support an imaginary of separate (and separable) bodies, where things can be withdrawn in ways that do not reconstitute the withdrawing or withdrawn-from body in the process. At the same time, withdrawal is opposed on the grounds that those withdrawn from are, in some way, undone; their wholeness and well-being dependent on attachments now lost or voided. This vulnerability also runs through justifications for withdrawal anchored in an anxious imaginary of the traces that contact can generate. In chapter 5, I take up these traces to think further about the erotic state. What is striking about these traces, however, is their bilateral quality. Providing a service (from a Gay Pride T-shirt to wedding photography) leaves something behind in the receiving body, but it also attaches something to the one who provides. Fear that gay-positive goods and services would constitute a form of endorsement,[95] with very real traces, was expressed explicitly in *Willock*, in which a photographer refused to provide services for a same-sex commitment ceremony on the grounds that, "as an artist, *she became a part of the events which she photographed.*"[96] Indeed, here the claim went beyond the fear of leaving a trace to a fear of becoming lodged and embedded in the undesirable event produced.[97] At the same time, conservative Christian litigants suggested they would also be contaminated by the contact. If the photographer became part of the events she photographed, the photographs of the event would (might?) also become a part of her—or, at least, of her professional corpus (see chapter 2).

Concerns about unsought leakages and things sticking disturb normative liberal imaginaries of clean divisions, as well as imaginaries of a controllable wholeness.[98] But it is not only conservative Christians who worried about discharges, adhesions, and leaking, porous bodies. Liberal public authorities expressed similar concerns. In the *Christian Legal Society* litigation, American law schools worried that registration and recognition of local CLS chapters, which refused to welcome gay students, would attach (or be seen as attaching) the societies to law schools in ways that would affect how both they and the society were seen (see chapter 3).[99] Likewise, Transport for London's refusal to carry "ex-gay" advocacy posters was anchored in concern that gluing such posters to its buses would, in turn, glue the public provider to right-wing Christian politics (see chapter 5).[100] Many liberal public bodies' concerns about stickiness related to their staff. While they worried about being attached to the out-of-office actions of conservative Christian employees (see Reyes 1995),[101] liberal bodies also fretted about what might, in turn, stick to them, carried into their organizations through their workers. Just as conservative Christian organizations objected to the contaminating effects from openly gay members, liberal state and public bodies agonized about the contaminating effects of off-color, out-of-office conduct sticking to employing subjects. Fear that divisions would not hold and that sticky animus would enter the workplace is interesting in light of the conflict over workers' labor discussed earlier. In this legal drama, liberal public bodies resisted treating workers' labor as belonging to individual workers, but they nevertheless identified such labor as colored by the wider life of the staff member in question. In this sense, they recognized labor as carrying with it not only the laboring person, but also the laboring person's outside-of-work life. So homophobic, racist, or misogynistic utterances on Facebook, or expressed in other visible non-work activities, could contaminate, or undermine, the "proper" work that staff carried out. Where liberal public bodies disagreed with conservative Christians was in refusing to treat the inhabiting of one's labor as giving rise to social property claims—that is, to an entitlement on the part of the worker to control the work performed.[102]

Concluding Remarks

On its face a mere subtraction from what once was, withdrawal is an important governmental and political technique. This chapter has traced its scope, form, and conditions within a legal drama that combined the *material* exercise of withdrawal's power through removing (or withholding) goods, services, and recognition, along with an asserted "I will not."

This assertion can be read as an expression of force or sovereignty; yet, typically in this drama, it drew on the subaltern power of bodies, voice, and labor, in claiming deference to one authority while another was resisted. The tension between asserting authority and asserting deference to another authority—in conditions in which conservative Christians wanted both to *be* the exception and to enact it—is an important aspect of this conflict. Equally important is the tangled, reciprocating, but also dynamic, character of power's exercise.

Power's exercise was certainly very far from equal. However, in conditions in which both the subjects and the objects of withdrawal were constantly shifting, the production of an exception cannot be reduced to a stable narrative of one sovereign body abandoning another to a paired-back miserable existence. Instead, constant shifts in power (and sovereignty) took effect. At one moment, the bodies subjected to withdrawal were lesbians and gay men; at another moment, they were conservative Christians; and in a third moment, they were public authorities. At one moment, withdrawal was anchored in the defense and pursuit of a seamless normative existence; at another, it related to narrowly circumscribed activities. At one moment, bodies appeared as joined or fused; at other times, they were discrete and separate entities, sometimes seeping and porous, and sometimes sealed and contained. At one moment, the sovereign authority was religious law; at other times, it was the liberal state (with both, in turn, fluctuating between being cast as obligatory or voluntary, orderly or excessive), as other authorities—employers, community organizations, workers, citizens—also came on stage. Finally, while power appeared at times as a top-down unitary force, at other moments it seemed far more dispersed, as different bodies demonstrated the goods they could make available, and the power they "held" in the social landscape, through exercising the right (which, of course, proved a contested right) to withdraw them.

We can read this legal drama of resistance to liberal gay equality for what it may teach us about right-wing dissidence when confronted by new state norms. As such, this episode is instructive for thinking about antihegemonic currents and the need for left theory to engage more deeply with *reactionary* challenges to progressive, hegemony-forming projects. But the conservative character of the opposition here demonstrated toward liberal gay politics is less important for my discussion of the state than the ongoing, dynamic shifts of status, access, and belonging; and the parallel, reciprocating, and sometimes mimetic movement of bodies withdrawing recognition, membership, and public goods. Emphasizing these parallels may prove unhelpful for a *critical* analysis keen to stress the location, specificity, and power of different social forces. However, if our aim is to reimagine the state in more plural, quotidian ways, the relationship between bodies and parts—in practicing care, responsibility, and activism—along with what gets entered, joined, retracted, and severed as bodies interact, becomes central. The discussion in this chapter may seem some distance from the realm of a reimagined state. The challenge for the chapters that follow is to show how this legal drama of withdrawal, with its subjects, authorities, properties, imagined worlds, and bodies, can open up new paths for thinking about what states could come to mean and be, paths with the potential to support a progressive, transformative politics.

TWO. Retrieving Dissident State Parts

We need to question the traditional figure of resistance as a subject who stands *outside* the state and refuses its demands. —TIMOTHY MITCHELL, "The Limits of the State"

What does a state feel like? Standard critical ways to address this question take the nation as the state scale. They explore the sensation of domination and control that oppressive states create as they churn through social life, sorting and selecting, creating detritus and chucking stuff (often stuff they once created) away. In the legal drama of this book, conservative Christians repeatedly denounced the state as authoritarian and overbearing. Speaking in the 2007 parliamentary debates against new British regulations to outlaw antigay discrimination, the Archbishop of York declared, "It now seems that a legal sausage machine is being creat[ed] . . . requiring all of us to go through it and come out the other end, sanitized and with our consciences surgically removed."[1] For conservative Christians this was the overreaching state, using its power and authority to colonize communal and domestic life, to "vilif[y]" Christians,[2] and to impose "a new moral establishment . . . on dissenters" (Rivers 2007: 52). In the same parliamentary debate in which the Archbishop of York spoke, the Bishop of Winchester remarked, "I greatly regret the fact that the Government chose . . . to coerce the churches and others to accept as the norm for this society . . . patterns of living and of family life that many people conscientiously believe are less than the best, less than the most healthy, and less than God's will for humankind."[3]

Conservative Christian depictions of an overweening state have garnered attention; far less noted have been the normative imaginaries of British equality advocates. Here, notions of democratic legitimacy converged with normative expectations of compliance with top-down, institutional decision making.[4] As Labour Shadow Minister for Equalities Kate Green remarked, countering conservative arguments that public bodies should accommodate Christian "conscientious objections" to same-sex marriage:

> That is one of the things that goes with being a public servant. One is there to fulfil the requirements of the law as the law of the land stands at the time. . . . [T]he idea that someone might consciously apply for a job as a registrar with the full intention of not carrying out the role in full, because it conflicted with their religious beliefs is not conscientious objection, it is deliberately setting out to subvert the employment to which one is applying. . . . *My fundamental point is that, if one wishes to be appointed by the state and employed by the state to carry out the functions of the state, one does not have the choice to pick and choose which of those functions one will or will not fulfil.*[5]

Performing state functions as a public official is to participate in maintaining a consistent machine in which the lumpiness of different human working parts has been minimized. While conservative Christians denounced state-enforced "moral mono-culturalism" (Parkinson 2011: 294–95), progressives, such as Green, argued for uniformity and discipline in the management and delivery of public services.

Yet despite differences in their qualitative and normative assessments of what the British state was doing, and whether what it was doing was right, conservative Christians and advocates of liberal equality nonetheless converged in their understanding of the state as a vertical structure, able (rightly or wrongly) to reach out, exert authority, and advance its agenda.

In other words, both sides adopted versions of what in this chapter I call the standard state perspective (ssp) on (neo)liberal contemporary state formations. What I therefore want to do in the discussion that follows is take up this legal drama of withdrawal as an opportunity to think away from this perspective and, so, to think about the state in other ways. I am interested in ways of recomposing and relocating the state that move toward an account of it (recognizing the very idea of an "it" here is problematic) as socially embedded: as society in its governing dimension.[6] Taking the ssp as my "straw polity," I want to think *against* its assumptions, rereading the claims and actions of participants in this conflict (which at first glance may seem to prop up and support a standard perspective). Instead of taking participants' assertions and experiences as reinforcing a bounded, hierarchical conception of the state—a state that reaches out to colonize civil society—I want to read their claims, and the legal episode more generally, in ways that orient it to a more horizontally embedded, heterogeneous conception of the state. This is not a claim about what the state *really* is; nor is it a claim necessarily about an overarching best interpretation. When it comes to critique, the state conception I am advancing may prove less useful, diffusing the extent of coercive state power and blunting some of the ways governmental authority is exercised unequally. But this book starts from the premise that different conceptions of the state are needed to support different endeavors, projects, and conversations. Since my particular focus is how to fashion a conception of the state that might be productive for a progressive transformative politics, the state's *potential* relationship to equality and social justice is asserted rather than denied, even as this requires different imaginings and enactments of what it means to be a state.

Making up the State

The composition of the state can be approached in various ways, and, of course, no definitive answer to its makeup is possible. It depends on how the conceptual cutting of the state is done: as the state gets imagined; enacted; and reorganized—a process usually entered in the middle. In chapter 3, I explore more deeply what it could mean to be a state, focusing on the differentiation of state from non-state bodies, as well as the tensions between internal diversity and external division that come to the fore when we think, in more plural fashion, about states. But here I want to delve into the institutional texture of nation-states, such as Britain's, to consider what makes states up. Assemblage perspectives, attuned to heterogeneous relations (see, e.g., Allen 2011; Müller 2015; Müller and Schurr 2016), and some of the state conceptualizing to emerge from actor-network theory (ANT) are helpful here.[7] Despite differences in orientation, both account for the diverse, contingent, sometimes surprising parts that assemble when states act. However, my aim is not to understand state *action*—to trace the elements that come together to produce stable practices or even unexpected events[8]—but, rather, to think about political bodies as sites of responsibility and what this may ontologically require. In other words, my aim is not simply to analyze *what is done* and so to determine which connections and divisions *really matter*. Instead, I want to consider different connections and divisions to trace a way of thinking about what *is*—oriented to the institutional assumption of public responsibility as something that is open-ended, forward- (as well as backward-) oriented, and reflexive.

Approaching states as social constellations, elements such as systems, resources, laws, things, spaces, policies, talk, fantasies, people, and norms play an important part. What I want to focus on here are those less dominant state parts, the parts often dismissed, which this legal drama of conservative Christian withdrawal interestingly foregrounds. While we do not *have to* think about them as state parts, my analysis is premised on, and advances, the value of doing so: of bringing fleeting, dissident, minority ideas, forces, and conflict into our conception of the state. Doing so supports a way of approaching the state oriented to heterogeneity, to bottom-up and horizontal effects, to the diffuse character of state power and opportunity, and to the ways states condense and are embedded within wider social relations. State embedding is often mentioned in academic work, but it is typically treated as meaning that states reflect the interests and agendas of dominant forces (where the balance of forces gets reduced to the forces that "win" the balance, albeit often in a particular apparatus) rather than the bric-a-brac arrangements and encounters of different forces, beliefs, and values—the weak, fleeting, and subjugated, as well as the strong, enduring, and dominant.

To explore the contours of a more heterogeneous, embedded conception, I want to juxtapose it, as I have said, with the standard state perspective (SSP) on contemporary (neo)liberal states, which I trace briefly before introducing an alternative account. My aim is to develop this alternative account through the legal drama of this book, focusing in particular on what makes up the state, what the state makes up, and the character of the relationship between the two. As the standard perspective has been exhaustively discussed, my account here will be brief, focusing on three elements that are central to the discussion that follows. The first is the normative presumption of an orderly and vertical approach to decision making in which lower-level actors carry out the policy decisions of superordinates, with senior officials in turn accountable to politicians. Keith Darden (2008: 37) writes, "It is widely agreed that the successful establishment of a system of administrative compliance is essential to all other tasks the state might perform. Without securing the loyalty and obedience of the officials in their various administrative hierarchies, states cannot collect taxes, make war, secure public order, or impose rule across their territorial domains, nor can they enforce law, property rights, or contracts." Democratic legitimacy, as well as effective state power, it is suggested depends on this division of labor and responsibility, organized around electoral accountability, professional expertise, and rational, lawful action.

The second key dimension of the SSP is the normative presumption that human state parts—as impersonal roles within routinized relatively stable systems—are stripped of particularity. While this claim usually refers to bureaucrats, its logic applies to other kinds of state workers, as well. Normative expectations of fairness and neutrality are also reinforced by depictions of their absence. Progressive critics, for instance, have long argued that civil servants are affected by the interests and perspectives of their role (Bevir and Rhodes 2006: 6); how, particularly as senior officials, they bring the agendas and outlooks of dominant classes *into* state practice. This critique has tended to focus on economic class. Nirmal Puwar's (2001) influential work on Britain's senior civil service exposes the power of racialized social markers, such as whiteness. In the legal drama over conservative Christian withdrawal, liberal state actors argued for the continuing significance of conventional notions of neutrality and fairness against Christian claims that new sexual political agendas had displaced them. According to the conservative writer Stephen Baskerville (2011: 97), traditional expectations of abstract impersonal roles were vanishing as "sexual agendas" altered "job descriptions to depart from the ideological neutrality with which civil servants are normally expected to perform their duties." Baskerville (2011: 98) tells the story of a gay police officer who arrested a street preacher for homophobic speech: "'I am a homosexual, I find that offensive,' officer Sam Adams apparently told McAlpine before arresting him." While the reported speech comes from the arrested McAlpine, what is important for our purposes is how such stories are used by conservative Christians as evidence of liberal state bias. They are also used to justify conservative Christian demands that their beliefs should have a place too within public services, such as social work (see, e.g., Hodge 2002).[9] In making such claims, conservative Christians highlight (if unintentionally) the relative absence in SSPs of minority interests, more generally, when it comes to understanding state formations' makeup (even as what counts as a minority will and does change). It is this absence and the value of making minor-stream, subordinate, and dissident interests visible that I take up in my discussion.

The third element of the SSP I want to address is how the *provision* but not the *receipt* of public regulation, services, and goods is depicted as a constitutive part of the state's composition. Receiving public goods (and the multiplicity of places where receipt happens), while extensively discussed within social policy, is rarely incorporated into accounts of state form—as forming part of what it is to be a state. Even the contemporary emphasis on public participation and coproduction, with its assumption and stress on bringing publics *into partnership with* the state, too often assumes their ontological separation and distinctness. Stripping service-based *relationships*, along with those people, things, and places subjected to state power and authority, from what it is to be a state is commonplace. Rarely remarked on, it nevertheless comes into relief when contrasted with standard liberal accounts of the *market*—a structure deemed to incorporate buyers as much as sellers and so treated as far more dynamic, interactive, and relational. Not all academic and other commentary on contemporary (neo)liberal states, of course, signs up to this standard account—an account whose territorial ambitions and normativity shape and assert themselves in the assessment of other states as well. Anthropology, organizational sociology, political geography, governance studies, and critical social policy, among other fields, have produced more richly inhabited, dynamically textured conceptions of the state, as this book explores. I therefore want to briefly trace three rejoinders to the SSP to emerge from these literatures, and then turn to the legal drama of this book to explore what it brings to these more critical accounts—specifically, how conservative Christian withdrawal can challenge us to rethink the relationship between dissident politics and the state.

In her critical account of Australia's federal interventions into Aboriginal communities in the Northern Territories in 2007, Tess Lea (2012: 110) describes the state as "inhabited by beings who think, feel, emote and make meaning within the worlds they are symbiotically shaped by *and which they help reproduce.*" Lea's account of off-piste official agency resonates with other studies of downstream policy-making, which read the routines, strategies and choices made in frontline service provision as part of the policy-*making* and not just implementation process (Barrett 2004) in conditions where street-level actors are also interpreted as decision makers. Street-level decision making is the first challenge I want to consider to a standard vertical state account. It suggests public sector workers (and other deliverers of public services, including for our purposes adoption and foster parents) assume some authority to determine how and to whom services should be offered in ways that deploy, and sometimes overstep, the formal discretion they are given.[10] Steven Maynard-Moody and Michael Musheno (2000: 332) describe how street-level workers "operat[ing] at the boundary between citizens and the state . . . profoundly shape the definitions of both through the actions they take and the norms they invoke."[11] In their account, street-level actors are officials whose formally limited authority does not stop them from making practical, improvised decisions involving "moral reasoning" and assessments of clients' needs as they decide who "deserves" help beyond the bare minimum and who does not (Maynard-Moody and Musheno 2000: 332, 350–51).[12]

What also emerges in Maynard-Moody and Musheno's (2000) account is how state-centered scholars and elite government figures perceive policy formation very differently to the understandings of street-level actors themselves. While the former treat frontline workers as carrying out policies made elsewhere, Maynard-Moody and Musheno (2000) describe workers as perceiving things otherwise. For them, state systems constitute a "shadowy and diffuse" presence in their own frontline decision making. "To our surprise, the cops, teachers, and counselors whose stories we collected rarely, if ever, referenced policy or rules when making normative judgments. Moreover, they rarely, if ever, described themselves as policy implementers or even government workers, although all of the street-level workers in our study received their paychecks from government organizations" (Maynard-Moody and Musheno 2012: 17). Policy and law provide resources and constraints, and while elected officials can be helpful, their "meddling" may also be experienced as obstructive to staff making decisions.

Accounts of street-level action unsettle an SSP which assumes street-level workers are little more than an operational conduit for higher-up others. Emphasizing the impact of frontline workers reframes accounts of *how* policy happens, foregrounding the unexpected influence of those expected merely to "deliver." But what makes this finding particularly significant are the normative (rather than purely causational) questions it provokes about the "proper" distribution of governing roles.[13] Arguments about democracy go both ways. Local discretion, particularly when "grabbed," may seem to thwart representative democratic decision making "higher up," as the quoted remarks of the once Shadow Minister for Equalities Kate Green suggest. Yet academic work also presents the devolution of policy and governing as valuable, allowing local and minority needs to be more effectively expressed and realized while also encouraging creativity, responsive judgment, and ethical self-regulation (see, e.g., Goss 2001).[14]

Frontline, non-elite actors make a difference to policy, and what it is that states both are and do.[15] Yet, as the legal drama over conservative Christian resistance to gay equality demonstrates, much of the discussion surrounding religious actors' refusal concerns its normative legitimacy. This discussion is important. However, questions of "what should be" need to also make room for the mediating factors and conditions that affect what is possible and thinkable. My interest here is in whether we should consider such refusal as making up part of the state, and how we should think about the objections (and other reactions) that conservative Christian refusal, in turn, generated. Certainly, we can think about the withdrawal of religious registrars, teachers, social workers, therapists, doctors, police officers, and firefighters from gay clients as doing policy on the ground. However, what precipitated many of these conflicts, or caused them to escalate, was the refusal of colleagues and managers to "let things go."[16] Rather than accommodating or ignoring withdrawal by their coworkers, their interventions constituted a further twist in the operation—but also in the meaning and form—of state policies and procedures. In other words, if street-level action constitutes policy, then the vigorously contested interactions around street-level action constitute—or, at least, contribute to—policy also. And if this follows for policy-making, it arguably follows for the composition of state procedures and form as well. But if a range of actors contribute to making up the state, what about the *non-elite interests, beliefs, and commitments* (religious and political, as well as role-based) that such actors bear? How do they shape and get inserted into state formations?[17]

Work on contemporary feminist and gay state activism has explored the presence of non-elite interests and beliefs within public bodies. Janet Newman (2012a) addressed this in her research on three generations of British-based feminist activists moving politically and professionally over several decades between nongovernmental organizations, grass-roots activism, and state institutional spaces. Newman's work traces how feminist political commitments informed state projects and action, from stimulating new pro-feminist policy agendas to being carried as personal beliefs by feminist workers into state arenas.[18] In the related case of state sexual orientation policies, particularly at municipal levels, minority identifications as lesbian or gay not only provided staff with an impetus to act,[19] but the very identifications themselves came to function as a state resource or part. In some cases where councils refused to act or dragged their feet, the energy of openly gay officials proved an important resistant or challenging state part. In other cases, gay officials' personal experience and confidence in the "issues" constituted an authorized, in-house municipal resource.[20] *R on the Application of Core Issues Trust v. Transport for London and Another* illustrates this well.[21] Discussed further in chapter 5, the case arose after Transport for London turned down Christian "ex-gay, post-gay" advertisements for its buses.[22] In the course of reaching a decision about whether to run the ads, a senior gay employee at the Greater London Assembly was asked for his views in order to ascertain how offensive other gay people might find them: "Mr. Harri explained in his witness statement that he thought 'Mr. Ritterband, as a gay man, would be able to bring a helpful perspective to the acceptability of the advertisement' so he emailed him . . . asking him 'how offensive do you find it?' Mr. Ritterband emailed in reply . . . saying 'Very offensive. You can't be "cured" of being gay. And to even hint it's an illness is pretty foul.'"[23] There is a lot we might question here, including the presumption of gay immutability and the responsibility placed on a gay official to speak expertly on behalf of a diverse population. We might also question the extent to which workers appreciate having aspects of their social identity requisitioned by their state employers. In their work on the experiences of lesbian and gay public sector staff, Fiona Colgan and Tessa Wright (2011: 565–66) describe how the staff they researched, at times, felt pressurized to act as unpaid "out" policy champions in conditions where leveraging their sexual identities also fed opponents' claims that policies were not neutral but reflected the "special interests" of those developing them.[24]

I return to the insertion of minority beliefs into state processes later. However, the third key challenge to the SSP concerns the omission of clients, users, and user spaces from a state account. In their groundbreaking anthropology, Veena Das and Deborah Poole (2004: 3) ask how the margins, "with all their practices and politics of life," come to "shape . . . the political, regulatory, and disciplinary practices that constitute, somehow, that thing we call 'the state.'" I want to ask: should we think of these margins, and the people and things that make them up, as *part* of state formations or as independent external entities whose actions merely have an impact on the state or on what it does? Joe Painter's (2006: 765) influential work on the "prosaic state" highlights the labor regular folk undertake in supporting state processes, including as witnesses and jurors, "enrolled as participants in processes of statization," in an analysis that identifies how porous and enveloping the state can be read as being. We might also think of service *users* and not just service *providers* as elements in the state's composition. Talking about "users" alongside other "enrolled participants" and staff is important because, as I discuss below, it opens up pathways for discerning how dissident values and beliefs become part of the state. Focusing on users also draws attention to the many places where regulatory processes are *felt* (see McDermont 2019), including among actors enacting state norms and state imaginaries in their more-than-institutional encounters.

Street-level actors, dissident beliefs and commitments, and the users and many places where public provision and regulation are experienced and felt—the parts not normally given a part in ssps, to use the terms of Jacques Rancière (2010)—suggest the need for a more textured conception of what makes up the state. This is not to negate systemic or structural factors (see Jessop 1990, 2016). Routinized and institutional dimensions of the state will typically prove more powerful than fleeting, dissident parts. However, turning *toward* the fleeting, dissident parts is important to appreciate the presence, capacity, and effects of minority and oppositional forces. In thinking about the state's contribution to transformative progressive politics, this presence is an important source of counterhegemonic as well as antihegemonic practice. In other words, it may advance and extend new norms, but, as the legal drama over conservative Christian withdrawal reveals, it may also resist them. As I stressed in the book's introduction, my aim is not to support or romanticize antigay religious withdrawal. However, its consideration is fruitful for thinking about the place of antihegemonic state action. Here, we are not talking (at least, not primarily) about street-level discretion being exercised, as in Maynard-Moody and Musheno's work, to better assess and respond to the presenting client's needs.

Rather, non-elite, subversive (if conservative) identities are engaged in downstream decision making and policy in ways that create bumps and disruptions in the everyday life of the state and in ways that also seem to make a (fleeting) difference—not least by providing an impetus for other state parts to reassert what and who they are. Conservative Christians' downstream decisions are not private "decisions" but institutional and policy ones as participants bring personally valued norms and attitudes to self-style their mode of working in conditions in which refusal rather than action constitutes a "doing." If behaving *inclusively* as a marriage registrar, family panel magistrate, police officer, and doctor have become routine (albeit in ways that are precarious, uneven and politically vulnerable), withdrawal has now become the *event* (see chapter 1). Indeed, in relation to procedures such as same-sex marriage, which have become highly institutionalized in a number of jurisdictions, causing discretion to be limited and hard to officially don, *embodied* refusal or withdrawal may be the only effective (if short-lived) way to exercise street-level policy-making.

Dissident Identities and Beliefs: Politics in the State

In their critical account of "public servants" claiming (and assuming) a legal right to withdraw from providing services to gay people, Bruce Mac-Dougall and Donn Short (2010: 152, emphasis added) suggest such refusal "injects those *religious attitudes* beyond the particular employee and into the government itself."[25] State officials, such as marriage registrars, insert more, then, than just their own objections or refusal. According to MacDougall and Short (2010), in the process, they also insert their "religious attitudes" or, we might say, their values and beliefs more generally. Across the book's many episodes of withdrawal, Christian beliefs and values erupted onto the scene in different ways.[26] But what appears in many of the cases relating to Christian state employees and clients is their quiet arrival, carried in by state actors who cannot (or who refuse to) "take them on and off."[27]

One case to demonstrate this is *Johns v. Derby City Council*.[28] The Johns were a married Pentecostal couple who wanted to become respite foster carers but refused to assure Derby Council, the English Midlands municipality responsible for their foster placement, that they would present gay and hetero sexualities as equally valid alternatives to children in their care.[29] The written record of the assessing social worker and her manager note their concern that the Johns' "views did not equate with the Fostering

Standards which require carers to value individuals equally and to promote diversity."[30] As a result of their concerns, the local council suspended the Johns' application, a decision the court upheld. While the Johns promised to "love" regardless of a fostered child's sexuality, their affective claims failed to make headway against the thick regulatory edifice of national minimum standards, statutory guidance, legislation, and case law. Following the legal decision against them, the Johns wrote a public letter formally requesting that the council reinstate and progress their application to become foster carers. They wrote: "You know that we would love and care for any child in our care and you are aware of our views on sexual ethics."[31]

The Johns' repeated turn to "love" echoes the warm emotions often uttered by conservative Christians in this legal drama, paradoxical in many ways since professed claims to love are being here used to justify exclusion, discrimination, and abandonment (see chapter 1).[32] In this foster care case, we might think of the promise to love as a kind of charm, a device intended to magically reorient and reanimate proceedings.[33] But it is not only love that is brought from the sphere of domestic intimacy into public life. The explicit, publicly claimed inability to treat gay sexuality as a valid choice also caused the Johns' Christian beliefs about child-raising to no longer be of solely personal concern. If we treat their refusal to care for gay sexuality as a "street-level" policy limit, establishing what is and is not possible for the Johns to do on behalf of (and in the place of) the state, we can see how religious rationalizations come to be stitched into the detailed microfabric of the fostering process. If expressing gay animus had remained uncontroversial, if law and policy had continued to discriminate against openly gay foster parents and teenagers, their stance would have had little effect. However, inserting religious beliefs in this particular time and place caused minor consternation. The Johns' application was closed, reopened, and then suspended; letters between social services and the Johns were exchanged; phone conversations were held; meetings were undertaken, and further reports were produced. Meanwhile the Johns gave media interviews, taking up their part in a wider Christian litigation movement.[34]

I want to draw on Rancière's (1999) account of the relationship between politics and police to consider how the misplaced expression of love led to the suspension rather than advancement of the Johns' fostering application. Rancière (1999: 29) uses the concept of "police" to identify "an order of bodies that defines the allocation of ways of doing, ways of being, and ways of saying." Police, in Davide Panagia's (2018: 51) words, "govern the movement and flow of energies."[35] As such, "police" resonates with those conceptions of the state that emphasize doing rather than being (see Chambers 2011).[36] Working with terms other than Rancière's, Marc Stears (2012: 10, 38) describes the state as "an agent of standardisation . . . creat[ing] order out of disorder." In this episode, the order and classificatory frameworks of national standards, statutory guidance, and legislation met the Johns' "love"—an affect we might align with Rancière's conception of politics. Rancière treats politics as the challenging of the police order, its verticality and smooth flow, by those who are not counted (or, at least, not in the terms they choose or prefer). Police and politics might suggest distinct processes, each in their own proper space. However, more useful for our purposes are perspectives, such as Samuel Chambers' (2011), that treat police and politics as interactive and entangled. Politics does not happen *outside of* the police order, within its own separate terrain in relation to its own separate objects, but is bound up with the police order as the unplanned, often disruptive encounter between egalitarian and police logics (Rancière 1999: 31–32). In this sense, like the Johns' repeated professions of love, politics constitutes the making "impure" of institutional governing (Chambers 2011: 305). This impurity doesn't necessarily produce a new hybrid unity (Chambers 2011: 310)—with its particular mix of politics and police. Rather, what it produces is an ongoing dynamic of confrontation where the distributions that the police order generates are reframed and restaged.[37]

The staging of a confrontation between police and politics, through inserting dissident norms and affect into state networks, runs through many episodes of conservative Christian refusal and withdrawal. By refusing to provide a service as the law seems to require, conservative Christians oppose the law's classifications and distributions. They challenge the inclusive "benign" cataloging wrought by antidiscrimination law, which claims, as in Britain, to protect everyone according to such "characteristics" as gender, race, marital status, age, disability, and sexuality. Conservative Christians question the law's proclaimed certainty (on the grounds it masks the provisional and changing character of protections and their grounds); they also question its proclaimed coherence (in denial of its own immanent inconsistency). If equality is a commanding principle, then this should include equality for them, too.[38] "Taking part in an activity that doesn't belong to them" (Panagia 2018: x), even as they are expected to take part, conservative Christians demand their concerns, and the religious tenets they follow, be heard as reason rather than as "noise." In so doing, they assert, even *prefigure*, a world in which their arguments and qualification "to speak" are recognized as valid, while knowing as they make their claims (and, indeed, make their claims to demonstrate that they know) that their status is one that has grown fragile within liberal political discourse.[39]

Writing on dissent often assumes its left-wing character. By contrast, this book centers conservative challenges to a "police order" of liberal antidiscrimination codes, as Christian magistrates, public sector managers, and foster parents bring their heterodox beliefs about religious sin or children's developmental need for "complementary" gendered parental roles into state formations.[40] As the Johns' case illustrates, unauthorized viewpoints do not have to enter the state through force. For the most part, conservative Christians have not pushed their way into state formations or processes; their beliefs and commitments are present through highly authorized formats, introduced as applicants in a procedure or as employees. While the beliefs themselves may have proven less welcome, once present (having accompanied ostensibly welcome bodies into state processes), conservative Christian beliefs become part of the tangled network of state action, shaping what happens. But conservative Christian beliefs can also be read as becoming part of the state in another respect: when action based on conservative Christian beliefs is held up by, and takes shape through, states as a result of actors drawing on the resources and opportunities state formations make available.[41]

The support that state activity and officials provide for unauthorized practices (whether deliberately or otherwise) has been extensively discussed in relation to the global South and postcommunist nations.[42] Less attended to are those state-permitted or -supported "illegalisms" or unauthorized activities within (neo)liberal states of the global North.[43] Yet state facilitation of dissident action occurs there, too, as this legal drama reveals. Support does not have to take the form of *explicit* assistance, empowerment, or endorsement. Instead, dissident projects may draw on a range of state resources, including the residue produced by long back stories of state formation (see, e.g., Martin and Pierce 2013). Conservative Christian withdrawal reveals the dissident use of access, audiences, and formal authority, made available by state processes. From incidents in which teachers refused to affirm gay equality to a roomful of students to magistrates who refused to sit on family panels dealing with gay applicants, to police officers who refused to provide cover for Gay Pride (see chapter 1), state action and systems provided the means for dissident beliefs, expressed through institutional withdrawal (and not just institutional provision), to leave a mark. We could say that conservative Christian forces *within* the state drew on state capacities, but this creates an unhelpful distinction that presumes some things (the durable, systemic, and dominant) are part of the state and others are not: that the police who cover Gay Pride are acting as part of the state but not those who refuse to. Yet why should the state consist only of its compliant parts? Why should we not think about those other, dissenting configurations of role, belief, commitment, opportunity, and place as also part of the state?

What the State Inheres in Inheres in the State?

What is the relationship between being part of the state and finding the state part of one's own domain? Conservative Christians directed much ire at the latter. In the liberal city of Brighton on England's southern coast, conflict erupted in 2008 when the City Council withdrew a £13,000 grant from a Christian home for the elderly on the grounds that the care home was not making the progress required, under new antidiscrimination laws, to become accessible and welcoming to potential gay residents.[44] Speaking in 2007, against the passage of these same antidiscrimination provisions through the upper legislative House, Lord Pilkington of Oxenford remarked, "The regulations question the right of a small or large voluntary society to exist with its own rules, doctrines and ways of behaving. . . . To my knowledge, during the past 150 years—200 years, almost—the state has given grants to church and other voluntary societies. It has never said that because it pays them money, it should be able to alter the rules. . . . That is a very dangerous step to take."[45]

Yet the state's presence in, and permeation through, British social and domestic life is far more pervasive than Lord Pilkington's remarks suggest. As Patrick Carroll (2009: 591) describes, "Every aspect of the built environment, from the sewer trap under every kitchen sink to the roofs over our heads . . . can be seen . . . to constitute the reality of the state." Traces of the state can be found everywhere, from spoken and written English to household insulation and road surfaces. To the extent these processes are normalized, the presence of the state remains largely invisible, appearing at most as inert marks carried by the things of everyday life but with little life itself. Yet when it comes to cases of conservative Christian refusal, such as guesthouses demanding the right to turn gay visitors away, the state rears back into life.[46] Gay couples then appear with state equality entitlements on their backs, hailing reluctant religious owners through a juridical grid that, from a conservative Christian perspective, does not belong in their homes.

Turning gay visitors away can be seen as an attempt by guesthouse owners to keep the state—*at least in its gay equality guise*—out of their properties. But can this state be shut out in this way? At first glance a seemingly empirical question, it also raises conceptual issues about what it means to be a state. To suggest the state (or this modality of the state) can be kept out—or, in Lord Pilkington's frame of reference, stopped from altering voluntary society rules—invokes an image of the state as an actor-thing, a defined, bounded entity that, if inadequately reined in, will use its power and resources to invade, colonize, or crush.[47] This is a state that has grown out of control as it bears and gives expression to excessive appetites and desires.[48] Such a depiction of the state, on the part of conservative Christians, is, of course, not *intended* to be performative in the sense of bringing into being that which it describes. Nevertheless, it poses a conception of the state (and of the proper state/non-state boundary) that is intended to have critical effects (see also Gupta 2012: 100).

Timothy Mitchell (1991: 90) describes how "producing and maintaining the distinction between state and society is itself a mechanism that generates resources of power." It should therefore seem straightforward to suggest that, in this episode, conservative Christians depicted a monstrous state to assert, and materially support, the rightful independence (in their view) of domestic and community life—a part of society perceived as properly beyond the activist equality state's domain. But what their characterization also critically evokes is a state acting on a domain, or inhering within it, *without the domain, in turn, becoming an influential part of what makes up the state*. In other words, the state can harmfully and wrongly affect (or make up) other entities without those entities, in turn, affecting (or making up) the state. At least, this is conservative Christians' fear in relation to certain state guises, such as the "social equality state," which they identify as having become troublingly dominant. Yet if our aim is to conceptualize the state in ways that are oriented to more participatory democratic forms, identifying—and forging—the *reciprocating* character of state-other relations becomes significant. These relations might be approached in terms of constitutive or performative effects or in the contemporary terminology of "coproduction." However, I am interested in a way of thinking about this reciprocating character attuned to the changing morphology of bodies in relations with others, including the evolving ways in which bodies make up others' parts.

Being part of the state, of course, does not necessarily mean making a significant contribution to state action, and in a sense, it is this power-lessness or passivity that conservative Christians fear. They recognize how what the state inheres in may, in turn, become a state part, but, in Bruno Latour's (2005: 58) terms, this may be as an intermediary not as a media-tor: a state part that simply supports existing agenda rather than chang-ing what the state does.[49] In other words, conservative Christians' activity, as guesthouse owners or foster parents, may work to *extend* the equality-promoting state rather than to reshape, thwart, or transform it. This might seem politically beneficial from a left perspective. However, the capacity of incorporated parts to make an *active* contribution to what the state does is also important in developing a state imaginary that foregrounds demo-cratic forms of embeddedness. Democracy here is not a simple matter of greater public consultation or voting. It is a matter of the complex ways in which different state parts *affect*. To the extent that conservative Chris-tians' actions are able to influence, or get taken up by, other state parts and projects, they may become *active* parts of the state as it is.[50] But they also contribute to something else: to the wider shape and condition of public governance (see chapter 3).

For many years, conservative Christian organizations have participated in partnerships with state bodies within a broader structured governance network, where the state provides support without domination or engulf-ment.[51] Christian organizations here hoped to remain distinct individuated participants—benefiting from the flow of resources while they pursued their own governance agendas, and benefiting from the status, recognition, and governmental influence that it was hoped partnership could bring. This was a partnership, Christian advocates argued, that also benefited state bodies, giving them the "personableness, rootedness, accessibility and flex-ibility" that comes from working with Christian organizations (Boucher 2010: 62). Yet as conservative Christian organizations discovered, part-nerships and governance networks can prove precarious,[52] as state bodies pulled out and back, canceling contracts with Catholic adoption agencies, removing subsidies and public resources from Boy Scouts organizations, and denying recognition to Christian student groups. We might treat these instances of disappointed partnerships as demonstrating the limits and difficulties of states working on an equal footing with other bodies, given the huge discrepancies of power and authority between them. Alternatively, we might use them to understand states' own compensatory actions, terminating contact in those minor cases where they can exert power. Bob Jessop (2002) describes how, in many contemporary governance networks, public bodies have found themselves outpaced by private corporations (see the introduction). In other contexts, states have found themselves unable to disentangle from non-state bodies in conditions where they wished to do so.[53] However, in the final part of this chapter, I want to consider something else. If conservative Christian bodies sought to form an active element of "gathered" states while also shaping the wider terrain of public governance, can we draw on their ambitious project to think about the place of responsibility in shaping what it means to be a state?

Assuming Responsibility

This book develops a conception of the state that faces *toward* the shape and condition of public governance, while foregrounding the gathered state as a densely articulated, heterogeneous formation. Bringing public governance and states together forms a staple of much academic work, even as accounts of their relationship vary. In some cases, the state is treated as itself a governance network; in others, the state is identified as one part or player within a wider network, supporting and enabling other bodies (or dependent for its operations and power upon them), but not necessarily at the network's core (Shearing and Wood 2003: 403–4). In a third set of discussions, governance networks are seen as the key ontological and analytical form, and as one that frequently bypasses the increasingly diminished state.[54] Thinking about what states *could come to mean* in order to support a transformative progressive politics gives value to a more open, process-oriented account of governance. At the same time, recognizing the existence and possibilities of more densely articulated states remains important. For work intent on critique, the gathered state identifies a hugely troubling assemblage of control, force, stability, power and action; it provides a focus for (and indeed animates) damaging relations of attachment along with exclusionary fantasies of the "we." For work oriented to reimagining the state, the gathered state is also important, albeit in another way.

Corporealizing the state, treating it as an entity—albeit one that is porous, constantly being assembled, heterogeneous and internally fraught—

supports a notion of public responsibility as something that particular bodies can hold and take up, where what is done is not the entirety of what *could* be done. In conditions where responsibility has been increasingly privatized, individualized, and institutionally disavowed,[55] reclaiming and growing public responsibility for the well-being of ecologies and social actors, both proximate and at a distance,[56] seems vital. This is not solely a retrospective or ongoing responsibility for damage caused and traced back, important as this is (particularly when state culpability for actions at a distance is easy to obscure).[57] Rather, the responsibility I am interested in relates to a readiness and willingness to act in order to support relations of social justice, ecology, and the more equal distribution of work and care. Arguing for greater state responsibility is tricky, given the ways powerful states have deployed responsibility's terms to justify violent and subordinating forms of international and domestic intervention (e.g., see Noxolo et al. 2012; Raghuram et al. 2009). One challenge is how to consider the contribution of institutional bodies toward more socially just forms of life without recuperating calls for powerful nation-states. Certainly, responsibility is not the purview of gathered states alone. It does not have to conform to a zero-sum relationship in which take-up by one entity evacuates responsibility held by others. However, if a governmental responsibility is to be relied upon; if it is something that can be imposed as well as being critically and reflexively assessed and replenished, it needs to be held (rather than reduced to its exercise). This suggests the need for bodies, in some form. Treating the state as simply the improvised or endlessly distributed effect of loosely networked governance relations is not enough.

I want to think about gathered states as formations whose multidimensional responsibilities are given and in creation, as they get revisited, redefined and developed. But how can a legal drama involving conservative Christian withdrawal assist in thinking about states in this way? At first glance this drama is a drama of nonresponsibility. Conservative Christian refusal—voiced as "I cannot help, but someone else will," or "I'm not going to assist but someone else might"—asserts a powerful refusal to take responsibility (see chapter 1).[58] In the process, anticipated beneficiaries of the responsibility (that would have been) are dismissed and discarded, a process which does not cause owed responsibilities to vanish, but externalizes them. For withdrawal does not make what is abandoned disappear but places it in a new relationship to the one who has withdrawn. At the same time, this legal drama witnessed conservative Christian bodies assuming a particular governing responsibility. Frequently, Christian organizations presented themselves as private bodies,[59] and so as responsible to and for "their own."[60] Yet, alongside their claimed obligations to God and their community, conservative Christian bodies also stressed a broader secular responsibility. The British Catholic adoption agency Catholic Care, for instance, argued for the right to change their charitable objects so they could legally exclude gay prospective parents.[61] However, an important part of their legal case was the necessity of exclusion to remain financially viable (through accessing resources within the Catholic community), and so to enable them to continue finding families for "hard to place" children (see chapter 3).

Public bodies that withdrew grants and subsidies from conservative Christian antigay organizations also framed their acts in terms of responsibility: the moral and legal obligation upon them to support gay equality, and the political culpability they would feel and be accused of if they continued to work with bodies that discriminated. By refusing to permit others to make an exception, by demanding that their staff fulfill in full the obligations placed upon them, and by requiring disgruntled employees to undertake awareness training, state bodies performed their responsibility through the laboring bodies they inhered in and worked through. The pathways and mechanisms that state bodies use to cultivate and advance their own public responsibility are important. In this legal drama, governments used a variety of techniques, from orders, instructions, and penalties to mediation, role play, and training. But what this drama of withdrawal also foregrounds is the composite and plural character of state action. State take-up of public responsibility is not something driven by elite institutional actors alone. Other forces also play a part. This chapter has explored how non-elite, dissident state actors might assume responsibility through, in Rancière's terms, staging politics in the place of police. By resisting what is asked of them, refusing to act as policy conduits for the top-down development and implementation of others' policies, conservative Christian state workers demonstrate how bodies can take responsibility in conditions where they are not supposed to. But religious refusal, alongside the counternudges and interventions of colleagues, also provoked action from other institutional parts in contexts where—it was feared or at least claimed—the provocation expressed in refusal would otherwise become a part of what the state was. In these relations of provocation and composite action, we can find state agency—not as a unitary voice, or as a project that finds itself hegemonic, but as punctuated, gritty lines of action.

Acting *as if* state agency is possible is important for thinking about public responsibility. Equally important is capacity—that bodies can *take* responsibility. Much of the discourse on neoliberal states asserts their diminishing capacity. Conservative Christian refusal, by contrast, demonstrates the unexpected resources that can be mobilized, including by subordinate actors: from the interjection of disruptive speech to the refusal of presence—whether one's own or that of others. The minor character of these acts, and the fact that they were largely overridden by state disciplinary procedures, brings a note of caution to any suggestion of their political force. At the same time, it foregrounds questions about how the development of institutional responsibility might be reimagined, given the complex and heterogeneous character of state power, on the one hand, and given the risks, on the other, of its take-up being expressed in ways that control, discipline, and coerce subordinate others or that assert paradigms of responsibility in line with dominant political projects (see Noxolo et al. 2012; Raghuram et al. 2009). In the chapters that follow I consider some ways of responding to these challenges. In particular, I address how more democratically embedded forms of institutional responsibility might be approached through free-running, commoning, and role play. But first, I want to question the notion that state responsibility means nation-state responsibility by exploring different ways of pluralizing the state.

Concluding Remarks

What makes the state up, and how should we approach its relationship to other dimensions of social life? These questions are important in orienting a conception of the state toward a progressive transformative politics given the methodological presumption, discussed in the introduction, that different conceptions of the state make different relations and politics thinkable (and so also unthinkable). If the state is aligned with what is stable and dominant, its place within left politics becomes that of an object of enduring critique or an apparatus over which to gain control. Critique and institutional success have their place; but my argument in this book is that they need to be supplemented by a different approach, anchored in the state's reimagining. In pursuit of this endeavor, this chapter has focused on questions of composition, approaching the state in ways that incorporate the minor, fleeting, and dissident. Such an approach does not disregard or underestimate the harms and significance of dominant and systemic processes and forces. Recognizing their power is acutely important for understanding what needs to be dismantled or changed. However, in light of state theory's routine discounting of the fleeting, dissident, and minor, I have foregrounded these elements, both to expose the opportunities they generate for a resistant or counterhegemonic politics and to imagine the state in more horizontal, polymorphically democratic, and responsible ways.

Incorporating what is minor and dissident offers a different image of the state to the prevailing depiction of an entity apart from its populations: defined, bounded, and in a relationship of looming power over them. Conservative Christians in this legal drama depicted liberal secular states in these terms. Yet their actions provide an entry point for a more heterogeneous conception of the state, as state-engaged activism—that is, activism in the state and activism intent on recalibrating wider public governance formations—brought politics, in Rancière's terms, to the heart of the police order. In this conflict over gay equality, dissident forces were not just engaged in resistance; they did not just say "no" to power. Through their own acts of withdrawal and through actions that, in turn, precipitated withdrawal by others, conservative Christians took up and deployed the opportunities, access, and resources that state-based roles and partnerships offered them—from the teacher who used his presence in the classroom to belittle gay relationships to the youth organizations that used state subsidies (in the form of venues, transportation, and publicity) to renormalize and protect a nationalist, binary-gendered heterosexuality.

In the final part of the chapter, I turned to the question of state reach. Gathered states touch everyone in some way (see chapter 3), but this does not mean that other activities and action networks do not also exist. People, things, places, and nonhuman forms of life participate in state and non-state relations simultaneously. In their work on feminist organizing, Janet Siltanen, Fran Klodawsky, and Caroline Andrew (2015) explore how associations can be enrolled in state projects while simultaneously taking up critical positions "outside," from where they oppose governmental decisions and participate in other networks of action. Newman makes a similar argument in *Working the Spaces of Power* (2012a) when she traces how activist feminist commitments sit alongside, even as they also inflect and are inflected by, activists' take-up of official government posts. Social forces can be simultaneously part of many network flows. At the same time, identifying the reach of gathered states, and what they inhere in, matters. Identifying such states as present when a customer, turned away from a guesthouse or bakery, cites unlawful discrimination could be understood in terms of state "effects"—the impression of a state brought into being through its hailing. It could also be understood in terms of the reach of state regulatory instruments. But I am also interested in what this relationship brings back to the state, including in the development of public responsibility as those turned away demand that other bodies—including institutional bodies—act. I have suggested that the relationship between social life and gathered states can be thought of as a democratic challenge: should what states inhere in necessarily inhere in states in turn? The legal drama over conservative Christian withdrawal foregrounds some of the complexity of this question. But posing the question of how social life should make up states also raises some fundamental questions about what it could mean to be a state. In the next chapter, I explore these questions further to think plurally, and not just heterogeneously, about the state.

THREE. **Pluralizing a Concept**

World society remains a pluriverse of different forms of organizing political authority and statehood. —MATHIAS ALBERT, "World State"

The nation-state is a borderline case of statehood, a very specific historical case that is by no means the perfect form of *the* state. —HAUKE BRUNKHORST, "The Co-Evolution of Cosmopolitan and National Statehood"

In 2001, Trinity Western University (TWU), a Christian college in British Columbia, won its case in the Canadian Supreme Court against the provincial teaching authority, which had sought to deny the college accreditation for a fully in-house teacher education program.[1] The teaching authority had refused to accredit the program on grounds of its "discriminatory practices," a key aspect of which was TWU's Community Standards document that students and staff were required to sign.[2] The document included a paragraph relating to "practices that are biblically condemned," including the "sexual sins" of "homosexual behavior," from which signatories must refrain.[3] Fourteen years later, TWU was back in court, this time fighting legal battles across several Canadian provinces in defense of a planned new law degree that several provincial Canadian law societies had voted not to recognize, again citing the college's Community Covenant (the successor to its Community Standards), and thus its discrimination on sexual orientation grounds.[4]

In this chapter, I take up the legal drama over conservative Christian withdrawal to explore in more depth the plural character of political and governance authority. Moving away from the standard state perspective, discussed in chapter 2, where vertical structures govern national domains, this chapter explores what a pluralist state account might entail. In chapter 2, I traced the state's compositional heterogeneity and reach; identifying how dissident and other minority actors, beliefs, and spaces might be deemed part of the state; and how what the state inheres in might inhere also (in passive or more active ways) in the state itself. This does not mean that everything is the state—or, at least, not *just* the state. Other relations and networks also exist, layered across, against, and sometimes apart from, relations of state governing. Yet in focusing on the composition and reach of the state, what chapter 2 bracketed was an account of state plurality. This is something that, while extending the concept of the state, paradoxically also becomes a way to *disturb* imaginaries of an all-powerful state. In this chapter, I develop such an account to explore how differently scaled and sorts of state and state-like formations coexist in tangled, overlapping ways.[5] A plural state account is not always helpful for a critical reading focused on relations of domination and exploitation, since it creates equivalents where, to a state critic, nothing—or, possibly, too much—is held in common. However, the aim of this book is less to provide a critical reading of present state practice and structures than to trace some productive lines for conceptualizing what it *could* mean to be a state in ways that resituate the state within a transformative progressive politics (see the introduction).

To suggest that a more plural approach can help us think the state in ways that counteract and diminish its set-apartness, exceptionalism, nationalisms, and dominations can be read as a normative claim: that states *should* take a plural form.[6] This is not the approach taken here. Rather than suggesting that states should become multiple and overlapping as if that were a goal to be accomplished, I am interested in where *thinking* the state plurally might take us. What issues and questions arise; what practical and imaginative possibilities are made available? Certainly, the legal drama over conservative Christian withdrawal lends itself to thinking about the state and sovereignty in this way, as some actors struggled to assert, while others sought to contain, the governmental authority of Christian beliefs and institutions. But this does not mean that the pluralist reach and purchase of this conflict is straightforwardly available; that it exists like buried or locked away treasure, merely needing to be dug up or freed. Rather, it requires us to read this legal drama in ways *oriented to* pluralism, where the at times obdurate quality of this reading is part of what it contributes. Arguing that a plural account of the state *as it is* provides helpful entry points for thinking about what states *could come to mean*, this chapter addresses multiplicity in three interconnected respects.

The first concerns how formations other than nation-state formations might be identified as states (or as state-like). In contrast to writing on conservative Christian withdrawal that draws clear distinctions between state and civil society associations in order to make legal or normative claims about what state bodies should (and should not) do as against the expectations imposed on non-state associations (see chapter 2), this chapter explores parallels between states and other governance formations. To do so, it draws on legal pluralism as a loosely analogous conceptual framework that extends what counts as law to take in rules and norms beyond the regulatory and constitutional structures of the nation-state. Central to state pluralism, as with legal pluralism, is the overlapping presence of multiple, differently scaled authorities within the same domain, where (in its strongest form) no one authority acts as political foundation or meta-authority. However, state pluralism, like legal pluralism, confronts some difficult questions: if law is not just state law, and the state is not just the nation-state, what criteria should determine what counts or is to be recognized as law or state? How can we know whether the law or state is *plural*? What particular kinds of separations, divisions, or shape-shifting demonstrate plurality, since some kinds of division and variation can exist within a single formation? Finally, how do the separations, invoked by and constitutive of plurality, coexist with other, overlapping, connections so that entities are simultaneously both separate entities and parts of other states (or legal orders)?

One line of thinking to address these questions, and the second kind of plurality I discuss, concerns processes of state enactment. States are not just made and in existence until they are dismantled or overthrown; they are constantly forged and re-forged. Against an approach that recognizes only top-down or systemic modes of reenactment—electoral victory, revolutionary overthrow, the structural logic of fundamental economic change—this chapter considers how both state formations and other governance authorities are continually remade through everyday micro-practices: a guesthouse that turns gay people away; a police officer who refuses to participate in a Gay Pride march; a regulatory body that will not accredit a Christian college. In chapter 2, I drew on street-level policy analysis as a way to think about the diffuse character of state formations—that neither state decision making nor the state's reproduction emanate from a center alone. In this chapter, I draw on sociolegal lines of thinking. Sociolegal analysis has, for some decades, stressed everyday life's influence and effects on the formation and re-formation of law. What might an analogous state account entail? Paying attention to small-scale, impossible to fully know aspects of continuous state re-formation signals, in turn, a third kind of plurality: that of perspective. The standard state account, especially in political science and law, approaches the state as if it can and should be properly viewed from some Archimedean place, where all who look see the same thing. This chapter takes a different approach. It suggests that we approach the state multiperspectivally, recognizing that how the state *appears* depends (among other things) on how and where one is situated. So what appears a single state from one perspective may appear as a multiplicity of states or state-like formations from another. But the argument in this chapter also goes further to question the conventional epistemological reliance on optics—that knowing the state comes from *seeing* it. Instead, I consider whether we might know the state through feeling (and being felt by) it. Writing on haptic forms of everyday knowledge, Kevin Hetherington (2003: 1939) describes how "we enter our homes through our slippers"—a process of sensing and knowing that also may involve "making" our home familiar through our slippers' comfortable tread. Here I want to consider how a shift in sensory registers might change the ways state formations are known, imagined, and performed. Can a legal drama over conservative Christian withdrawal help us to think about the haptic state?

Withdrawing Books, Venues, and Children

At first glance, litigation in official national courts appears an odd ground from which to explore state pluralism, particularly given the way a formal state optics (and haptics?) subordinates and disempowers non-state law and non-state governance authorities, refusing to treat them as state equivalents and obliging them to present and forge a convincing and relevant case in state law's terms. However, aside from the plurality inherent within judge-made law, as Margaret Davies (2006) has discussed, litigation in state courts provides a useful vantage point for thinking about state pluralism. Litigation and legal judgments reveal how different governance authorities are recognized, and rendered intelligible, from one *explicitly situated perspective*, and they reveal how, through this situated legal frame, governance formations become aligned, defined, ordered, and separated. State and legal pluralist approaches do not deny the work performed by formal state law. What they do is denaturalize its norms, logic, and perspective as the only ones available. In the cases discussed here, much remains outside the state's legal gaze. But exploring how state law produces this conflict on one particular set of stages—albeit formal legal stages with powerful performative effects—not only offers glimpses of other more shrouded perspectives, authorities, and claims but also captures some of the tensions and challenges that competing forms of authority pose, even when incorporated by, and expressed through, state law.

In chapter 1, I traced the different incidents to arise in this legal drama. Here my focus is three specific scenarios: withdrawal by school boards; commercial refusal; and liberal state pullback. The first is illustrated by two school board cases in which books showing gay parents in normalized fashion were excluded or withdrawn from school use on the claimed grounds of parental concern. In the mid-90s Canadian case, *Chamberlain v. Surrey School District No. 36*, an early years teacher asked British Columbia's Surrey School Board to approve three books showing same-sex families for use as supplementary learning materials for a curriculum component relating to family life.[7] The board declined on the grounds the books would create controversy, given parents' religious objections to same-sex relationships.[8] On appeal, a majority of the Canadian Supreme Court found that the school board had overreached the statutory limits of its power and authority by, among other things, giving undue weight to religious beliefs: "The requirement of secularism means that the school board must consider the interests of all its constituents and *not permit itself to act as the proxy of a particular religious view* held by some members of the community, even if that group holds the majority of seats on the board."[9] In a lengthy dissenting judgment, Justice Gonthier disagreed. Comparing the school board to a democratically elected legislature, he emphasized the reasonableness of its decision to withdraw the books, given its decision-making autonomy and legislatively envisaged "shared authority."[10] Justice Gonthier's judgment emphasized the board's accountability to parents who, he said, had a privileged governance role when it came to children's well-being and rearing: "Parents are clearly the primary actors, while the state plays a secondary, complementary role."[11] Within the provincial framework, Justice Gonthier wrote, "consensus is developed locally, a reflection of what parents deem is in their children's best interests."[12]

A related incident occurred in the Davis School District of Utah in 2012. There, a school board withdrew the book *In Our Mothers' House* from the open shelves of elementary school libraries. This action followed complaints by several parents that the book "normalized a lifestyle that we don't agree with."[13] The book told a story about three adopted children raised happily by a lesbian couple. After the withdrawal, the book was placed behind the library counter, available only on special request with parental authorization. The minutes of the district's Library Committee signaled that other books with "homosexual themes" would be treated similarly if complaints were made.[14] The American Civil Liberties Union challenged the withdrawal of *In Our Mothers' House*, and the Davis district settled.[15]

My second scenario concerns the withdrawal of venues for weddings or related celebrations from gay couples and individuals by conservative Christian organizations and small businesses. Liberal discourse typically depicts individuals and corporations as sovereigns of their land, a form of control that is essentially state-like (see Ruggie 1983; 1993: 157). At the same time, while property owners can routinely make decisions regarding access, setting out to provide a *commercial* service brings venues within the auspices of national, provincial, and other human rights and antidiscrimination measures that work to limit owners' dominion (see chapter 1). In a Canadian case, a lesbian couple in British Columbia sought to rent a wedding reception hall owned by the archdiocese and operated by the Knights of Columbus, an international Catholic men's society.[16] The Knights claimed that, because the Catholic church did not "promote, solemnize or celebrate same-sex marriages," and "the Knights [were] required to be in conformity with this core religious belief," it was impossible for them to rent the hall for a gay wedding event.[17] The British Columbia Human Rights Tribunal disagreed, stating, "The Archdiocese owns the Hall and the Knights operate it on its behalf. These facts alone do not protect it from scrutiny. . . . A religious organization may own property, which it rents, but which has no relationship, other than ownership, with the religious organization."[18] At the end of the day, this was what scuppered the Knights' case. Aside from the fact that the Knights had not accommodated the couple "to the point of undue hardship," they also could not show that their use of the hall was closely tied to their own "religious affiliation."[19]

Religious claims to determine the character of a space also came to the fore in the U.S. case *Bernstein et al. v. Ocean Grove Camp Meeting Association*, in which a couple sought use of an open-air boardwalk pavilion in New Jersey for their civil union ceremony.[20] The pavilion, along with all Ocean Grove land, had long been owned by a Methodist organization,[21] which in 1989 promised to make the pavilion "open for public use on an equal basis" to acquire a tax exemption.[22] Investigation into its use, in the course of litigation, identified a mix of activities, with religious and nonreligious rentals taking place alongside wider improvised public undertakings: "The Boardwalk Pavilion is used by the general public in a variety of ways, including as a place to sit, congregate, picnic, play and to seek shade and shelter from the weather."[23] Nevertheless, the pavilion's owners refused permission for it to be used for a same-sex civil partnership ceremony on the grounds that the pavilion was part of their "ministry" and thus inherently religious, since "marriage is a sacred institution ordained by God and exclusive to one man and one woman."[24] Their refusal was rejected by the state.[25]

As discussed in some detail in chapter 1, the acts of withdrawal arising in this legal drama have involved not just conservative Christians. Equally important were the reactive withdrawals of liberal state and regulatory bodies, pulling back a range of public benefits in response to conservative Christian antigay action as well as inaction. While there are many instances of this withdrawal, including in the Canadian law societies' refusal to professionally recognize TWU's new law degree program described at the start of this chapter, I want to briefly mention two others. These also highlight how Christian bodies can get caught between conflicting governing authorities. One concerns the refusal of some U.S. law schools and other university bodies to recognize heterosexual-only Christian student societies. In *Christian Legal Society Chapter v. Martinez*, Hastings College of the Law denied funding and registration to the local chapter of the Christian Legal Society (CLS) because it excluded students on sexuality (and faith) grounds.[26] Hastings CLS's policy, in line with the national organization, required members to sign a "Statement of Faith"; this barred individuals from becoming members if, among other things, they engaged in "unrepentant homosexual conduct."[27] Hastings argued that this contravened its nondiscrimination policy, which required a registered student society to open membership and leadership positions to any student, regardless of his or her beliefs or status.

Catholic adoption agencies faced similar dilemmas resulting from their position on same-sex adopters. Thanks to new protections against discrimination on sexual orientation grounds in the provision of goods and services, local authorities in Britain terminated partnership agreements with Catholic agencies that were unwilling to consider gay adopters. Councils argued that contracts and resources could not go to religious bodies that operated an antigay policy. In response, conservative Christians claimed the state was overreaching (see chapter 2). In a letter to British prime minister Tony Blair, the Archbishop of Westminster, Cardinal Cormac Murphy-O'Connor, asked for an exemption for Catholic agencies so they would not have to "consider adoption applications from homosexual couples."[28] He wrote, "We believe it would be unreasonable, unnecessary and unjust discrimination against Catholics for the government to insist that if they wish to continue to work with local authorities, Catholic adoption agencies must act against the teaching of the Church and their own consciences by being obliged in law to provide [gay couples with] such a service."[29]

Local Catholic adoption agencies found themselves caught between two powerful authorities imposing incompatible conditions on affiliation, recognition, and cooperation.[30] Some Catholic charities chose to terminate adoption services altogether rather than officially welcome or provide services to gay couples.[31] In other cases, adoption bodies tried to find legal ways to continue to exclude gay applicants. The British organization Catholic Care embarked, without success, on a series of legal appeals in order to change its charitable objects and so bring itself within a statutory exemption that would allow exclusions to continue.[32] Other British Catholic bodies, however, decided to comply with the law, but with fraught institutional consequences. The Catholic media describes the case of Catholic Caring Services (ccs), a Catholic adoption agency in Lancaster, a city in northern England, which decided to consider gay couples as adopters, against the Bishop of Lancaster's demand that they refuse to cooperate. Following their decision to open up their service, the bishop resigned from the agency's board of trustees and withdrew recognition of the agency as belonging to the Diocese of Lancaster.[33] The ccs could no longer call itself a Catholic charity; Catholic churches, schools, and other bodies could have no formal association with the ccs; and the agency could no longer benefit from diocesan collections.[34] In a letter to the community in response to the ccs's breaking links with the church, the bishop wrote, "How can I allow the Catholic church to be associated with a body that has chosen a path that cooperates with actions that are against the explicit moral teaching of the Church?"[35]

Yet despite these different attempts to withhold services, conservative Christian acts of withdrawal have proved legally fragile when challenged on discrimination grounds. While some Christian litigants win, many more—notably, in Britain—seem to lose. However, defeat and the growing liberalization of public bodies' attitudes toward gay equality do not undermine the value these cases have for thinking about the state. While they are hard ground, for reasons I discuss, in many ways it is their inflexibility and stubbornness in illuminating the plural state that make them productive for postnormative political thinking in a (neo)liberal context, supplementing those sites or dramas that lend themselves more easily to such work (see the introduction). More generally, the complexity in using this drama to think state plurality speaks to the book's wider challenge—namely, to work from the fraught ground of conservative Christian activism and (neo) liberal state politics to reimagine what it could mean to be a state in ways oriented to a progressive transformative politics.

Unsettling the Single State

Early European claims to political sovereignty invoked a variety of recognized forms including as kingdoms, cities, and church states (Brunkhorst 2012). However, what subsequently came to dominate liberal political thinking was a normative imaginary of isomorphic nation-states.[36] While extensively criticized and challenged, not least for being very partially applied, this image of a "nearly exclusive unit of sovereignty . . . [with] state power . . . projected to the very edge of its territory" (Scott 2009: 11) still exerts a powerful grip on political imaginaries. Contemporary state fantasies evoke a global mosaic of large and small states, bounded, contiguous, and mostly touching. In this way, states are mapped along a horizontal plane. While states may vary in power and size, fantasy renders them all members of the same nation-state class. States are also imagined vertically as a set of nested relationships in which local state governments reside within provinces or states, which in turn combine to constitute federal states or supranational regional federations, such as the European Union. In this "Russian doll" framework, determining where particular bodies are placed is subject to contestation, and changes over time (witness Britain's current relationship to both its devolved countries and the European

Union); nevertheless, one state level is typically recognized as the dominating scale of the nation-state.

The pluralist account developed in this book unsettles both horizontal and vertical imaginaries of orderly political power, proposing a much more contested, improvised, and varied account of government authority. As such, it responds to a cluster of literatures that, in different ways, unpick notions of a coherent sovereign state. One cluster of work includes twentieth-century pluralist writings, which in different ways questioned the monist state as both fact and virtue.[37] Attentive to the need to recognize, support, and develop diverse forms of associational authority and life, political pluralism treated nation-states as able to assume an institutional shape in which no one unit dominated or provided the exclusive basis for loyalty, attachment, or authority. From this perspective, states also lost their exceptionalism and instead, as associational structures, coarticulated with other related forms.[38] Political anthropology, law, international relations, and governance studies have also contributed to thinking about state plurality, including in relation to nonstandard states (see, e.g., Albert 2014; Aretxaga 2003; Caporaso 1996; Fisher 2013; Scott 2009; Wendt 2003).[39] Yet despite the presence of diverse academic literatures unsettling the notion of a single state structure governing relations at home (and often also abroad), state pluralist frameworks have not been extensively adopted or developed, analytically or normatively. Much political and legal theory, for instance, continues to rely on a conception of geographically exclusive, sovereign, bounded, "thing-like" states. This chapter therefore traces an alternative account, drawing on *legal* pluralism to do so. Despite the fact legal pluralism typically assumes a clearly defined territorial state (so as to distinguish official state law from non-state legal and normative orders), helpfully, for our purposes, legal pluralism confronts some of the difficulties and challenges that emerge from decentering the paradigm of formal, official institutions in order to think plurally. Three aspects of legal pluralist thinking are particularly fruitful: the distinction between strong and weak pluralisms; accounts of how legal and normative orders interact; and the question of determining what counts as "law."

The distinction drawn between "weak" and "strong" legal pluralism is a useful starting point for thinking about state plurality (see, e.g., Griffiths 1986). Weak legal pluralism recognizes that subjects and spaces in a given social field can be subject to different legal norms emerging from disparate sources. However, subordinate sources and systems of law are assumed to acquire, *and depend on acquiring*, superordinate permission from a judicial system, central legislature, or governing constitutional text. In weak legal pluralism, different sources of authority fit together to form a single coherent framework that looks (or should look) broadly the same, irrespective of where it is regarded from. Strong legal pluralism is different. Here, disparate legal orders and their legitimacy do not depend on, or receive, recognition from a single superordinate body, text, or authority; instead legal orders are rooted in diverse, often competing sources, each claiming authority or sovereignty.[40] From a strong legal pluralist perspective, what the nation-state may consider illegal according to its laws may be deemed legal or legitimate according to the "laws" or normative expectations of another body or order, such as a religion, association, or social movement (see chapter 1). Thus, strong legal pluralism challenges mono-perspectival depictions of law and legal authority. This is not only because perceptions of the authority, legitimacy, and normativity of particular laws or organized bodies may diverge,[41] but also because there may be no agreement on the authoritative source or procedure for *determining* the respective authority of different laws and bodies within a social field, or even on what constitutes authority or law—empirically or conceptually.

Applied to states, we might think of "weak" state pluralism as a situation in which the coexistence and interrelationship of different "states" and governance authorities is framed and organized by an overarching, power-allocating constitutional structure or sovereign figure. This leads regional, local, micro-, or supranational states (and other forms of political authority) to have defined resources, powers, responsibilities, and functions alongside those of nation-states. Weak state pluralism suggests that dominant state formations and subordinate others recognize the existence of variously scaled bodies exercising power, according to accepted or clear principles or authoritative demarcations, within the same geographical space.[42] From this perspective, a settled and recognized geometry of statehood functions as at least a normative ideal. Powers and responsibilities may shift, and they may sometimes be fought over, but the distribution of power is (or should be) determined in a way that the dominant state level accepts or authorizes (as should other levels also). We can see a weak state pluralist stance in the gay family storybooks case of *Chamberlain*, with its close parsing of the school board's autonomy and authority. There, the majority judgment declared, "Like legislatures and municipal councils, school boards are elected bodies, endowed with rule-making and decision-making powers through which they are intended to further the interests of their constituents. *However, school boards possess only those powers their statute confers on them.*"[43] Legal discretion and authorized variation exist,[44] but they are contained and managed. The school board is required to operate within the context of a coherent statutory framework intended to make governing effective. Although majority and dissenting judgments differed on the niceties of school board autonomy, and the degree to which the board could legally prioritize (conservative Christian) parents' wishes,[45] all judgments took for granted the presumption that the school board had to operate within a wider state-based legal framework.

This judicial response is not surprising. Administrative law assumes that a proper division of power and responsibility exists even as litigation demonstrates the contestedness of such divisions. It is this contestedness that resonates with John Griffiths's (1986) characterization of "strong pluralism." Applied to state or other governance authorities, strong pluralism suggests a situation in which governmental powers, obligations, and legitimacy are not derived from an agreed source but are *claimed and asserted* through divergent and sometimes *competing sources* of authority and accountability. In conditions of strong state pluralism, states (and other political governance formations) sharing a geopolitical space not only may acquire, but also may fight to assume and retain, the same or overlapping powers, legitimacy, or authority, whether in relation to taxation, adjudication, policing, welfare, or something else. Begoña Aretxaga (2003: 398) describes this process in her account of private companies, warlords, and nongovernmental organizations acting as if they were states or in state-like ways.[46] Discussing the borderlands of political authority, she writes, "There is not a deficit of state but an excess of statehood practices: too many actors competing to perform as state" (Aretxaga 2003: 396).[47] Aretxaga and others describe a form of strong state pluralism in conditions where unofficial sources of state-like power are enacted (although de facto acceptance by states or other powerful political entities may leash these authorities back into a weak state pluralist framework).

Strong state pluralism can turn into weaker forms (and vice versa). Nevertheless, sustaining the difference between them has tremendous normative significance in contexts where the respective legitimacy of different sources of statehood and governance authority is at stake. This is evident in the claim that federal states, such as Australia and Canada, cannot *give* sovereignty to Indigenous communities since Indigenous sovereignty, predating colonization and colonial settlement, already exists.[48] To the extent that Indigenous claims to sovereignty are read as practically trumping and displacing colonial state rule, they may seem to challenge strong state pluralism. At the same time, as a matter of practical politics, and as an analytical perspective on the present, strong state pluralism foregrounds the assertion and practice of competing forms of sovereignty by overlapping nation/state formations. This is captured by Audra Simpson (2014) in her account of contemporary members of the Iroquois Confederacy enacting their own conceptions of territory, boundaries, and political authority, and facing down the ongoing and competing claims of American and Canadian officialdom.

If the legal drama over conservative Christian withdrawal demonstrates some of the frictions associated with weak state pluralism, as the *Chamberlain* case reveals, to what extent does it also reveal strong state pluralism? Played out in official nation-state courts, the existence of strong state (and legal) pluralism is unsurprisingly dismissed in the judicial assumption that litigants' claims are subject to a coherent legal framework in which authoritative resolution can be achieved. At the same time, the situation is more complex, as legal discussion over TWU's Community Covenant demonstrates. At first glance, the rules of the Community Covenant seem to illustrate limited (and thus weak) legal pluralism: the authority devolved to a private religious university to govern membership terms and conditions without triggering public regulatory sanctions. Yet, as the case of *Trinity Western University v. Law Society of Upper Canada* suggests (challenging the Ontario law society's refusal to accredit TWU's proposed new law school), Community Covenant rules also held a different status.[49] Presented in court before being judicially subordinated to secular liberal norms, covenant rules were depicted as expressing norms incompatible with wider public values of gay equality.[50] As such, from the court's perspective, their presence was less an example of lawfully devolved regulatory discretion than an intrusive, inequitable set of requirements whose wider public discrediting provided a good lawful reason for the law societies to *deny* professional recognition to the new degree (see also chapter 5).[51] But is this denial evidence of strong pluralism's *impossibility* (as secular state governance trumps and displaces religious governance) or, conversely, of its presence (that college principles anchored in Christian doctrine resist state equality norms)? In a sense, both are true.

Even when they defeat alternative legal claims, judicial decisions do not so much negate as underline the importance of a multiperspectival approach. From the perspective of religious individuals and organizations, those governance authorities articulating theistic claims and obligations are independent of, and can (at least morally) trump, liberal regulatory demands. Some religious claims may be rendered insubstantial in official state courts (despite "stock" judicial gestures of respect) as religious authorities become defined as private organizations subject to, and so subordinated by, state law. But their presence demonstrates a plurality that cannot easily be cast into a neat and orderly form even when, as with TWU, court decisions lead bodies to revise their principles in order to access state resources.[52] What, then, does this mean for how we think about the state? If authority is plural and contested in ways that go beyond weak pluralist accounts, if how rule is organized depends also on perspective, when should governance bodies be understood as states or state-like? Many of the judgments discussed assert a bright line between state and private institutions, but the work involved in producing this distinction foregrounds a core question: What is it to be a state, and how should this be determined?

What Does It Mean to Be a State?

Legal pluralist scholars often deflect excessive attention from the "What is law?" question by referring to legal *and* normative orders.[53] Likewise, "state and political governance authorities" can be a way to avoid a similar rabbit hole wrought by the imperative to determine exactly which authorities are state authorities while also avoiding an approach that treats stateness as a matter of intensity and degree, with its implication of greater and lesser states.[54] State and political governance authorities offer a broadbrush, encompassing phrase that includes public bodies as well as those governance formations, such as churches, that do not simply engage in administrative or technical determinations but also make, operationalize, and adjudicate on politically inflected matters. Of course, some may argue, being a public authority or governance structure is not all it takes to be a state (see Kinna 2019). Analogizing churches (and similar institutional formations) to states, particularly liberal capitalist states, is problematic, because it negates (or obscures) the critical significance of states in coordinating and securing dominant interests, managing capitalism, having defined responsibilities, and constituting an abstract principle of power, authority, and coercion (see the introduction). A similar argument can be made about legal pluralism when micro-normative orders, such as the rules internal to a group, club, or workplace, are included within legal pluralism's analytical gaze. The written constitution of a university is, surely, not analogous to the codified constitution of a state; the norms within a family are so far removed from the regulatory structure of state law that analogizing becomes absurd.

What comes within the remit of "legal and normative orders" is varied, and discussion about any particular regulatory framework, whether state-based, religious, or organizational, may have a specificity that is not extendable. But in some respects, official laws and rules parallel and share ground with unofficial or sectoral rules and norms. As an interpretive tool, legal pluralism opens up ways of understanding informal or unofficial law that benefit from the analytical tools developed in studying state law (and, it should be said, vice versa). Much of the work undertaken within legal pluralism is not invested in law's isomorphic character: that everything called law looks and works similarly or that different kinds of legal orders have comparable force (see Davies 2017). Treating law, instead, as a heterogeneous and hybrid field, studies in legal pluralism explore how official legal orders interact with other legal and normative orders: how they clash, collide, borrow, and sometimes displace one another (Merry 1988). Legal pluralism recognizes that state law typically (although not always) exerts greater force on hesitant subjects than other law-like and normative orders. However, legal pluralism remains alive to those contexts in which state's law capacity to saturate, determine, crush, or control seemingly less powerful orders proves far less totalizing (and far more precarious) than anticipated.

We might adopt a similar approach to state pluralism, as state and other governance formations demonstrate a complex mix of similarities and differences.[55] Many contemporary Christian denominations, for instance, have lawmaking and adjudicating (penalty-setting) bodies, as well as welfare functions and bureaucratic procedures. They also have members or subjects for whom they claim responsibility, and on whose behalf they claim to speak.[56] In other ways, of course, they differ from (neo)liberal nation-states. For instance, the physical territory of many churches is less clearly defined or less weighty; their legal status is significantly different from that of recognized states; their ability to make explicitly territorial grabs is limited (although not completely negligible); and the difficulties they face in imposing certain kinds of sanctions, particularly detention-based sanctions, contrasts with the coercive "ease" of nation-states in organizing custody, as well as with churches' more readily available penalties of loss of resources and membership (see chapter 1). We could go on in identifying differences. But doing so, in this way, assumes that the properties and attributes associated with statehood—like law in legal pluralism[57]—come from nation-state genealogies.[58] Thus, territory, institutional apparatuses, lawmaking, coercion, deferential attachments, political rationalization, dominant class interests, social provision, and militarism are high on the list. But this conceptual turning toward the nation-state is not settled and invariant. Just as the church contributed to early European state imaginaries, future state imaginaries (and contemporary imaginaries of future states) might draw more closely from formations other than today's nation-states, from global, shadow, or local states, for instance. Indeed, if the concept of statehood is to have a progressive future, certain dimensions that are currently read as core aspects of the state by many left-wing critics, such as coercion, domination, and the coordination of elite interests, need to be conceptually severable so that they are not treated as *essential* features of what it means to be a state (see also Dhawan 2016). Coercion, domination, and elite control are also not exclusive to *nation*-states. They are found in other political governance formations—"illegal" military parastates, for example—that may also lack more progressive governing characteristics, such as participatory membership, ecological stewardship, and welfare responsibility. In contrast, left-wing urban authorities or radical "micro-states" (Hancox 2013) may display more progressive state qualities, downplaying hierarchy, coercion and aggression in their governance practices.[59] The challenge, then, is how practically, as well as interpretively, to recut and reconfigure what it is that states are and do. But does this mean that entities with *any* state-like quality can usefully be considered states?

There is no right or certain answer to this question. It depends on what we want a conception of the state to do. In light of this book's orientation toward progressive transformative politics, one response is to focus on acting *like* a state. While this might suggest that there are authentic states and copies, I am more interested in different ways of acting like a state in the absence of an original state that others merely mirror. So we might consider ways of state-acting that are officially recognized, including by other states; those unofficially acknowledged and asserted by certain domestic constituencies; those that conform to prevailing or liberal notions of what "proper" states should be like (relatively autonomous with territory, a population, governmental apparatuses, elections, and so on); and those that invoke or fashion counterinstitutional forms of stateness. Taking up this last option does not mean that the state should be narrowly *redefined* around care and democracy, rationalized by political philosophies of social justice rather than, say, the social contract. Rather, it suggests we might loosen the terms of statehood to include governance formations that demonstrate more prefigurative state qualities. Focusing on bodies that act *like* states emphasizes the importance of plurality. While it invests in some kind of distinction between state bodies and others, it recognizes this is contested, changing, and performative.

A different way to reorient what it could mean to be a state, in ways that bracket the anxious drive to distinguish state from non-state forms of governance, approaches the state as the shape and condition of public governance. This opens up the concept of the state to many different ways of organizing public governance and to many different kinds of bodies and practices, including commoning and mimetic state play. It means recognizing that particular forms, such as the nation-state, and particular attachments such as nationalism, are not primary or essential in constituting statehood. As such, it resonates with critical work that treats the state as a relation or effect, attuned to "spaces of flows" rather than "spaces of place" (Blatter 2001: 176). It also echoes older meanings, such as those Quentin Skinner (1989) has traced, including within republican discourse.[60] Thus, it supports ways of thinking about government and representation that are more horizontal and embedded, where the state comes to stand for society in its public governing dimension. However, from the perspective of the present, defining the state exclusively in this way has shortcomings. In particular, for my purposes here, it risks undermining the ties I want to foreground between progressive stateness and the assumption and obligations of public responsibility (see chapter 2). As a result, this book works with two interconnected state conceptions.[61] First, it faces toward an understanding of the state as the shape and condition of public governance: as a broad, evaluative approach that allows different kinds of governance networks to be described in these terms. Second, it focuses on gathered states as particular institutional forms within wider governance networks. As tightly articulated, differently scaled formations, gathered states express and cultivate wide-ranging responsibilities, underpinned by a political relationship (formulated in different ideological keys) to people, other spaces, and things.

Finding Plurality or Making Different Cuts

Whether operating at a micro, local, regional, or global scale, gathered states and legal orders take diverse and overlapping forms. But how do we know when entities, whether law or states, are *plural*? Attentive to expanding the definition of law, legal pluralism can sometimes neglect the troubling question of plurality, assuming that it follows from law's broader conception; that if law embraces state law, associational rules, and everyday lived norms, multiple legal orders will invariably exist. But how do we know whether the specific distinctiveness that plurality depends on is present? Certainly, if legal orders are depicted as internally organized, unified, and bounded, their separation from other legal and normative orders may seem a fairly clear-cut affair. But if, as Margaret Davies (2006) describes, official state law is internally pluralistic, and if states are porous and heterogeneous (see chapter 2), determining whether we are looking at internal diversity or external plurality stops being a straightforward matter.

How to understand the shape that political bodies take is not a purely ontological matter. In the case of governance formations, it is also a conceptual, strategic, and politically contested affair as to whether the connections are sufficiently significant and valuable to be read as producing a single (larger) entity or whether they demonstrate relations between different (smaller) ones.[62] If entities do not have clear, unequivocally agreed shapes; if their form varies depending on proximity, perspective, and relationship (even as their sociomaterial makeup and context will contribute to the perspectives formed); and if differently imagined and materializing forms coexist, then determining and separating one plurality from another (and from assertions of unity or other forms) becomes difficult and contentious. Timothy Mitchell's (1991) influential work on the state recognizes how boundaries are contingent and political, produced in particular historical conditions to do particular work (see chapter 2). Equally important is recognizing that different imaginaries (institutionally generated and otherwise) locate and define these boundaries in infinitely varied ways as different cuts and connections get rendered salient.

The conflict over conservative Christian withdrawal demonstrates the importance of perspective, and of different perspectives, as fraught questions about whether bodies are separate entities or part of a common system overflow the logic of legal doctrine, even as they are addressed in legal terms.[63] Across the different cases of this legal drama, courts and even individual judges make different cuts, drawing boundaries around entities—or drawing important animating boundaries around particular institutional parts—in different ways. Here, competing notions of what belongs, and is part of what, struggle for authority. For instance, is a school board primarily a subordinate part of a vertical state or a political formation with some autonomy and accountability downward or sideways to constituents? Is Trinity Western University part of a wider educational system (and thus legitimately subject to overarching social agendas) or an "arm of the church," as it later described itself?[64]

These questions reveal lines of political and legal conflict. In the litigation over Christian Legal Society's response to prospective gay members, court judgments differed widely over the status of individual chapters, their right, freedom, or obligation to be treated as part of the law school, and the conditions that could be legitimately placed upon their activities and rules as a result. In *Martinez*, Justice Kennedy suggested that treating student societies as integral to a law school's educational mission could justify legitimate constraints.[65] Justice Ginsburg accepted the school's claim that it would not use public money to subsidize conduct of which Californian residents disapproved, a framing that accepted a contingent line being drawn between a nonconforming society and a democracy-deferring law school.[66] Justice Alito, by contrast, in his dissent, presented societies, such as CLS as "private, independent . . . organizations" that, nevertheless, depended on their campus "world" for the resources necessary to flourish.[67] Value-based considerations in determining how and where to draw the cuts and joins can also be seen in *Catholic Care (Diocese of Leeds) v. Charity Commission for England and Wales*. Justice Sales followed earlier tribunals hearing this case in referring to the "adoption *system*,"[68] a framing that recognized diverse provider parts while emphasizing the importance, and collective responsibility, of the system as a whole. Although Justice Sales shed doubt on the claim that antigay discrimination in a religious part of the adoption system would lead same-sex adopters to withdraw from the system altogether, he nevertheless recognized that harm in one part could have knock-on effects in others.[69]

Plural State Enactments

How and where judges place their cuts demonstrates different sociocultural understandings and commitments. It also has performative consequences.[70] Boundaries and divisions are not simply *revealed*; they are *constituted* through court decisions, as asserted judicial imaginaries bring new forms into being—at least, to some degree. Treating a student society as part of a university, for instance, may justify imposing limits on how the society can behave (and who it can exclude); conversely, it may require the college to provide the same "recognition-based" benefits that other college societies receive.[71] Treating a Christian charity as part of an adoption *system* rather than an independent body may limit the charity's discretion, thwarting its organizational decisions about which families it is prepared to work with, given the values declared by the system as a whole.

The performativity of judgment also raises some parallel questions about how states, in all their divisions, separations, and connections, evolve through everyday institutional practices. For legal pluralism scholars, *non-state* legal orders take shape in two principal ways: through the top-down assertion and imposition of rule-based frameworks as with religious law; and as lived community norms, where what is proper depends on what is properly and routinely *done*. I want to stay with this second approach as one that recognizes the enabling capacity of social action and ask, What do such everyday processes mean when it comes to shaping political governance's evolving forms? This is an important question for thinking about how gathered states, including nation-states, might change. Traditionally in Britain, for instance, the mainstream left has focused on influencing or taking over dominant state positions, where winning elections constitutes a primary strategy, and ad hoc campaigns for reform a secondary one. While anarchists and other radicals look outside of the gathered state for innovation and change, I want to draw on this legal drama to consider other ways of remaking differently scaled state formations.

Legal pluralism has something to offer here. While its focus is how *non-state* legal frameworks resemble and interact with state legal frameworks, it also allows us to revisit *state* law and see how it resembles or borrows from other, non-state normative orders. The same move is possible with the gathered state. Thus, while state pluralism may principally demonstrate how governance formations perceived as non-state formations parallel and resemble state ones, this relationship can be reversed. In other words, in conditions in which different kinds of governing formations have characteristics in common, exploring non-state formations may shed light on state formations also. This reversal both challenges and repurposes court decisions that, certainly in this area, as I have discussed, insist on a distinction between the two—between state and non-state bodies. The capacity of states to be affected and reshaped by the exercise of informal powers and authority—*that is, to be too like non-state governance formations*—is often presented as a symptom of weak states and, as such, something to be avoided. But while courts in this drama have repeatedly insisted on the distinct specificity of state form—treating state bodies as subject to an interlocking chain of *already existing* powers, duties, and freedoms—what, if anything, can be drawn from legal depictions of other bodies in thinking about the changing character of *responsible* states?

One cluster of cases in which the courts engaged with the question of non-state bodies' makeup—their character and composition along with where the conceptual cuts should be made—was the wedding venue cases mentioned earlier. While owners claimed that the primary character, purpose, and use of their spaces was religious in nature, legal opponents emphasized the secular nature of the spaces—that they had *not* been tightly rolled into the advancement of denominational faith, in large part because *secular* activities regularly took place there also. Courts tended to agree. As the tribunal stated in the Canadian wedding reception case involving the Knights of Columbus, "The Panel is not persuaded, by the Knights argument, that the Hall was exclusively a place where Catholics put their faith into practice. It was much more than that."[72] Court assessments of the heterogeneous character and identity of religiously owned, *mixed-use* venues suggest a sturdy form of religious governance, able to withstand secular intrusion—indeed, tacitly welcoming of it to the extent that religious and commercial imperatives enhance each other (see chapter 1). This depiction of healthily heterogeneous bodies provides a different interpretation of religious governance from that posed by the gay membership cases, such as *Boy Scouts of America v. Dale*, with their depiction of easily contaminated, mixed-up bodies—mixed up from being mixed.[73] The venue cases usefully reveal how the legally recognized shape and character of bodies—a shape that includes material parts, such as halls, pavilions, and guesthouse bedrooms—is structured by narratives of usage, particularly those narratives that, in contested conditions, prevail.[74] Here, the courts read past decisions, actions, and policies about usage as determining what these spaces *are*: whether they are domestic or commercial, religious or secular. In the process, the legal tension over how to name the relationship between venue and owner reveals a tension about the relationship between part and whole. For conservative Christian organizations and owners, the part is both constituted by and a contributor to the whole (and so saturated by a religiosity that it also nourishes). Court judgments, by contrast, read these "venue" parts as distinct. While plausibly part of a larger entity, they remain a distinct and heterogeneous part, whose character is constituted not by ownership or the "whole" but by their own, discrete, everyday activities.

Considering how court judgments interpret the shape of non-state entities may seem some distance away from the question I am concerned with—namely, how the emergence of other entities informs our understanding of how gathered states develop and change.[75] But what judgments in this legal drama of withdrawal demonstrate is how routine, seemingly banal, or minor decisions and practices regarding usage can affect how entities are recognized, and what shape is recognized as being their shape in particular contexts. Might this suggest that changing forms of contact and usage can change what states become? What, if anything, can we take from these cases to help us think about the banal everyday processes through which the embodied form of states changes?

The criteria states apply to recognizing other states, particularly in their narrow, legally embodied form, have been well examined. Far less attended to are the vernacular principles non-state others apply, especially when the states in question lack official status. Recognition is not just about whether an entity is recognized as being a state (or part of one). Equally important is *how* the state is recognized—the practices through which (meaningful) recognition takes place, but also what the state is recognized as being and entailing, and the qualitative assessment made as a result. These intertwined processes have important effects on the *ongoing makeup* of states, as demonstrated by the paths that conservative Christian withdrawal precipitated. One path tied antigay action to the criminal law, as when a Kentucky marriage registrar refused to recognize the court's authority and was jailed for refusing to issue licenses to same-sex couples,[76] or when a gay couple, turned away from a guesthouse, chose to involve the police (although, curiously, this seems to have involved finding alternative accommodation rather than as an entry point into the criminal law).[77] Other paths perform and replenish what it is to be a state differently, including through the acts of refusal discussed in chapter 2, and the playful simulation of states explored in chapter 6. In the final part of this discussion, I want to explore the everyday performance of states from a further angle to ask, drawing on the experience of different kinds of governance bodies, Can "feeling" the state contribute to redoing and remaking the state that is known?

Knowing States by Touch

Recognition of new states or new state forms may follow their self-declaration—even as recognition may also be withheld or given by parties who are unable to hegemonize or institutionalize their approval. But to the extent knowing that states exist and, more particularly, knowing their shape and texture does not come through processes of declaration alone—how else can we know what state and governance authorities are like? In other words, what allows us to recognize formations as state formations? Optic idioms have tended to dominate the sensory toolbox when it comes to how states are known, as well as what they "know."[78] James Scott's *Seeing Like a State* (1998) is one of the most influential accounts of the relationship between optic modes of knowing and state rationalities of discipline, standardization, and governing at a distance.[79] In her discussion of "seeing like a city," Mariana Valverde (2011) usefully explores different forms of governmental sight—from the two-dimensional representation of zoning cartographies to the more relational, immersive, and situated form of nuisance law.[80] Valverde is critical of Scott's assumption about how states see, although she also remains with the language and idioms of sight. So too do Stuart Corbridge and his colleagues (2005), who reverse the gaze to focus on how the Indian state came into view particularly among the rural poor. Their work recognizes that how the state is *seen* is shaped by how it is experienced. Thus, optic processes of seeing the state are always mediated, including by touch.

While I stay with the directional gaze of Corbridge and his colleagues (2005), this book decenters the prevailing focus on vision for other aspects of the sensoria. My aim is not to exclude the visual as a way to understand or know states but to supplement an analysis organized around idioms and technologies of vision with haptic (or touch-based) forms of knowledge, recognizing in the process that different sensory rationalities may align with divergent, even contrasting, conceptions of the state.[81] The nuisance law Valverde (2011) discusses is quintessentially about how place is known through the intrusive, distracting, uncomfortable "impact" on the senses of unwanted smells, noises, obstacles, and vibrations, among others.[82] Thus, Valverde's (2011) account resonates with Hetherington's (2003: 1935) discussion of the relationship between "proximal thinking" and touch as an "embodied, sensory . . . out-of-sight approach to knowing the world"—that is, "unfinished," "approximate," and "partial" (Cooper and Law 1995: 239).[83]

Foregrounding touch emphasizes the emergent, evolving character of gathered states. It is not a fully built and static state (or governance authority) that is felt but something in flux. Indeed, it is change that typically impresses itself on experience. In his phenomenological discussion of touch, Matthew Ratcliffe (2012: 423) writes, "As I lean my elbow on the table and think about what to write next, the experience does not incorporate a clear elbow/table contrast. The same goes for the clothes on my body and my bottom on the seat. It is only when I feel discomfort that the boundaries become salient."[84] Knowing states through touch, and through changes in its pressure, often signals coercive forms of contact. Amid the complex ways in which institutions and systems touch is the touch of particular actors. Keith Woodward and Mario Bruzzone (2015: 543–44) describe the touch of a police officer upon a protestor, who freezes; her body responding corporeally before she (or he) consciously knows what has happened. But states do not touch only in repressive ways.[85] Elsewhere I have explored how the British Labour government's early twenty-first-century equality agenda drew on countless idioms and technologies of contact (Cooper 2014: chap. 3). While I do not claim that these were unproblematic, they nevertheless provide entry points into thinking about what more tentative, sensitive, and reflexive forms of governing might entail—even as a "touchy-feely state" may not be widely desired. Here I want to briefly consider two ways that touch produced particular kinds of knowing in this legal drama. I address both in more detail in the chapters that follow.

The first concerns withdrawal. Removing (or withdrawing from) particular books, bodies, agencies, commitments, commercial arrangements, clubs, and venues is often read simply as an absence. Something that once was present is no longer. In some cases, it would seem, nothing much was ever present—a tentative booking of a guesthouse bedroom or wedding venue, but little more. What reading these relations as *withdrawal* highlights, however, is how processes of withdrawing are also processes of contact and touch. Whether or not the posttermination point sustains ongoing connection, getting there often involves intense interactions, touching the legal, social, and biomaterial bodies of others through letters, telephone conversations, emails, meetings, and court time (see chapter 5). Pulling out is *felt* as subjects *lose* accreditation, service partners, books, jobs, halls, and recognition. The feelings that pulling out generates are vividly staged in the legal performance of this drama, as litigants describe their disappointment, stress, upset, anxiety, and frustration at losing what they thought they had gained (see chapter 1).

But it is not only unhappy litigants and their supporting networks that come to know other bodies through their withdrawal. By withdrawing, religious, state, commercial, community, and laboring bodies also come to know themselves. In chapter 5, I explore how state bodies perform who and what they are through what they are prepared to touch. More generally, we might say that bodies know themselves through, and as a result of, the haptic decisions they make, in conditions where withdrawal demonstrates religious purity and conviction or, conversely, a deep, unshakable attachment to liberal equality norms. But, of course, this is also where bodies' managed self-presentation—for instance, as religious—can prove unsuccessful, confronting judicial unwillingness to confirm the religious identity of particular spaces and uses, as I have discussed. Sometimes, a malfunction in identity confirmation occurs because organizations have relied on vision, and it has proved to be a failed technology, as when conservative Christian litigants unsuccessfully argued that the religiosity of their buildings, halls, and guesthouses was clearly evident.[86] In the *Knights of Columbus* wedding venue case, they pointed to "the crucifix, a picture of the ascension of the Virgin Mary, a picture of the Pope and pictures of the leaders of the Knights."[87] The trouble, in such instances, as the adjudicating panel here described, was that "the complainants . . . did not take notice of these items," perhaps because their attention was focused elsewhere.[88] Thus, the insignia were not *felt* by the customers who, not "feeling" the religious character of the venue, consequently failed to "see" it. And because they failed to see something that was not previously made visible or uttered, the venue owners' attempts to withdraw the bookings to sustain a particular sense of self was rejected in court.[89]

Conflicts over withdrawal demonstrate how knowing governance bodies through touch, and what is felt, can supersede or clash with optic forms of knowledge. This is important for thinking about states, given that many states emphasize self-presentation (good "optics") as a way of countering or overriding what is felt as a result of their actions. Knowing the state through dramas of withdrawal is not a passive cognitive act—experiencing an institutional formation that remains unchanged in the process. Rather, what takes place during or after withdrawal contributes to the stitching and cutting work that creates state parts, gathers them together, or causes them to split or change. The episodes of withdrawal discussed in this book are also, importantly, part of larger dramas. As a consequence, withdrawal can lead to new or more intense forms of contact, such as when adoption agencies or venue owners fall back into the arms of their religious progenitors. How and why new forms of contact take place may be due to fear—of the withdrawal that will happen if religious bodies do not pull out. But it is not only about fear. In chapter 4, I explore how gay activists played with the reluctant edges of state formations, drawing on superordinate state bodies' official commitments to gay equality to authorize their contact with resistant local states—a contact that also changed the local states involved. Thus, in asking how we can know states through touch, I am interested in the capacity of contact to revise and reconfigure political formations, where knowledge is not simply about knowing something that is already formed and fixed. It is also about knowing something that is changing, including in and through relations of contact,[90] where ways of understanding what the "other" is, as Nick Gill (2010) describes in relation to refugee activist organizations' conceptions of the state, also shape the contact (and, to some degree, the bodies) taking place.

But are there dangers in focusing on these micro-touches to understand and explore the replenishment of the state? Do they, like microscopic forms of viewing, risk overamplifying what is new? The aim of this book is to develop conceptual tools oriented to change.[91] This does not mean exaggerating political transformation. What it may mean, though, is changing scale and sensory register to *notice* the politically minor and visually submerged; to pay attention to *felt* processes of political formation, and reformation, as well as to those processes where, it may seem, potential alone is what is felt. There generally seems to be a reluctance to recognize state formations that cannot be seen or heard,[92] that are invisible and silent because they lack the recognized paraphernalia and rituals of nation-states, with their flags, anthems, spectacles, speeches, legislatures, constitutions, and laws; stuff that facilitates recognition from other states; the reciprocating gestures on which states practically and juridically depend (see chapter 6). Might a haptic approach allow us to notice other kinds of states and other forms of state enactment? Might it open up paths for imagining states and state relations differently, including through the improvised touch of certain forms of play or the intense, vibrant touch of erotic practice? These are the questions to which I now turn.

Concluding Remarks

Discussion of state pluralism often takes shape in contexts where states are seen as weak or failing. This chapter, by contrast, has explored pluralism not as a way to explain or understand the incapacity of official bodies to govern, but as a way to explore what becomes thinkable once we dislodge the conceptual primacy of nation-states. What does it mean to think the state plurally in terms of its overlapping forms; conceptual definition; processes of re-formation; and multiplicity of ways, including performative and haptic ways, through which it is known (and felt)? I have approached this question through the legal drama over conservative Christian withdrawal. Yet I have done so attentive to the rejoinder that, while this legal drama may have much to say about contested forms of authority (secular and religious), to the extent that it has taken shape in official national courts, in seemingly stable governmental jurisdictions, it does not seem to be an intuitively productive site from which to explore *state* plurality. But it is the *difficulty* of thinking about state plurality through such a legal drama which gives rise to much of its value, for it gestures to a state plurality that is small-scale, modest, and easy to miss. Indeed, plurality's forms may be so faint in this legal drama that their significance, and even their existence, is called into question. Yet it is the relentless judicial depiction of a singular state, clearly distinguished from its non-state counterparts, that incites us to ask: What ways of knowing are obscured and denied by this stock judicial approach? What would it mean and do to find something other than the depiction that the judgments unwaveringly provide?

Pluralism is a difficult issue for a critical left politics. When taken up analytically and descriptively in relation to the state, it can negate the deep structural or systemic inequalities and power associated with (neo)liberal nation-states. As a normative framework, it can also appear to offer too much: suggesting that democracy, equality, and a more vibrant society would be possible *if only* political constitutions were designed for plurality rather than for monism. This chapter's engagement with plural state thinking takes a different path. Rather than saying that the state *is* or *should be* plural, I am interested in what being *oriented* to plurality can do. And I think its value here is several-fold. To begin with, it allows us to identify a wider range of state-like entities and to understand how they interact, parallel, and exchange features with the typically understood states of the nation-state. Many writers have explored how the organization of authority, power, and internal hierarchy within the church and Christianity came to function as an important influence on the development of many states. The drama of this book underscores how borrowings and assertions of equivalence between state and religious bodies continue, including through moments of sharp conflict. At the heart of conservative Christian withdrawal is the repudiation of state law's supremacy. At moments in which the two legal orders appeared or proved incompatible, Christian litigants asserted the preeminence of religious law (chapter 1). While a standard state account treats the authority of religious law as dependent on state law, a pluralist account treats them both as law emanating from divergent governance authorities. This supports an analysis that *follows* rather than assumes the different kinds of power, recognition, or legitimacy that different governing bodies exercise and possess. But recognizing the state-like character of other bodies is not just analytically useful. It also disturbs the exceptionalism of the nation-state, shaking its grandiosity and taken-for-granted centrality and eminence. Whereas states in the standard account are associated with hierarchy, sovereignty, discipline, and power, a pluralist approach "cuts" the state down to size, as the nation-state becomes just one kind of state among others in a contemporary list that includes guerrilla states, micro-states (or "statelets" [Scott 2009]), para-states, city states, shadow states, regional states, and even global states, alongside other bodies that share some of the characteristics associated with states.

Reading states so plurally may prove counterproductive for certain forms of critique (given the dangers of underestimating the specifically organized concentration of political and governmental power still exercised at the national scale). However, if we are oriented instead to the contribution states might make to a progressive transformative politics, plurality in what it *means* to be a state can prove helpful, making it possible to imagine not only other entities as states (or state-like),[93] but also other ways of being a state, akin to Eve Darian-Smith's advocacy of legal pluralism "for its potential capacity to imagine diverse realities and new possibilities" at varying scales (Goldberg-Hiller et al., 2011: 285). Orienting to plurality foregrounds the variability and contingency in how states are imagined. If there is no single conception of what it means to be a state, the political question then becomes: what work do different state conceptions carry out? One approach might be to develop prefigurative conceptions of the state that take their definition, say, from radical local experiments rather than from (neo)liberal nation-state formations (see Cooper 2017). Reimagining what it means to be a state in this way, and enacting these meanings in the current moment, may seem to promote a fiction. At the same time, it may be one with performative effects. Changing the state we recognize, can give presence to new institutional forms as I discuss further in chapter 6.

In this and the previous chapter, I have sought to develop a conception of the state that, while not explicitly prefigurative, is oriented to thinking about statehood and stateness in ways that recuperate the state conceptually. I have suggested that we move *toward* a definition of the state as the shape and condition of public governance while holding on (for now) to the gathered form that states, at different scales, can take to avoid responsibility's "empty place." Recognizing state responsibility for people, animals, ecologies, things, and places, beyond any defined and delimited list of functions, obligations, or tasks, offers a way of thinking about states that supports revitalized practices of democracy, social justice, and care (see chapter 2). In other words, it provides a conceptual grammar for thinking about left-wing forms of public governance and statehood without definitionally limiting the state to these progressive forms.

How people conceptualize the state depends on the work they want it to do. In this legal drama, courts approached the state as a clearly defined entity even as they diverged in how to trace its contours, and vacillated over how other, non-state entities should be defined—sometimes treating spaces and things as part of one system or body and sometimes as part of another. What I have taken from the courts' focus on defining other spaces and things is the part everyday uses can play. One of the difficulties in bringing the state into everyday politics, conceptually and practically, is its tendency to spring back into a discrete, remote, vertical relationship to the places, people, and things it participates in governing. But if gathered states, at different scales, are just one kind of governing formation among others, then they—like other kinds of governing formations—are constantly being re-created through small-scale, often banal, quotidian actions. This claim gives weight and meaning to a politics that tries to re-create the state in ways that do not depend on taking ownership of its apex but instead involve dense, repeat efforts to re-perform governing practices and systems, and the connections between them, differently. Approaching state reform in this way highlights the value of the plural sensorium. When it comes to the senses, state scholarship foregrounds vision and, with some exceptions, uses it to emphasize relations of vertical separation and distance.

Yet remaking states through practice depends on immersion and context. Here a haptic register is useful because it focuses on how states are known, and thus remade (since touch is invariably double-sided, at least), through experiences of contact and what is felt. Critical scholarship unsurprisingly has focused on coercive and punitive forms of contact. But if the state is to offer a relevant concept for a progressive transformative politics, other forms of touch may also be relevant—forms that may be pleasurable, light, and stimulating, and forms that may be initiated by bodies and networks that are not quite, or not exactly, state ones.

FOUR. **State Play and Possessive Beliefs**

I want to now turn to play: to work from the glimpses that this legal drama provides of state-engaged play to think about play's place in reimagining the state. To do so, I consider the state from quite a different vantage point from that of the previous chapter. Chapter 3 sought to pluralize state thinking in a number of ways, including through questions of scale, form, everyday refashioning, and perspective. As I discussed there, states may seem divisible from one vantage point and joined from another depending on how material practice combines with perceptions of significance—the joins and cuts deemed to matter. This chapter takes the joined-up nation-state as its focus to explore how the connections among different state sites and "levels" get mobilized through play. Conventionally, the assertion of hierarchical connections and the reining in of subordinate state forms is read as directed from the top. The account in this chapter does not dismiss this reading but explores how grassroots activists can also deploy superordinate political resources, including as a means of compelling lower state levels to comply with liberal gay-equality norms in conditions in which conservative local state actors refuse to do so. Play offers a useful concept for studying the rejection and subsequent mobilization of superordinate state authority. In addition to offering a framework for thinking about what state governing could be like, it provides a language to think and talk about the teasing, testing, delicate dance in which political bodies engage with one another.

Play, however, is not normally associated with states, particularly nation-states. Indeed, for many, state cultures of bureaucracy, gravity, legibility, and instrumentality seem entirely opposed to the for-its-own-sake expressive norms of pleasure, pretense, ambiguity, and levity that play invokes. As M. Lane Bruner (2005: 148) remarks in his discussion of activist satire, "The humorless state has a very difficult time dealing with absurdity, symbolic protest, and the curious blending of the fictive and the real—people becoming turtles, elves becoming 'real.'" State criminalization of airport "bomb jokes" (Martin 2010) also demonstrates states' lack of humor when it comes to the reckless or foolishly ludic behavior of others. Yet play can be conducted seriously (Statler et al. 2009, 2011); it can do social work and have consequences—intended and otherwise. States are also not immune from the competition, banter, risk taking, and disorientation associated with many forms of play. We might think of the staged battles between opposing politicians performed publicly in Parliament and then laughed over privately in the bar afterward; or the tactical game-playing of nation-states.

There is no shortage of play when it comes to (neo)liberal nations, but outside of game theory (with its emphasis on calculated strategic action) such play has received little direct study.[1] Certainly, there is a long-standing literature on politics as a dramatic, staged, or theatrical performance (see, e.g., Edwards 2013; Hallward 2006; Huizinga ([1949] 1970), but this often brackets states.[2] Rather than associating drama and performance with the institutional texture of public governing, the agonistic appearance of bodies and talk within the public sphere tends to get foregrounded. Performance-based concepts have not been kept entirely apart from public policy and its deliberations (see, e.g., Anderson 2014; Hajer 2005). Writers have used improvised art forms, such as jazz, to explore the creative and unplanned dimensions of state decision making and legal adjudication (see, e.g., Jeffrey 2012; Kamoche and da Cunha 2003; Ramshaw 2013). Nevertheless, particularly in relation to this book's core states, legal and political scholarship tends to downplay role play, fantasy, and the mischievously playful.

One place where these state qualities have received more attention is in anthropology. Begoña Aretxaga's (2000) tale of Spanish police officials who acted like terrorists to fight Basque terrorism illustrates how make-believe can be rolled into state practice. She describes how the state, through its actions,

> imitates the landscape and actions associated with [the Basque separatist group] ETA in cinema, fiction, and the media: the obscure frontier passes in the Pyrenees, the hide-out in the mountains . . . , the secret contacts and meetings, the hidden documents charting events, even the seal and acronym. . . . There is little rational about this state. It is suffused with affect: it gets excited, exhilarated at trespassing on the fantastic space of terrorism, carried away by its own fantasy of the terrorist's supposed omnipotence, uncontained by the rule of law, unrestrained by the symbolic rules defining the "civilized" reality of parliamentary democracy. (Aretxaga 2000: 49)

Role play also emerges in Yael Navaro-Yashin's (2012) compelling account of Northern Cyprus, which she describes as simulating statehood. Official documents and practices were treated internally *as if they were real*, yet lack of international recognition generated a sensation of make-believe and so anxiety in residents. State mimicry has been explored in many other contexts.[3] However, as Aretxaga's and Navaro-Yashin's accounts reveal, these copyings are not typically read as playful, horizontal, or progressive.[4] Can state play be approached differently?

Certainly, we might paint an idealized future in which different kinds of gathered states (see chapter 3) not only enable and support much greater play (and play time) among citizens but engage in cooperative and pleasurable play themselves. To think about states playing more, and playing differently, however, raises questions about the kinds of states they would be. Is the state that plays well more likely to be a micro-, local, or regional state, for instance? Would it necessarily be egalitarian, democratic, socialist, or liberal? What conditions are required for state bodies to play with humans (and other animals) in ways such living subjects would enjoy—a question we might also re-pose to ask, How can people play well with others in the process of governing? In approaching these questions, this chapter does not seek to map an imagined ideal future of state play but to think about how states currently play in a manner that orients state play toward more just possibilities. Thus, in thinking about states playing, my account focuses neither on the best nor the worst aspects of current play. Instead, it foregrounds instances that reveal state play's quotidian and multivalent character.

Chapters 2 and 3 argued for moving toward a conception of the state as the shape and condition of public governing, a conception that incorporates (but also exceeds) the gathered forms that help to compose it. This chapter focuses on the articulated form of the nation-state, with its rolled-in provincial and city forms of governance. Thus, it brackets informal micro-state or para-state forms (see chapter 6). In part, this comes from the chapter's concern with institutionalized rights regimes; in part, it comes from my focus on play's presence within those formal state terrains in which play may seem most oddly placed. A more idealized approach might locate state play within a very differently imagined state. But I am interested in what we can learn about play and governance and what play can do, politically and socially, when it emerges within the formalized domain of bureaucratic and public policy practice. Certainly, the conflict between conservative Christians, openly gay subjects, and (neo)liberal states may not seem to be an obvious ground for exploring state play. Yet as I explore, various glimpses of play can be found, foregrounding, in turn, the very different ways states play, from engaging in play's design and acting as its referee to providing a terrain, subject, and object for play undertaken by others.

Beliefs as Possessions

In addressing play, I focus on one specific aspect of the legal drama over conservative Christian withdrawal. It concerns the formal depiction of "identity beliefs" (i.e., beliefs anchored in and about identity) as *belonging*, in deeply constitutive and intimate ways, to those who hold them.[5] For the Christian litigants of this book, beliefs come from many sources and take different forms.[6] However, the depiction of beliefs as a specific set of truth claims or tenets about the world (as well as about God) that can be identified, asserted, and lived has become an important component of how religion is treated in equality and discourse by both religious litigants and public bodies. Also important, and underlying this discussion, is the specifically *other-oriented* character of the religious beliefs I am addressing. These beliefs are not about the origins of the universe, life after death, or how to dress and eat but evaluative beliefs about the ways others live. As such, they include the claim that gay sexuality is sinful; marriage should be exclusively heterosexual; sex is proper only between married people; and children need a mother and father.[7] This other-oriented focus can have damaging effects when imposed on religious community members. It also becomes problematic when it is institutionalized in protective legal frameworks, so that such religious beliefs are analogized to other social categories or relations, including gender, ethnicity, or sexuality. The effect of this is to suggest that *not allowing* the condemnation or rejection of others' ways of living (on grounds of belief) is equivalent to not allowing people to express their ethnicity, gender, or sexuality. In the legal drama of this book, the tensions (and absurdity) these legal analogies generated came to the fore in the iced-cake wars. In *Masterpiece Cakeshop Ltd. et al. v. Colorado Civil Rights Commission et al.*, the Supreme Court eventually found in favor of the baker who had refused to make a wedding cake for a same-sex couple. In his judgment, Justice Gorsuch argued that there was a clear equivalence between declining to bake a "gay" wedding cake and declining to bake a cake iced with antigay biblical remarks since both were expressive forms of action. If a pro-gay baker could refuse to make the latter, then a Christian baker should have the right to refuse to make the former.[8]

While the Christian beliefs in this legal drama are other-oriented, human rights and equality law nevertheless construct them as property[9]— that is, as things that belong. As such, they should be recognized and given value by a state law that is attentive to its assumed responsibilities for members and their possessions. Regularly, in litigation, conservative Christians referred to their "conscience" or "belief system" as something they possessed and over which they were entitled to exercise control and expect protection.[10] In his influential account of "possessive individualism," Crawford B. Macpherson (1962) describes how this paradigm of private, exclusive property ownership, in which individuals functioned as the owner of their person and capacities, came to dominate Western liberal thinking (see also Carens 1993).[11] Macpherson's account has been criticized on various grounds,[12] including for erasing the racial, colonial, and gendered character *and conditions* of self-ownership within liberal thought and practice,[13] as well as for his overly restrictive understanding of property in the self.[14] However, what is important for our purposes is the way identity beliefs came to be enrolled in this possessive paradigm as things owned and invested in.[15]

Identity beliefs have long had legal and political value. However, determining this value has not remained stable. Property in beliefs is continuously subject to significant recalibrations.[16] Today, explicitly acting according to certain beliefs, such as male superiority, has been de-propertied in many jurisdictions. However, manifesting religious (or related) beliefs about the lesser status of other social identities, particularly heterodox sexualities, remains legally protected (at least to some degree). In early twenty-first-century Britain, the propertied character of Christian beliefs was resettled in part through equality legislation, culminating in the Equality Act 2010. The act confirmed the prohibition on discrimination on religious grounds (without giving Christianity any greater protection or status than other faiths),[17] but it also did the same for sexuality.[18] In swelling recognition and protection for these different identifications,[19] neither the act nor its predecessor legislation adequately confronted the consequences of multiplying rights, a neglect that became directly targeted in litigation over conservative Christian withdrawal. As conservative Christians, liberal public bodies, and gay-equality proponents tested the value and weight accorded to their own and others' rights, British (and other) courts found themselves engaged in property thinking as they addressed the problem of seemingly colliding rights. If Christians had property in their beliefs, did antigay sentiment constitute a "core" aspect of these beliefs (and so part of its necessary estate)?[20] Was determining a belief's theological significance subject only to the judgment of religious believers, or could the courts form their own, independent assessment?[21] And how far should property-like protections extend—to "social" remarks made about homosexuality on an employee's personal Facebook page, for instance; to emails sent from a work account to external organizations; or to evangelizing remarks made to a colleague?[22] For the most part, British courts worked to limit the reach and force of religious beliefs about sexuality in terms of *how* such beliefs could be manifested and *what* they could be used to accomplish.[23] At the same time, court judgments tacitly confirmed the normalized status of property and its application to identity beliefs.

The problems of treating beliefs as *property-like* are several, and lie specifically in their privatizing, depoliticizing, and individualizing effects.[24] We may not want conservative Christian beliefs to constitute collective or state property (as I discuss below). However, treating beliefs as *private possessions* reinforces a worldview of stable, unitary subjects set apart from each other, and holding tight to their beliefs,[25] beliefs on which they should be free to act (provided *unacceptable* harm is not caused to others) and on which, when they collide with other beliefs or identity statuses, the courts will adjudicate.[26] The problem with treating beliefs in this way is that, outside their framing in liberal legal discourse, they are not that individual, private, or reified.[27] Many beliefs, including those at the center of this drama, are highly politicized, and when they are concerned with *other* people's ways of living, they are, unsurprisingly, deeply contested. In this respect, they seem fundamentally different from claims for property-like protection for other cultural beliefs, such as those held by minoritized communities, where property frameworks may be useful in challenging their colonial appropriation or "theft." Minoritized knowledges, beliefs, and other cultural goods bear, tacitly or otherwise, complex embodied histories and struggles for meaningful survival. These struggles can be erased or compromised when cultural knowledge and beliefs are taken up, mixed, and misrepresented by outsiders.[28] But the context of the discussion in this chapter is quite different. Here, beliefs are claimed as property to protect ways of thinking aligned with historically powerful belief structures and to legally rationalize the unequal treatment of others. Property discourse in this legal drama orders and classifies values and social relations. While this may not always protect traditionally higher-ranking knowledge claims, it nevertheless hollows out the content of these claims so that they become simply *things that belong*—whether to individuals or to the (religious) body politic.

State Play

In the rest of this chapter, I explore how the conflict over possessive beliefs became enacted as and through play. Driving my analysis is the question, Can play unsettle the depiction of beliefs as fixed properties belonging to individual and collective subjects? Can it contribute to the political task of unsettling possessive attachments? And do the forms of play glimpsed here confirm play's destabilizing qualities, or do they instead show play's capacity to reinforce already settled beliefs? While many writers tend to pin down play in particular ways—to determine what play really *is*—my interest in thinking about play is to illuminate distinctive registers of state engagement. Central to play here, then, is its "as if" quality. By this I mean that play reenacts being, desiring, thinking, exercising authority, and undertaking activities in ways that seem to convert the "real" into something else, including as its copy or simulation (see chapter 6). Johan Huizinga's ([1949] 1970) famous concept of the "magic circle" is often used to identify the separate, make-believe space of play. Stephen Nachmanovitch (2009: 15) writes, "Pretend-play, theater-play, music-play, sports-play, and mythology are all about parallel universes and alternate time-streams that work according to their own laws and patterns different from the everyday." Others suggest that play is far less discrete. Beyond the expressive enactment of other worlds, play—conceptually and empirically—troubles divisions between worlds while inserting new forms of imitative practice into existing "reality" (see chapter 6). This intermeshed aspect of play is particularly apparent when play is understood as a *qualitative dimension* of social life and not just a *kind* of activity. But even in the latter case, play does stuff and has consequences (Thompson 2014). In an Arendtian sense we might think of play as "little deeds" performed with and for others.

One important dimension of play is its relationship to its subjects. The notion that play's *subjects* engage willingly is a staple element of much play theorizing.[29] However, it takes on a particular counterfactual prominence in relation to state-engaged play, where participation may seem inherently pressured or compelled and where, importantly, participants risk becoming the terrain or object of play rather than its players. Willingness to play is also associated with the desire or expectation of pleasure. Play's pleasures may not be benign. They can injure those objectified by play, and even those who imagine themselves play's subjects can end up hurt. But being a player is associated with feelings (or, at least, *anticipated* feelings) of enjoyment or satisfaction, even if this is only a melancholic satisfaction on the part of those playing. Satisfaction and pleasure are typically important drivers of play and so worth stressing in normative accounts. Yet when it comes to state-engaged play, positive affect is less clear-cut. Other more critical feelings may arise and displace feelings of pleasure, including a sense of play's unreality or of its triviality and insignificance. Thus, while feelings are important, state play in this narrative does not assume particular feelings on the part of its players; nor does it assume players' self-awareness that they are playing. What it does assume, however, is a kind of mutability as play stretches, tests, repurposes, and reuses what is around.

At one level, mutability is about play's relationship to order, something play can affirm and produce anew, as well as transgress. This relationship is where much of play's creativity lies. Whether playing involves people, things, or spaces, its creative dimensions emerge as objects (and sometimes subjects) get stretched, absorbed, transformed, redeployed, broken, and filled up.[30] But the mutability and toying quality of play is not just about creativity and change. What play also captures is the simultaneity of challenge and confirmation as play supports and expresses competing ideas: the nip that both is and is not a bite (see Bateson 1987: 185–86),[31] the ostensible governmental commitment to gay equality that others dismiss as mere spectacle. Play reveals the simultaneity of opposing positions; it also reveals, in accordion-like ways, the capacity for contradictions to be exposed and stretched or collapsed and hidden—something Christine Harold (2007) also explores in her account of "culture jamming."

How, then, do states play? It should be said that states in the standard state perspective (ssp), discussed in chapter 2, do not tend to play kindly. Strategic "game playing" among nation-states through bargaining, diplomacy, and war or among officials, politicians, service users, contractors, and others suggests a kind of play that is often provocative, combative, and cruel. Even when it is not cruel, state-engaged play, in the ssp, is usually framed as sharply competitive. But not all state playing is combative. Governments today also use play, in the form of organized games, to incentivize and structure public participation in planning and resource allocations (see Lerner 2014). Playfulness also appears in the everyday joking of teachers with students and in those more relaxed, if differentially experienced, moments where state officials joke with users or clients.[32] Self-satire is an interesting dimension of state play, often used to demonstrate a state's good humor and liberal confidence. Through supporting or engaging in self-parody, governments and publicly funded bodies set out the stall of their national (or local) character: this is what and who we are in our ability to laugh at ourselves.

Recognizing the pervasive character of competitive, strategic, sometimes cruel, sometimes friendly or funny state play is important, as is its vacillation among authorized, semiauthorized, and unauthorized forms. However, given the focus of this book, my primary interest is in what state-engaged play can bring to a progressive transformative politics. Thus, I bracket explicitly combative or sadistic forms of game playing to explore other kinds—particularly mimetic and role-based play, that is play in its "as if" guise. At the same time, to avoid romanticizing what state play could become (as well as what it is), it is necessary to stay mindful of certain risks:

that celebrating state play can seem to trivialize important state functions;[33] that it may appear to accept the residual, "becoming-insignificant" impression of contemporary states within neoliberalism (where play is all that is left to them); and that state play can prove an improper register of governing when gravity is called for[34] or where relations of domination and need are too acute. It seems doubtful that a homeless person, for instance, could play (in any meaningfully equal way) *with* their housing officer.[35] In such instances, play may appear disingenuous, pretending a bonhomie that masks state government's far more coercive, oppressive, or failed character (in its capacity and readiness to take responsibility for peoples' well-being). My argument is not simply that we need *more* state play. Rather, I want to explore the relationship between state-engaged play and possessive beliefs to consider what state play looks like in this context and what it can offer as a pathway into thinking more generally about the conditions, value, and potential for "better" state play.

Belief-Directed Play

Being stopped from playing, refusing to play, challenging others' refusals through play—play has an interesting relationship to withdrawal. At one level, many of the episodes described in this book involved recreational activities (to put play at its broadest) as lesbians and gay men sought to enact their committed beliefs in same-sex equality through staying in guesthouses, going to youth camps, taking part in parades, attending school proms, having wedding parties, and even, in one case, if the news story is accurate, bringing prewedding munchies and champagne into a bridal store.[36] Yet as these leisure and pleasure pursuits indicate, even lawfully authorized forms of play require support—from accommodation and membership to firefighters, photographic records, printed T-shirts, wedding dresses, and permission to enter. This need for support renders gay forms of play vulnerable to others' withdrawal. But play "stoppered into solid, repeatable forms" (Shields 2015: 304) is not the only form of play produced in this conflict. A different play-form emerged in the accordion-like movement between two conservative Christian stances. In the first, conservative Christians assumed a mimetic sovereignty, role-playing the ruler authorized to say "no" in the face of those (liberal secular) sovereigns who had said "yes." At the same time, in their creative expressive work as florists, wedding-cake makers, calligraphers, and photographers, Christian litigants represented themselves as *playing* (and so, it would seem, not governing) when they argued that the state-mandated requirement not to discriminate undermined the *legitimately artistic* dimension of their work.[37]

Play's mimetic qualities also emerged in a series of tactical actions by both conservative Christians and those opposing their withdrawal. Reacting to the litigation that followed a bakery's refusal in Northern Ireland to ice a cake with a pro–gay marriage message,[38] a customer in Dublin requested a cake iced with the message, "BY THE GRACE OF THE GOOD LORD, I [name redacted], that in my honest opinion—'GAY MARRIAGE' IS A PERVERSION OF EQUALITY and the 34th Amendment to the Irish Constitution should be REPEALED." [39] According to news stories, the aim of this wordy request was to reveal liberal hypocrisy, how those objecting to Christians who refused to make gay (or gay-positive) wedding cakes wanted to be able to refuse to print distasteful iced messages themselves.[40] The simultaneous wanting and not wanting of a service displayed in this form of play is also evident in two other plays, similarly intended to reveal the illegitimate attachments of others.[41] In one, a British journalist underwent a treatment session with a therapist "with a Dictaphone taped to [his] stomach," after presenting himself as an unhappy gay man seeking to be cured, in order to expose the heteronormative conversion strategies some Christian psychotherapists practiced.[42] In a second example, customers "played" with a conservative Christian cake shop in the United States to unmask its antigay bias.[43] As part of the action against the Masterpiece Cakeshop, in Colorado, for refusing to make gay wedding or commitment ceremony cakes, Stephanie Schmalz (one of several people whose request for a cake was rejected) described, in her affidavit, how she subsequently contacted the shop saying she was a dog breeder planning a dog wedding celebration. "I specified that for the 'dog wedding' I wanted a cake large enough to serve about 20 people, in the shape of a dog bone, and lettered with the names Roscoe and Buffy. Mr. Phillips stated no objection to filling this order."[44]

Across these diverse instances, play and beliefs remain closely attached. Certainly, play takes different forms (including forms that seem far from happy ones, even for those deemed play's subjects). At the same time, play works here to confirm and *stabilize* rather than undermine the possessive quality of subjects' relationships to their beliefs. While certain beliefs may be played with, these forms of play establish—indeed, they are undertaken to expose—the illegitimate attachments of others, as with the psychotherapist engaged in conversion therapy or the baker unwilling to make wedding cakes for gay couples. Framed in the terms of liberal legal discourse, acceptable beliefs—and, of course, what constitutes them is contested in litigation—become possessions. Subject to attack by others, to the extent they function in propertied ways, the legal question is not whether they, as beliefs, *should be* protected but how and where their propertied contours should be drawn. In the episodes involving the therapist and American cake shop, activists used play to demonstrate how conservative Christians were exceeding the parameters of what religious antigay views should legally be able to accomplish. However, the success (or otherwise) of their actions depended on declarations subsequently made by official legal bodies. Can play work in other ways, so that it is not merely foreplay to law's "real event"?

Play is often described, at least in its potential, as disarming, interactive, ambiguous, creative, and open-ended. As such, it contrasts with more coercive, top-down modes of intervention that (neo)liberal states use or have considered using to control and penalize the hateful expression of "unacceptable" beliefs, such as the criminal law. Play then might seem to offer a register through which possessive beliefs can be unraveled, reallocated, or transformed in ways that do not depend on court penalties or mediation. But can play move beliefs between players, enrolling nonplayers in the process? To explore this terrain further, I want to turn to three different registers of state-engaged play. In the first, public bodies use role play to help protagonists move beyond fixed oppositional standpoints; in the second, gathered states take up activist beliefs as if they were theirs, while activists express radical beliefs as if they were state ones; and in the third, liberal provincial state beliefs give gay activists the necessary traction to "free-run" city bodies.

1. Role Play and the Caretaking State

Can play, particularly role play, help conflicting forces to (temporarily) bracket their beliefs to understand the viewpoint of another? While left academics debate the question of whether it is possible to "stand in someone else's shoes" (see, e.g., Young 1997), progressive governments have used recreational modes of contact to improve understandings between different groups.[45] In Britain, the legal duty placed on public bodies to promote "good relations" generated local initiatives to develop contact, including playful contact, as a way of minimizing intercultural hostility. In other policy contexts, promoting better relations or outcomes between different interests has also led government to draw on play and games.[46] We might think of these strategies as forms of responsible caretaking work, embedded in wider state projects of responding to welfare needs, supporting populations, stewarding resources, and "tending" to local ecologies. These are processes that left-wing scholars have often approached skeptically, attuned to the authoritarian, paternalistic, biopolitical ethos of much state care. But if care and responsibility are important features of progressive forms of governing, how might they be done differently? Can play here play a part?

Discussing the challenge of developing governmental policy over water conservation in California, given the presence of sharply conflicting interests, Judith Innes and David Booher (1999: 16) explore the contribution that role play can make. "Participants come to the table representing stakeholders with different interests. It is each one's job to play the role of that stakeholder in the discussion, just as in games where one person may play a vampire and another a werewolf." In this instance, Innes and Booher (1999) suggest, playing together over a period of time allowed participants, with divergent concerns and perspectives, to arrive at shared solutions. Facilitators encouraged participants to draw on nonofficial, more personal roles (e.g., as a cyclist rather than a water board employee) to establish some distance from their official positions and interests and to consider solutions from other contexts.[47] The hope was that, rather than simply understanding one another's perspectives better, new perspectives would emerge through play.[48] As Erik Olin Wright (2010: 161–62) writes, "If actors can for a time suspend their attachment to specific conceptions of their interests and get down to the practical issues of solving problems, then in the course of deliberation and experimentation their interests [and, we might add, their beliefs] are likely to evolve along with their discovery of solutions to problems."

Applied to the legal drama of this book, we can imagine different state bodies—schools, local authorities, hospitals, police forces—bringing parties with competing beliefs on sexuality together over periods of time to explore ways of managing or avoiding conservative Christian withdrawal.[49] Such a strategy is far from utopian, extending already used initiatives in the public sector to develop more mutually respectful working relations between gay and conservative Christian antagonists.[50] However, while the prevailing logic of tolerance and respect for different possessive beliefs directs participants to *talk through* their differences, a playful approach might use role play, games, imaginary outcomes, and stories to—at least temporarily—relax people's ties to their normative commitments, moral understandings, and narrowly hoped-for futures. Can this work? Aside from the question of whether conservative Christian and liberal equality beliefs can be meaningfully "suspended,"[51] even for a short while, to experiment with other outlooks through play (it is notable that several instances of conservative Christian withdrawal in fact concerned a refusal to participate in gay-equality education, cultural, or training initiatives),[52] the use of games and play to create institutional agreement has other shortcomings.

Consensus politics has been extensively criticized by feminists and others for assuming a horizontal relationship between forces that are often unequally positioned and for prioritizing agreement. In the conflict over gay equality, public bodies may assume a caretaking role, designing games to generate consensus or agreement among staff, service users, or those they regulate (see, e.g., Lerner 2014). But this exercise of responsibility—tacitly oriented to the orderly arrangement of different interests and the avoidance of dissent—can neglect (or dismiss) the productive tension that interventions in the name of new (or suppressed) principles of equality offer even when they take shape as satirical, mischievous, or challenging forms of play (see also Rancière 2010: 42–43). Instead, instituting top-down, safe, directed play narrates the gathered state (and its bodies) as separate and hierarchical, with participants play's targets or objects rather than active agents who are also engaged in play's design.[53] I therefore want now to turn to how play's design can be appropriated and redirected as participants become players, playing *with* (and not just *in*) the games that have been set for them.

2. Playing with Equality Beliefs

When it comes to equality beliefs, liberal states in the global North have undertaken a massive program of nationalization—or, at least, this is the claim of much conservative Christian legal politics. This is a nationalization that does not remove private property rights but instead reinforces them as the state takes co-ownership in gay equality beliefs. The parameters and effects of this nationalization become apparent when we consider critics' claim that conservative Christian beliefs have been accorded very different treatment.[54] Christianity may be publicly affirmed as an important, even national, religious belief system. However, when it comes to specific beliefs about sexuality and marriage, critics argue, commitment to heterosexual norms has been legally reconstituted as private rather than publicly shared.[55] In some cases, its status has even shifted to a form of dangerous property.[56] And so, like other kinds of dangerous possessions (knives and guns, for example), religious antigay beliefs must be legally constrained in what they can be used to do.[57] This is the state in activist mode, taking on a role more commonly associated with civil society organizations. Unlike the guardianship role described above in which state bodies attempt to bring holders of competing sexual perspectives together in ways that ostensibly favor neither side, here state bodies are seen as actively advancing particular beliefs. But in what sense does the deliberate nationalization of belief in gay equality involve play?

For a number of writers, play is an experimental mode of action. Matt Statler and his colleagues' (2009, 2011) work on "serious play" identifies it as a nondirectional method that simulates solutions to design problems. In commercial contexts, serious play typically takes a top-down, management-driven form to help generate innovative products. However, as a concept that combines creative improvisation with strategic, purposive action, serious play has also been taken up in noncommercial contexts. Lauren Leigh Hinthorne and Katy Schneider (2012), for instance, explore how serious play can enhance critical reflection, participant interaction, and innovative problem solving in international development (see also Mann 1996: 466). Serious play allows for mistakes, recognizing, too, that a focus on process does not deny the possibility of outcomes (since these will inevitably emerge) but treats outcomes as integral to a dynamically recursive process rather than as its terminal effects (see chapter 6). Playful experimenting with new ideas is an important aspect of innovating, but when taken up by state bodies, in the course of pursuing a political agenda of sexual orientation equality, suspicion often follows.

In her discussion of Hegelian self-consciousness, Judith Butler (1997) considers the lord's disavowal of his body in the injunction to his bondsman to "be my body for me."[58] In sexuality-focused state activism, this utterance seems to reverse as social forces demand that gathered states take up their political projects, embodying them as if they were the state's own. In the Hegelian story, which Butler tells, the bondsman does all the labor yet owns nothing of what is produced, stamped by the master with his own name. In the rather different story told here, "be my body" is an invocation that the state stamp controversial agendas and programs, such as sexuality equality, with its own name.[59] The desire for beliefs to become public property, given the institutionalization and security that it is hoped will follow, is an important aspect of state engagement. Instead of gay equality simply being recognized as a legitimate belief for gay people to hold, state bodies are impelled to act *as if* the beliefs are their own. But while gay activists hope that their ideas or beliefs will become part of the state fabric (see chapter 2) integrated with other public governance commitments, they remain fearful.

Left-wing writers and activists have long expressed concern that incorporation leads state bodies to defuse and water down radical politics, even as state bodies mark such politics with their own signature. As Amy Lind and Christine Keating (2013: 529) write, discussing LGBT policy reforms in Ecuador, "There is . . . reason to worry about the fragility of these gains, as the state is a notoriously fickle and unstable partner when it comes to rights for marginalized groups." In part, worry comes from states' seemingly contradictory character—that they support competing projects, express divergent rationalities and logics, and embody contrasting agendas. But it also comes from inevitable processes of translation as beliefs get transferred to, and taken up by, institutional bodies in ways that involve slippage and reframing (as when sexual liberation becomes gay rights). This reframing is not just done by state bureaucracies. If states and particularly nation-states are complex formations, activists attach to them, create conduits into them, and in some respects function as part of them[60] by deliberately making their own beliefs state-friendly. This can involve its own form of simulation as activists express beliefs that *they do not necessarily hold* to facilitate state take-up. In his work on mimicry, Michael Taussig (1993: 77) describes baby talk as "the adult imitating the child's mimicry of the adult's mimicry"—in other words, adults copying infants copying adults copying infants (or, perhaps, the reverse). In the case of sexual politics, similar processes are evident. Social movements have adopted simplified (presumed-to-be) state-friendly frames, such as "one in ten is gay" (Cooper 1994). They have also drawn on analogous state-based race and gender frameworks. These are frames (and analogies) that themselves came from state bodies copying, and so translating, social movement discourse that, in its own turn, developed mainstream approaches (alongside others) attentive to the value of congruence with state-based law.[61]

When it comes to gay equality, state beliefs cannot be treated as emerging from public bodies alone. However, running through much LGBT engagement with public authorities has been an anxiety that national, provincial, and local states are playing when they should not be, make-believing their own attachments and ownership of gay-equality norms. Acting as if they are committed to gay equality, states seem, to some, to offer a signature that is dramaturgical rather than productive, enacting a performance that is not intended to have performative effects (see also Ahmed 2012).[62] Yet accusations of play, when it comes to gay rights and equality, do not come only from the left as conservative Christians characterized states' assumed ownership of beliefs in gay equality as an irresponsible form of play. Here, derogatory references to play were not about the absence of consequences but, rather, about their excess. In the British case of *McClintock v. Department of Constitutional Affairs*, in which a magistrate refused to sit on family panels that would be assessing adoptions by potential gay parents, the tribunal noted, "The basis on which the appellant had sought to refuse . . . was that he thought that children were being *treated as guinea pigs in what was part of an unacceptable social experiment*."[63] According to McClintock, "Insufficient research had been undertaken in relation to whether this was desirable," and children should not be used "in the name of politically correct legislation."[64] From a conservative Christian perspective, sexuality was too risky and contentious to be treated as a terrain of innovation, indulged in by state bodies playing at political correctness with no thought of the consequences.

Both right and left, then, have dismissed state attempts to support gay equality as play, either because the initiatives forged (or remained within) a world of policy make-believe or because they sought to intervene in the only-too-real world according to a set of make-believe facts. In the first case, the nationalization of beliefs was doubted; in the second, it was treated as entirely reckless. But in both cases, activists mobilized to protect property in their beliefs. At the same time, exceptions did arise as property frames became displaced and the explicitly political character of beliefs emerged. Play here can be read as a register for reclaiming beliefs as *political provocations*. So if, at times, activists ask states to "be my body for me," this transaction can also be reversed. Then activists embody (or ventriloquize) state-assumed beliefs, doing so in ways that form not simply a transmission but also a translation, playfully, even *mischievously*, remaking the public property such beliefs might bear. Just as employees use a wily kind of play to cope with or challenge oppressive, controlling, or tedious employment contexts,[65] those ostensibly enrolled in supporting state property may mischievously convert it into a different kind of discourse.

Let me give an example that surfaced briefly in the British media. It concerned an experienced educator and campaigner for gay equality in schools, who gave a presentation at a staff training day for teachers.[66] According to the story later told by an unhappy teacher, at some point during the day the trainer remarked, "What makes you all think that to be heterosexual is natural?"[67] At that point, the unhappy teacher, along with several others, walked out.[68] The teacher was later suspended, in part for his comments, relayed after the event to the organizers, describing God's wrath toward homosexuals, comments that, in a sense, vandalized state-held property in liberal sexuality beliefs. However, the trainer's remarks are interesting as an instance in which a state-contracted activist failed to act exactly as she was supposed to, stepping outside the liberal terms of antihomophobic training by problematizing and so denaturalizing heterosexuality. Taking up the state educational pathways made available to her, the trainer expressed beliefs outside the logic of possessive belonging. In other words, she did not refer to the propertied character of her beliefs (that they deserved to be institutionally recognized, protected, and empowered *as things belonging to her*). Rather, in her role as an educator employed to give voice to publicly authorized beliefs, she played with this position, translating state equality discourse, to assert a more contentious and political set of claims.

We can read the intervention in other terms, but what play illuminates, in an incident such as this, is the kind of mischievous risk taking that can occur when utterances are expressed outside (or against) the terms of expected and authorized speech. In the process, a creative, unanticipated use of a position (here as a trainer) is exposed. This is a position in concertina-like relationship to state authority, as lines of access and opportunity allow players to move in and out of proximity and identification with their public role, oscillating between their authorized position and the less authorized beliefs expressed through it (see also chapter 2). Role play, in the sense of playing with a role, means it would be a mistake to see an episode such as this one as contained by play's "magic circle." It may have developed its own tempo, rhythms, and spaces, but the trainer's statement led to moves that proved increasingly un-play-like, as disciplinary action and sanctions took hold. Provocations such as the trainer's may appear modest, but they can precipitate a series of events that end with dismissal and litigation. As a way of destabilizing specific beliefs, the limitation of the "wise fool" remark (Anderson 2014) lies also in the fragility of its challenge. As one game move leads to another and institutional processes take over, the playful force of the original provocation, "What makes you all think that to be heterosexual is natural?" quickly gets lost.

So far, I have discussed the movement of beliefs through play where others' beliefs are experimentally taken up as if they belonged to those bodies playing or, in the case of the trainer just discussed, as if the player's beliefs actually belonged to or were authorized by the state. My final discussion turns to a different scenario. It involves gay groups in Canada using superordinate state commitments, derived from provincial codes, to engage recalcitrant City Councils and compel them to act as if the "superior" state commitments (and beliefs underpinning them) were their own. I want to use this episode to think about the embedded state and the performative practices of activists who act as if such a state exists. In chapter 2, I suggested that a democratic politics might ask, How does what the state inheres in inhere in the state in turn? The following discussion explores one form this indwelling can take. Here, the local state's imprint on community politics, through their refusal to support gay projects, caused activists to temporarily entangle themselves with, and so become part of, local City Councils by attaching to and seeking to mobilize municipal procedures. In this instance, activists sought to become an *active* component of a renetworked form of local state authority rather than a passive extension of the City Council. But, as I discuss, this attempt was also resisted. Play may overtly unsettle the boundaries between inside and out (as it also unsettles the boundaries between what is yours and mine), but play is also anchored in the ongoing life of these divisions, as this episode reveals.

My example concerns a dispute in the late 1990s in which gay groups in Ontario and British Columbia challenged the refusal of city mayors to issue pride proclamations in contexts where proclamations for other causes were routinely given.[69] Repeatedly these mayoral refusals were struck down by the courts. Homosexuality was a legitimate property that mayors could not refuse to "endorse." Nor could they deny it "pride" and pride's property, given the particular history of its attachment.[70] The mayoral proclamation cases pivoted on the celebration of Gay Pride as a communal rather than merely individual property, to which a mayoral proclamation added value. Here endorsement not only enhanced gay equality as a legitimate belief for gays to hold but placed the property of city approval in it. But these proclamation cases also demonstrate something else; namely, how provincial gay rights norms can get taken up by activists to play with local states. In this case, activists attempted to inhabit public bodies in order to redirect them, aligning city authorities with gay rights as if this was a property these city authorities also wished to value and protect. I want to read this inhabiting or contact, with its improvised tactics, energies, rhythms, and "as if" quality, as a form of play, specifically as a way of "free-running the state."

3. Free-running the State

With roots in early twentieth-century France and Martinique (Atkinson 2009), free-running and its sibling form, parkour, took off in the late twentieth century as a highly skilled recreational activity of running, tumbling, scaling, and mounting predominantly urban, human-engineered landscapes (Saville 2008).[71] According to Maria Daskalaki and her colleagues (2008: 62), parkour constituted "an expressive medium of individuals who view the city as a playground," where alienating physical terrain could be made stimulating and challenging rather than grim and depressing.[72] In this discussion, I want to extend the concept of free-running beyond its familiar terrain of city landscapes to consider it as a way of making contact with state apparatuses. Specifically, I want to consider free-running as a play-like way of doing politics and a political way of sometimes doing play.

Let me give an example. In the Canadian case of *Hudler v. City of London*, a gay support organization, HALO, sought a proclamation in support of "Pride Weekend" from the city of London, Ontario.[73] First, HALO approached the mayor, whose office was formally responsible for issuing such proclamations. When the mayor refused, HALO contacted a city councilor who had a track record in assisting the lesbian and gay community. The councilor spoke to the mayor who explained that she would "never grant this proclamation."[74] The councilor then approached the city clerk, following which HALO asked for the matter to be placed on the agenda of the city's Board of Control meeting. However, the report from the board advised that neither they nor the council had "jurisdiction to consider HALO's appeal of the mayor's decision."[75] Following this, the councilor submitted a resolution to the City Council asking that particular days be recognized as "a celebration of Pride." The motion failed.[76]

What state free-running usefully emphasizes, in cases such as this, are the dynamic, mobile, changing ways in which activists who have not received the touch they desire touch back, moving across administrative procedures and personnel as they search for the crevices and protuberances that might make a productive grip possible. Like water running over ground searching for a way through (Atkinson 2009), community activists in the mayoral proclamation cases crossed city authorities swiftly, if not always surely.[77] Adopting an improvised form of political dance (see also Saville 2008: 899), they went from the Mayor's Office to sympathetic politicians to bureaucrats and City Council committees, and eventually to the courts, seeking their proclamation. I want to come back to this desire for contact shortly. But there are also other ways in which state free-running resonates with parkour's more familiar urban form of tumbling. Like parkour, state free-running does not wait for state formations to change; nor does it prioritize campaigning for states to reform.[78] Instead, state free-running takes up institutional networks as bodies to inhabit and landscapes to reuse. Nathaniel Bavinton (2007) describes how parkour refuses the social meaning borne by an object, such as a wall, to focus on how an object can be used to further a free-runner (or *traceur*'s) fluid passage through an urban environment. In the case of state free-running, political objects may render movement less fluid. Nevertheless as obstacles they force activists on. State free-runners do not necessarily reject the political meanings held by different state parts, of committees, procedures for deputations, policy decisions, or bureaucratic posts. Rather their intention is to use these parts, if necessary and if possible, to achieve specific ends.

State free-running is purposive and often instrumental, but I do not want to treat it as only that. While contact with City Councils in these instances occurred to obtain a different proclamation decision, I want to think about how the desire for a proclamation decision also made contact with City Councils possible. This is a voluntary form of contact anchored in the existence of superordinate gay rights commitments, as well as in the reluctance of City Councils to comply.[79] It is also a contact that foregrounds governing as a process rather than as just a source of outputs. Just as city free-runners do not cross space efficiently merely to efficiently cross space, state free-running draws attention to the value of contact as a way of thinking not only instrumentally about politics but also about the process-value of democratically embedded forms of state governance, a theme I explore further in the two chapters that follow.

How bodies embed themselves in others is a theme I return to at different points in this book, attuned to the contested character of fusion and separation. Michael Atkinson (2009: 70) describes how, in free-running, the "lines separating roads, buildings, cultures, selves, and bodies disappeared."[80] Can similar claims be made about state free-running? Does it provide a way of experimenting with different bodily relations, including that of merger, with all the challenges this poses for other conceptions of democracy? We might treat the free-running gay activists as bearing the equality provisions of superordinate state bodies as they sought contact and sometimes fusion with City Councils. That this relationship was far more than the passive provision of a conduit for the beliefs and norms of superior state bodies can be seen in the following example.

The case of *Cradle of Liberty Council v. City of Philadelphia* illustrates the struggle that can surround activist attempts to present themselves as part of the local authority structure in order to advance gay equality.[81] Rather than a pride proclamation case (involving the withdrawal of symbolic recognition by conservative city administrations), it concerned a liberal city's withdrawal of a long-running building subsidy from a local Boy Scouts organization as a result of the national organization's public antigay stance (see chapter 1). One aspect of the Scouts' case concerned the claim that a local gay group had placed improper pressure on the city solicitor, evidenced through a series of email exchanges made public in the judgment. One email from the group reminded the city solicitor not to do "a disservice to the LGBT community *of which you are a part*."[82] Repeatedly, emails asked that copies of draft letters from the city to the Boy Scouts be circulated to group members, threatened to go "public about the City's . . . secret agreement," and, in somewhat imperious tones, remarked, "Your recent communication with the Scouts may indicate a willingness on your part to move in the right direction. On the other hand, a meeting in the near future *really does mean the near future*."[83] Emails from the group suggest a bold attempt to temporarily blend with the city's authority, to be both outside and inside through the asserted bond of shared identity and beliefs (albeit in a context in which the group's governmental authority depended on being able to work *through* the city government). But this bond was also resisted, and not only by the Boy Scouts' litigants and ultimately the court. The *Cradle of Liberty Council* judgment includes the emailed replies of the city solicitor, demonstrating the discursive effort, however polite, that can go into reproducing institutional boundaries, resisting free-running's drive to meld bodies and authority through property in beliefs held in common.[84]

Free-running is a useful concept for thinking about more democratically horizontal state practice. While democratic state thinking tends to foreground participative institutional structures, this book explores other ways for social forces to become active parts of states. One means, discussed in chapter 2, is through state workers' take-up of governmental resources, opportunities, and authority in order to deny others public benefits, a form of policy-making that works through omission and refusal. Here, free-running constitutes a way to try to repurpose state commitments and practice through contact-oriented pathways, intervention as a tinkering that is not altogether dissimilar to the experimental and curious actions Michiel de Lange discusses in relation to the hackable city.[85] Talk of intervention and tinkering may seem to suggest a distinction between the state and the activist, and to some degree this distinction, and its boundaries, can get produced by conflicts in which particular state bodies appear impervious or highly resistant to change. At the same time, if briefly and narrowly, engaging with institutional processes and systems in ways that generate a response makes it possible to identify free-runners as part of the movement and flow of public bodies—against, but also within, their dermal boundary.

Concluding Remarks

The claim that personhood is subject to a property logic is far from novel. Various scholars have drawn on the work of John Locke and Thomas Hobbes to explore the relationship between ownership and self-belonging, while others, such as Rosalind Petchesky, usefully point to older and nonliberal traditions of self-ownership. However, little of the work on self-belonging has addressed the "propertization" of beliefs within contemporary polities, a process that leads certain beliefs (but not others) to become institutionally defined, extracted, recognized, protected, and enabled. In the common law jurisdictions of this book, this process acquired a particular form through antidiscrimination and human rights regimes. These legal frameworks enforced, even as they ostensibly sought to redistribute, property rights in identity beliefs, nationalizing some while enclaving (dangerous) others. Situated in its midst, the legal drama over conservative Christian withdrawal highlights the contestation that formally redistributing and reshaping property in beliefs can generate.

Focusing on play as mimetic and plastic—capable not only of changing its form and meaning but also of simultaneously carrying competing forms and meanings—this chapter traced a series of different play moves. In the first, role play offered a register through which state bodies could encourage people to temporarily suspend their attachments to particular beliefs (or interests) to find new shared outlooks or ways of resolving conflict. In the second, state bodies experimented with how to operationalize beliefs they had promised to nationalize in ways that some conservative Christians dismissed as foolishly reckless and some LGBT activists feared was merely make-believe. Yet, to the extent that new liberal beliefs were institutionalized, activists also kicked back, taking up channels established for advancing new public beliefs to express other opinions, including opinions that retranslated those the state had taken up. Finally, the chapter explored city free-running in cases where activists took up superordinate state beliefs to compel dissident City Councils to act, even as they relied on court judgments to demand that councils express ideas they explicitly refused to hold.

Teasing out these complex relations highlights the exchange-like character of play as players move beliefs among themselves, acting in turn as if the beliefs now held are theirs or as if their beliefs now belong to another. Yet while this may seem like an elaborate card game, its value is far from trivial. This chapter has explored play's take-up as a term of opprobrium and as a practical activity for unmasking others. However, my primary focus has been on play's plastic, "as if," concertina-like qualities, because it is these qualities that seem to underpin play's capacity to disarmingly challenge settled interests and norms. This is something many activists are well aware of when they use satire and parody, pretending to be animals and elves to disturb authoritarian regimes. Seeking to remove or devalue what people identify as theirs risks generating huge resistance. In such contexts, play may offer a mode of engagement that defuses, unsettles, or, at least, diverts antagonism because play simultaneously recognizes attachment and detachment as it plays with the relationship between the two.

This stretching and condensing of contradiction has been developed in other scholarship on playful politics. What has received far less attention is the capacity (or otherwise) of play to present us with a different state ethic. In this chapter, I have used the conflict over possessive beliefs as an entry point to explore the different ways gathered states engage in play—designing, managing, and taking part while also providing a terrain and (ventriloquized) object for play by others. Certainly, not all state play is beneficial. It can be cruel and harmful to those who become its objects; it may distract from and trivialize important political objectives; and for it to operate in more progressive ways, players need to be able to participate willingly and not out of necessity. At the same time, while state play can garner criticism, as I have discussed, it can also support new ways of thinking about states. In addition to providing a ground from which the conditions needed for states to play well come sharply to the fore, play offers a register for expressing and enacting the caretaking, activist, and democratically embedded dimensions of progressive statehood. In other words, play is not simply a trivial, ludic form of practice. While foregrounding the possible pleasures of public governing (see chapter 5), play also suggests ways to govern that involve responsibility for the well-being of others and experimentation with new social justice agendas. Finally, play encourages a style and ethos of participatory statehood that does not simply rely on communities "speaking to the state" but also includes ways for communities and grassroots forces to inhabit, repurpose, resist, and invoke the still and mobile parts of institutional life.

FIVE. **The Erotic Life of States**

Not simply a rise and fall, a waxing and waning, but movement, processes, transmuta-
tions. That is what constitutes the appeal and power of desire, its capacity to shake up,
rearrange, reorganize the body's forms and sensations, to make the subject and body
as such dissolve into something else, something other than what they are habitually.
—ELIZABETH A. GROSZ, "Animal Sex"

In our yearning for justice and care we reach for the good state.
—ANNA SECOR, "Between Longing and Despair"

How can the erotic help us think about states—what they are and what
they could come to mean and be? This chapter explores the erotic dimensions of the legal drama over conservative Christian withdrawal. My aim is
not to celebrate the erotic in general or to celebrate the erotic state practice
that currently exists. Rather, I read this conflict for its erotic dimensions in
order to support new paths for thinking about public governing and what it
could entail. One theme running through the chapters so far is that of state
form. I have suggested that we might think *toward* a conception of the state
as the condition and shape of public governing while remaining attentive
to the gathered or embodied forms both state and non-state entities (including organizations, clubs, religious institutions, grassroots movements,

parties, and everyday utopias) take. This chapter explores how the erotic helps to constitute this embodiment and give expression to it. Of course, the erotic can also contribute to processes of disembodiment, to the pulling apart of organizational forms. Yet since the erotic and embodiment are deeply entwined, the part the erotic plays in state embodiment is at the heart of this analysis.

Ideas of political embodiment have a long and complex history. In some versions, the state is imagined as a hierarchical composite body composed of different sections of society. In others, the biological body of the ruler (or leader) and the artificial body of the state are deemed to intricately coexist, from medieval notions of the "king's two bodies" (Kantorowicz [1957] 1997) to contexts where the bodies of leaders stand in for the state (see Laderman 1997).[1] The notion of an embodied state is not just a historical artifact; it continues to have mileage, as Claire Rasmussen and Michael Brown (2005) discuss. It is tacitly deployed by scholars when they critically depict the state as coherent, stable, and oppressive. More explicitly, it is drawn on by those who worry about the implications of seeing states as embodied; whether due to its associations with fascist or authoritarian forms of rule (see, e.g., Neocleous 2003) or, more generally, because notions of state corporeality seem too organic, functional, or reductionist in treating the state as a unified living thing rather than a disembodied (even disaggregated) idea.

In this chapter, I want to explore the sociomaterial dimensions of stateness. According to the anthropologist Uli Linke (2006: 206), "Modern states are . . . embodied forms. Political worlds have a visual, tactile, sensory and emotional dimension." This does not mean, as Linke acknowledges, that states take shape *only* in this register. States can be imagined and imaginary (see chapter 6), and the cultural, ideological and fantastical constitute important dimensions of sociomaterial state formations too. However, reducing the state to an idea can lose other more material dimensions. It can also undermine ways of thinking about states concerned with notions of responsibility, organization, and agency—important for understanding state formations *as they are* and for thinking about what states *could become*. Embodiment does not have to entail defined, bounded entities. Just as ideas about biological bodies have moved away from the notion of a coherent, contained, unified life-form, and ideas about humans have evolved through the influence of cyborg and posthumanist thinking, so state embodiment can also shed its anthropomorphic or animal shape.[2] We might think, instead, of the different (composite) elements that assemble in state formations—the roles, humans, other animals, laws, systems, buildings, texts, ideas, plans, vegetation, procedures, and places. These elements are not fully assembled in advance, such that coherently formed states go about the business of acting in the world. State embodiment is not something that simply *is* but rather something that is *done and redone*, where the embodied quality of state action—its relays, systems, sensations, texture, and agency stretching across and folding in distance—shapes (even as it also depends on) public governance's wider force and relationships.

It is in this context that I want to think about erotic state relations, focusing primarily on the gathered state (see chapters 2 and 3) while remaining attentive to the shape and condition of public governance produced in and through the common law jurisdictions of this book. My aim is threefold: to briefly trace uses of the erotic (or sexual) state in academic writing; to consider what a legal drama over conservative Christian withdrawal, with all its retractions, attachments, and pleasures, can contribute to this discussion; and tentatively to assess what the erotic might bring to reimagining the state for progressive politics. But what is the erotic when applied to states? Extensively theorized across cultural theory, philosophy, psychoanalysis, and sexuality and gender studies, the erotic has been pulled in various directions. This chapter approaches it as a relational charge or force involving desires, vitality, and sensations. Central to this framing is a depiction of the erotic as something broader than sex or sexual pleasure, and as something that foregrounds relations with both others and the self. The erotic is often juxtaposed with rationality, death, and performance; in this discussion, these elements also emerge as the underside of the erotic—what it carries with(in) it—and as that which the erotic negates or pushes away.

From Sex as a Scopic Form of Power to the Erotic State

The erotic provides a way into thinking about the sensory, vibrant, generative, and interactive dimensions of social and political existence. Yet despite the sensory force, desires, and interactions that states express, attract, and evolve through, the relationship of states to the erotic, as something other than a governable terrain of social life and activity, remains understudied.[3] This is particularly apparent in work on (neo)liberal polities. In contrast to writing on erotic economies, attuned to the mutual imbrication of desire and economic practice (see, e.g., Bennett 2016), when it comes to states, the erotic is typically depicted as the antithesis; that which states, in their laws, policies, and expenditures, try to suppress, destroy, or otherwise control. Yet in thinking about how the erotic runs through state formations, there are literatures on which we might draw. One is work on emotional governance, which foregrounds how people feel about state practice; the affective relations that develop in the course of public provision; and the feelings that both animate and get suppressed among state workers.[4] A second cluster of work focuses on popular deployments of erotic discourse to ridicule the state. Achille Mbembe (1992: 9) explores the mocking humor, centered on "the mouth, the penis, and the belly," used to satirize elite political power in the sub-Saharan postcolony.[5] Parallels with Mikhail Bakhtin's (1968) account of European medieval folk culture can also be found in other satirical challenges to state authority as they take up and redirect the attention paid by the erotic to the everyday sensory character of sustaining and reproducing life.[6] A third approach centers on the sexualization of sovereigns and sovereignty, drawing (implicitly or explicitly) on relations between the ruler's two bodies to explore what happens when at least one of these bodies becomes improperly sexualized—something Thomas Dumm (1998) vividly describes in his cultural analysis of Bill Clinton's impeachment.[7] However, the most prominent and extensive body of writing to locate the state within a sexual (if far from erotic) terrain concerns nation-states' use of sex and sexually coded body parts to dominate and govern.

Discussing the Turkish state's "fixation" with penile penetration, Asli Zengin explores its use of sight and touch to reproduce a conservative gender and sexual order. She describes how the state measured transwomen's vaginas to ensure they were sufficiently extended (and penetrable) so that their subjects could receive a "pink" identification card and be granted "legal recognition as a female" (Zengin 2016: 233). She also describes how putative gay male conscripts could be subject to anal inspection and compelled to include photographs of themselves being penetrated in order to obtain exemption from military service on "psycho-sexual disorder" grounds (Zengin 2016: 238–39). Begoña Aretxaga (2001: 10), likewise, writes powerfully about the random and terrifying use of strip searches on female political prisoners in Northern Ireland in the early 1990s, a scopic form of governance that combined sex, surveillance, and control to sexually shame and subordinate female activists.[8]

Yet while governments, through their human parts, touch and scrutinize the sexualized body parts of others, performing a sex that is violent

and unassented to, other work identifies a very different use of sex by contemporary (neo)liberal states. Echoing an older history in which colonial
narratives of conquered peoples' nonnormative sexual activities were used
to build and legitimate European state action (see, e.g., Povinelli 1994),
here, sexual attitudes come to provide a litmus test of the self and others'
civilized state as (neo)liberal states deploy savior/rescuer narratives to
deny membership and resources to those nations and individuals identified as backwardly antigay (see, e.g., Stychin 2003).[9] As I discuss in the introduction, tied to this move is a domestic project of incorporating certain
minoritized sexual subjects into the realm of the "normal" and so worthy
of care. In their discussion of Ecuador, Amy Lind and Christine Keating
(2013: 518) describe this move, in which "political actors harness the power
of the state to protect LGBT people from persecution and domination," as
one of "homoprotectionism." And it is this homoprotectionism, in legal
and policy form, that precipitated the legal drama of this book.[10]

Writing on the sexualized state provides an important context for the
account offered here. While I want to explore how the erotic might orient
us toward more progressive state thinking, I do so across and in relation
to a far more critical reading of state sexuality. This is a reading attuned
to the ways in which governments deploy (or permit) sexualized violence,
work to sustain hegemonic sexualities, produce stigmatized and unlivable
sexualities, and mobilize desire for coercive and oppressive ends (see,
e.g., Agathangelou et al. 2008). To ignore such a critical reading risks per-
petuating a view of states and statehood (or at least neoliberal ones) that
is overly romantic and sanitized. The challenge, though, is how simultaneously to sustain both critical and hopeful accounts. One means of doing
so, developed in this book, is to deploy different "cuts" in determining
what it is and means to be a state (also Barad 2003: 816), so that ways of
approaching the state oriented to transformational change do not depend
on conceptions of the state generated through critique.[11] Approaching the
state in ways oriented to transformative progressive change certainly require material cuts and joins that substantially alter state practices and
modes of organizing. But recutting also has an imaginary dimension in
terms of how and where the connections and boundaries that constitute
the state, as well as particular states, are drawn. Reimagining the state does
not mean taking states as they are currently figured and simply rereading
them. While glimpses of possibility can be found in what is currently recognized as state practice, the postnormative approach developed here also

involves reframing and reorienting our understanding of what it is to be a state. Previous chapters have adopted this approach to reimagine the state through principles of heterogeneity, plurality and play. In this chapter, I take it further by drawing on (and reworking) a series of erotic idioms.

Reading states through the figure of the erotic (or sexual) has been undertaken in pursuit of critical accounts as well as more ambivalent ones. Teemu Ruskola's (2010) account of the "rape" of China powerfully demonstrates the former. In it, Ruskola (2010: 1480) takes seriously the legal fiction of states as persons to explore "the homoerotic violation of non-Western states [as] a condition of possibility of fully realized (Western) sovereignty." More ambivalent is the portrayal of state sexuality in Carl Stychin's discussion of Quebec's relationship to the Rest of Canada (ROC).[12] He writes, "It is a cliché in Canada that the federation is a 'marriage' between French and English; a heterosexual metaphor in which French Canada (centred territorially in Quebec) takes on the female role. . . . But the construction of national identities is not limited to a heterosexual frame. The relationship between Quebec and the ROC long has been constructed in homosexual (and homophobic) terms" (Stychin 1997: 15–16). Hoping to show that "this 'relationship' is far more complex and contradictory than the [heterosexual] marriage metaphor would suggest" (Stychin 1997: 16), Stychin demonstrates what sexual idioms can bring to exploring political relations. In doing something similar here, I am also interested in challenging the presumption that the erotic is a *fictive* (or metaphorical) register when speaking about states. Idioms, such as the erotic, can consolidate and deepen boundaries and distinctions between things (particularly when the carriage across is seen as taking "real" meanings into places where the "fit" can *only* be an imagined one). But to the extent that metaphors identify new, less naturalized interpretations or names, they can also work differently. Drawing on Ricoeur, Mark Rifkin (2012: 17) writes, "The designation of a statement as figurative . . . can indicate . . . its effort to register something in being that *available discourses* do not count as part of reality" (emphasis added). In the case of the erotic, its (idiomatic) application to state bodies as well as human ones creates a provisionally horizontal ground that allows us to explore relations between bodies *qua* bodies (albeit different kinds of bodies). It also opens up useful questions about states—about the intensities that seem to craft and sustain particular state forms and about the tensions that arise when a state body enters or withdraws from another, trailed by sticky fluids that show "where it has traveled and what it has come into contact with" (Ahmed 2006: 40).

This book has explored encounters between very differently embodied entities, from Christian colleges to professional regulatory bodies, local states, firms, staff, users, and others. These encounters are some distance from the horrifying sexual violence and sex-based humiliation that critics rightly hold nation-states politically accountable for. Yet in this drama of withdrawal, with its everyday exercises of discrimination and refusal and everyday acts of political authority, sex and sexuality are repeatedly signaled. In some instances, they become the *reason* for withdrawal, as in those cases where guesthouse owners deny gay male couples a shared bedroom in case they have sex or, as in *Reaney v. Hereford Diocesan Board of Finance*, where the English bishop distrusted the applicant's promise to remain celibate—a promise required for the gay young man to obtain a job as a church youth officer for which he was the leading candidate.[13] In other cases, sex, especially what counts as sinful sex, gets rolled into the beliefs seeking protection from a state more concerned with axes of sexual orientation than with its everyday erotic manifestation.[14] But there is more to the erotic in this drama than the sex and sexuality over which conservative Christians, gay litigants, officials, and activists fought. This chapter is foremost about the presence of the erotic in the withdrawal, attachments, and forging of states and other bodies.

Withdrawal and the Activist State

Within penetrative registers of exchange, withdrawal typically forms the postponed or suspended moment, taking place once interest has subsided and the "main" event is over. But the withdrawal of this book is far from the epilogue or forgotten postclimactic moment. It is not about men pulling out of other humans or even about women and others doing so. Rather, it is about the public bodies and states that humans pull out of as they, in turn, pull out of humans and one another. We might think of these episodes, with their centering of withdrawal, as queer, premature, and maybe queerly premature. Like pornography, where early withdrawal is needed to scopically capture the moment of ejaculation, here, too, it is the untimely departure—of goods being pulled out or bodies pulling away—that demonstrates, even as it also sharpens and intensifies, the desire for those things and bodily connections that have become denied.

Withdrawal, of course, is not necessarily erotic. However, approaching it in this way draws attention to the sensual body-making (and body-expressing) dimensions of this conflict, to the fantasy and desires projected and expressed, and to the vibrancy and liveliness of matter (see, e.g., Bennett 2009)—especially when subtracted. Through withdrawal, bodily identities, boundaries, and connections are asserted. While this is felt by and projected onto those withdrawn from, it is also evident in the self-imaginaries of those pulling out. For some conservative Christians, withdrawal seems to impart a vibrant fantasy of independence: here I am, standing my ground, refusing to be part of a liberal consensus; I know who and what I am, where I begin and end, from pulling back and pulling away.[15] Similarly, for public bodies, such as the City Councils denying Gay Pride proclamations (chapter 4) or those state authorities denying conservative Christians the right to discriminate (chapter 1), withdrawal constitutes an act of self-naming and self-definition. Through withdrawal, boundaries are forged, but they are also contested.

The discussion that follows draws on three cases of refusal. They concern a marriage registrar, Transport for London, and sections of the Canadian bar. In the first, Lillian Ladele, a London marriage registrar, refused to participate in same-sex civil partnerships after they were legally introduced in Britain following the Civil Partnerships Act 2004.[16] Initially, Ladele changed rosters with colleagues so she could opt out of any work involving same-sex couples.[17] Subsequently, under pressure from unhappy colleagues, managers at Islington Borough Council demanded that she participate. Ladele refused, felt forced to resign from her post, and brought an employment tribunal case that eventually was decided against her by the Court of Appeal (a decision upheld by the European Court of Human Rights).[18] The second episode, which led to a cluster of cases, involved the evangelical Christian college Trinity Western University (TWU) in British Columbia and the new law school it proposed in 2012.[19] The university had, at this time, a Community Covenant agreement to which all staff and students had to adhere that prohibited, among other things, sexual intimacy outside of heterosexual marriage (see chapter 3). As a result, several provincial law societies refused to give the new law school professional recognition; TWU challenged their decisions, with uneven results across different provincial courts, subsequently appealing and losing in the Canadian Supreme Court.[20]

The third case returns us to London. It concerns Transport for London's decision in April 2012 to turn down antigay posters from "being paraded" on the outside of its buses. The posters read, "NOT GAY! EX-GAY, POST-GAY AND PROUD. GET OVER IT!"[21] They were solicited by a Northern Ireland charity, Core Issues Trust (CIT), an organization dedicated to advancing Christian scriptural beliefs and conservative family politics. The posters were intended as a response to earlier ones placed on buses by the LGBT organization Stonewall, which read, "SOME PEOPLE ARE GAY. GET OVER IT!"[22] While the advertising contractor initially accepted CIT's advertisement, the transportation authority and Mayor's Office expressed immediate concern about providing, in effect, a "mobile billboard" for religious interests.[23] The charity challenged the decision to reject the advertisement, arguing, among other things, that the ban had been introduced for an improper purpose—namely, so the mayor could retain the good favor of London's gay community in the run-up to his (hoped-for) reelection.[24]

We can read these three episodes as demonstrating a kind of state activism as governance authorities used disciplinary, accrediting, and advertising powers, against the grain of their conventional intended usage, to advance a liberal form of gay equality—a political project perched on the jurisdictional threshold of policy-normal.[25] Not yet fully enrolled within the everyday, unproblematic concerns of governing, the contested status of formal gay equality left it vulnerable to being depicted as a form of regulatory excess—enacted by overreaching, overreacting state bodies, including those described as the "statutory delegates of government" (see also chapter 2).[26] This depiction came to the fore in the Nova Scotia Supreme Court decision in *Trinity Western University v. Nova Scotia Barristers' Society*. There, the court remarked, over the refusal by the Nova Scotia Barristers' Society (NSBS) to recognize TWU's law degree, "It is hardly a pressing objective for a representative of the state *to use the power of the state to compel a legally functioning private institution in another province* to change a legal policy in effect there because it reflects a legally held moral stance that offends the NSBS, its members or the public."[27] Painting a picture of an overly libidinal bar association, excessively eager to support gay sentiment, the court went on:

> The NSBS argued that its decision was an effort to uphold the equality rights of LGBT people. It was not an exercise of anyone's equality rights. . . . *The NSBS is not the institutional embodiment of equality rights for LGBT people.* . . . Refusing a TWU law degree will not address discrimination against anyone in Nova Scotia. . . . The state through the NSBS does not have the authority to try to coerce [evangelical Christians] into changing [their] beliefs so that they conform to those of mainstream society.[28]

For the court, the NSBS had exceeded its authority, particularly its territorial authority, in attempting to give voice to its desires, "spending" its resources recklessly, as I discuss below. By seeking to control university policies in another province, the Barristers' Society was using its powers to compel a "private" university to touch in friendly, welcoming ways those the university chose not to.

What emerges in this and other judicial depictions of state bodies' giving excessive life and power to their political desires—touching too much and too intrusively—is a critical deployment of the erotic, closing down on the legitimate terrain of political desire and intensity. Yet, in doing so, what also comes to the fore is the sensation that bodily friction causes. Withdrawal is rarely a simple and clean act. The *Transport for London* case reveals the rapid, anxious swirl of sensory contact that can result from bodies attempting to pull out. Following Transport for London's decision to withdraw its agreement to carry the posters, an intricate lattice of meetings, emails, and phone calls across state agencies took place, involving the London Mayor's Office, the operations director for London Buses, Transport for London's managing director of marketing and communications, the director of external affairs at the Greater London Authority, the deputy mayor, a Transport for London commissioner, the advertising contractor, the Committee of Advertising Practice, the *Guardian* newspaper "sniffing around," and a series of other players.[29] With law demanding that any lattice of municipal contact take a properly authorized shape, this one became vulnerable to intense after-the-fact judicial scrutiny. Like the overly disclosing depictions that constitute pornography, here institutional openings, intensities, vulnerabilities, and bodily interactions were on display. But this was not just a scopic form of engagement, restricted to observing and witnessing the opened-up public body. Juridical events such as these, where questions of improper influence arise, also become subject to a prodding form of touch, digging and delving into previously hidden parts.[30] In contrast to end-oriented forms of scrutiny, judicial review can make the minute sequencing of contact matter,[31] however quickly or slowly it takes place. Bodies must prove they know where their parts are and what they are doing as the courts scrutinize the devolved proprioception of the state in painful detail.

In chapter 4, I considered a series of cases involving gay activists' crossing City Councils at speed, seeking openings that would allow them to effectively compel reluctant councils to provide Gay Pride proclamations. Focusing on the *erotic* dimensions of such crossings—the pleasures, intensities, desires, and sensations generated by fluctuating contact (including the sharp and rough contact of something being pulled out and pulled away)—brings questions of process to the fore.[32] The erotic is not just about what gets produced, about outcomes, effects, and outputs; it is also about the experiences and sensations of engagement, of taking part. This is important for thinking prefiguratively about the *pleasures* of collaborative governing, as I discuss later. It is also helpful in reassessing the meaning and implications of what typically gets counted as waste (or wasteful). In his discussion of libidinal economies, David Bennett (2010) examines those "unproductive" sexual expenditures—paid for, masturbatory, nonreproductive—where sex is written off as producing nothing of value. In the case of states, claims of waste are also commonplace, with welfare states in particular subject to neoliberal accusations of spoilage, squandering, and inefficiency.[33] If waste identifies nonvaluable uses, or if it identifies once valuable uses and things that have become residualized, lost or rendered superfluous (unattractive and out of place, perhaps, because what counts as rightly placed, or even as rightly timed, has moved on), one critical move is to reverse these calibrations—to show that those processes (or outputs) deemed worthless indeed have value. This is something conservative Christian advocates tried, using refusal and withdrawal to challenge new secular distributions of value with its attendant dismissal (or at least perceived dismissal) of their authorities and commitments.

Reversing calibrations of value may also mean *reinterpreting* certain kinds of state process—at least for the jurisdictions of this book. Instead of seeing the tense, elaborate, time-saturated interactions of staff and politicians in the *Transport for London* drama as a waste of time and energy, such interactions—and the internal libidinal energy they generated—might be seen as productive, establishing connections and contact among different nodal points (and producing these points as nodal ones). This reassessment speaks to the organizational worth of what often gets dismissed. Here, the creation and "spending" of energy in emails, phone calls, meetings, and memos is not simply a drain but can be read as productive in producing particular state "lines," as organizational pathways of meeting, seeing, hearing, and instructing contribute to forging state bodies and giving them a particular shape. This shape is not necessarily a progressive or horizontal one, although it can be. Like play, the erotic sidelines goals and instrumental action by finding value elsewhere. In this case, value might be found in feelings of aliveness; in sensitivity to other participants' feelings, thoughts, and actions; or in the excitement of impending, possibly avoidable, legal danger.

The nervous, desiring, anxious energy of organizational friction also has other effects. Sometimes it pushes bodies apart, relying on (and thus sustaining) the hazard of unwanted connection that contact and contact-based secretions threaten, something Dumm (1998) explores in his account of attempts to manage President Bill Clinton's sexual incontinence. In the legal drama explored here, the trace and flow of secretions was also read negatively and stickily,[34] as withdrawal became rationalized in contraceptive terms. In this sense, withdrawal constituted a preemptive means for conservative Christians, liberal public bodies, and gay equality advocates to avoid fertile secretions being left behind (see chapter 1). For Lillian Ladele, the marriage registrar, withdrawal from ceremonies involving same-sex couples was necessary to avoid some intangible part of her remaining with the gay couples that she registered. And because registering gay couples might contaminate her also,[35] withdrawal was essential as a form of protection. Yet withdrawal is not always the first choice, given the seductions of doing what is easy and least costly. Ladele may have resisted the temptation to conform, but Islington council initially gave in to the "easy money" (Bennett 2010: 100) by ignoring Ladele's practice of changing rosters to avoid civil partnerships.[36] It was only when the council faced growing pressure from Ladele's unhappy colleagues that they demanded she comply. Yet despite this early hesitation, Islington council argued in court that relieving the claimant of her duties—allowing her to register only relationships she approved of—would be to "connive" in discrimination.[37] What the council allowed staff to do (and not to do), when it came to their work, affected the message sent to employees about their commitment to equality.[38] In other words, not only would allowing Ladele to refuse mean Islington Borough Council was participating in discrimination, but some part of the council would be deposited in Ladele's act of refusal, in turn depositing the act back in them.[39] In the *Transport for London* case, similarly, a major part of the drama concerned the London mayor's apparent fear that antigay sentiment on bus posters would attach itself to him.[40] According to the director of communications at the Greater London Authority, "The Mayor was very clear in his reaction and I clearly remember him saying words to the effect that he was not having buses driving around London telling gay people that they are sick and can be cured."[41] Failing to withdraw from the agreement to run the advertisement, the court acknowledged, would attach large, prominent slogans not only onto London's municipal transport system but onto and even into its residents: "Advertising on the side of London buses is extremely intrusive. The advertisements are large and prominent: 6 metres long, ten feet in the air, facing the pavement. Buses dominate the streets of London. Millions of people who live in, or visit, London will be confronted by advertisements on buses, whether they are pedestrians, cyclists or motorists, and they will not be able to avoid them."[42]

In this legal drama, then, labor, bus posters, recognized law degrees, and, in other cases, cakes, books, and room rentals became subject to withdrawal to avoid the shedding (and movement) of bodily stuff that, without withdrawal, would attach itself to the service provider, as well as to the client. But the things withdrawn also reveal something else: the work mediating entities perform in bringing different bodies *into relationship*. We might read these entities (employee labor, posters, law degrees, and so on) as social propagation devices, promising (or threatening) to give rise to newly formed beings. For, if Islington council was sufficiently plastic to be implicated by the decision it eventually refused to make—namely, to allow Ladele *not* to register gay couples—and if giving Ladele *permission* to refuse would have "connived" in discrimination, then taking the "easy" route would have produced a different kind of Islington, an authority shaped by its *incorporation* of Ladele's refusal rather than by its rejection of it (see chapter 2). But mediating *things* (along with places and policies) are more than petri dishes in this conflict. They are also important in their own right. This drama of withdrawal is a drama of desire, love, and fantasy for (and about) the things and bodies that assertions of sovereignty or governance allow to be withdrawn. As thwarted or denied objects, these advertisements, accreditations, and marriage registrations, alongside iced cakes, T-shirts, and guesthouse vacations, take their place in a scripted enactment and representation of desire: the object other that "solicits, beckons, implores, provokes and demands" (Grosz 1995: 285).

We might think of these thwarted objects as "public gifts," things transferred or passed on that wholly or, at least, partially remain outside of market relations (see Hyde 1979). In some cases, what circulates cannot be bought; in other cases, buying remains incommensurate with (or defines only a part of) what is transferred (Hyde 1979). The "ex-gay, post-gay" ad on a bus, for instance, carried more than the cost of its purchase, and more than the revenue it would generate, which is why the exchange was inadequate for Transport for London and withdrawal unacceptable to CIT. For

Islington council, the value of Ladele's work as a marriage registrar did not make up for the loss caused by her unwillingness to participate in civil partnerships. Allowing her to refuse was not legally required and thus a gift the council was not prepared to make. In this way, liberal public bodies and conservative Christians pulled things from particular circuits where the money or benefits received did not seem equivalent to what was given and where the freedom to make (or not make) a good available exceeded the obligation (or, at least, the legally recognized obligation) to provide it. If the erotic character of gifts, as Lewis Hyde (1979: xiv) suggests, lies in the relations that bind donor and recipient,[43] here withdrawal draws attention, beyond its own economy, to those sensory circuits of injury and pain that shadow the gift. These circuits parallel their satisfaction-seeking counterparts—the chains of beneficiaries extracting value, for instance, from the movement of the "ex-gay, post-gay" posters.

Attachment and Minor Sensations

It would be wrong, however, to treat withdrawal as a rejection of contact or association per se. Withdrawal can generate new forms of association and enrollment as leaving or forsaking one body generates closer ties to another (see chapter 3). Withdrawal can also provide the opportunity and impetus for an adversarial or agonistic contact, as on those occasions where bodies withhold a public "gift" that others deem an entitlement. We witnessed this in the case of Canadian gay activists free-running non-pride-proclaiming City Councils discussed in chapter 4. Here, though, I want to consider something else—namely, how bodily attachments and entry generate, and are tied to, desire.[44]

The desire to merge, attach, or enter is an interesting counterpart to the fears, just discussed, about what might stick. Certainly, some bodies worried, as I described, that their actions would be contaminated by adhering to or being touched by gay, conservative Christian, or liberal state others. Yet in other cases, what got foregrounded was the desire to be a part,[45] to insert one's body into (or remain within) that of another, and to have a "carved out" space in which to dwell.[46] Previous chapters have discussed a number of examples: of gay staff wanting to remain part of Christian organizations; of student societies wanting to remain connected to (and so recognized by) their law schools; and of Catholic adoption agencies trying to stay attached to City Councils (despite their gay-equality policies) without this jeopardizing their place also within the body of their diocese. Sought-after attachments and habitations contrast with those involving "compelled" forms of contact.[47] But how does the desire to attach to or enter other bodies relate to questions of state governance, leaving to one side those state practices involved in regulating and brokering their distribution?

"To be sovereign is not to be rapable, and to be rapable is not to be sovereign" (Ruskola 2010: 1529). In his account of nineteenth-century relations between the West and China, Ruskola describes how a gendered, sexualized discourse provided the idiomatic terms through which "intercourse" became forced penetration as a result of China's underwhelming interest in economic and diplomatic relations with the West. An "extensive repertoire of legal strategies of informal empire . . . [produced] a shell of Chinese sovereignty, penetrated repeatedly from all sides so that its spatial representation looked increasingly like an elaborate latticework" (Ruskola 2010: 1526). In other cases, economic and diplomatic intercourse have remained a dominant frame for thinking about interstate state contact, legitimated through claims (albeit ones that critics question) of national autonomy, consent, necessity, and the practicalities of everyday state relations.[48] Typically, discussions of state intercourse focus on relations *between* nation-states.[49] How can an erotic reading of this legal drama help us to think about the governmental effects of other kinds of attachments, entries, and immersions?

Reading the book's legal drama in ways attuned to the erotic underscores the life-force that antihegemonic desires can bear. These desires enter gathered states in different ways. They often bypass the conventional routes on which democratic norms and procedures rely, since antihegemonic desires may not necessarily (or only) be presented *to* states through the participatory or consultative structures that give outsiders permission to speak and act. Instead, they are carried into states by the actors and partners that state bodies already have (chapter 2). While we can understand the presence of conservative Christian beliefs in gathered state formations in different ways, an erotic reading foregrounds their force and energy: the willingness of advocates to "spend" themselves not simply in pursuit of withdrawal but *in pursuit of remaining in place*, even if this destroys or harms them in the process, as with the Kentucky marriage registrar who chose imprisonment rather than resign or sign certificates for same-sex marriages.[50] The vitality of antihegemonic beliefs and desires reveals something of the processes that go to make up heterogeneously embodied states. At the same time, the animating presence of dissident beliefs also speaks to an *embedded* conception of the state as it reflects, mediates, and sometimes intensifies wider social tensions.

When it comes to dissident forms of state entry or attachment, there is a tendency on the left to take one of two positions: either to advocate for new hegemonies or to support their endless contestation through deconstructive antihegemonic moves. What gets routinely neglected is how these two processes might combine; how progressive *hegemonic* projects can be forged in ways that not only facilitate and sustain moments of immanent challenge but also benefit from them. Karen Ashcraft explores a similar interconnection in her work on feminist organizing, tracing the productive role of dissent in organizations seeking to advance feminist agendas (see Ashcraft 2000, 2001, 2006). From a Deleuzian-inspired perspective, Torkild Thanem (2004) also explores the contribution of "non-organization," of unpredictable forms of purposelessness, to organizational life. "Non-organization . . . subverts and resists, contradicts and interrupts, escapes, precedes and exceeds organization. It is part of the spontaneous, nonlinear and unpredictable movements of desire" (Linstead and Thanem 2007: 1494). Sometimes, we may want particular "unpredictable movements of desire" or moments of disorganization to succeed, and we will differ on when this is so. But at other times, these challenges—as the stuff and forces that fail to be captured by new hegemonic projects—can be fruitful *to the extent they remain minor*, if not for those who express them (and who grow disappointed by their subsequent lack of take-up), then for others instead. I therefore want to question the normative tendency to read the value of political projects as constant across scale—that is, if it is good (or bad), the same applies regardless of its extension or multiplicity.[51] What the erotic usefully provides is a positive register of the minor, those forces that may not be desirable scaled up but nevertheless, as micro-provocations or stimulations, intensify and enhance the desires, life force, and vitality of governing processes.[52] This is something that progressive governmental projects often miss. Decentralization and public participation agendas routinely fail to think about how to create sparks or how sparks can happen (when they exceed institutional modes of design). As a result, they miss the liveliness that often motivates wider involvement or instead seek to domesticate or gamify it through managed, overly designed participatory formats (see chapter 4).

The legal drama over conservative Christian withdrawal is a drama of micro-sensation, concerned with the attention and feeling that *undesired* refusals generate in conditions where bodies want contact and to dwell (temporarily or permanently) within the symbolic and sociomaterial embrace of another. Some critics might argue that micro-sensations already receive too much attention, that excessive political and institutional concern is paid to minor hurts and injuries—to wedding venues, photographs, cards, and cakes sought from one body rather than another. From this perspective, the force of sensation (especially the sensation caused by rejection) stands in the way of freedom and robust politics—a rope around the necks of those who simply want to follow their own, incompatible desires. There is a gendered quality to this critique in its encoded dismissal of small-scale sensation as too petty and inappropriate for states to attend to. But if we want gathered states to be embedded within everyday lives as responsive democratic entities, what kind of relationship to desires and feelings, including colliding desires and feelings, should such states have, and is there something valuable in the shared "spending" (see Bennett 2016: 54) that these minor moments expose? Unlike other relationships of donor and donee, producer and consumer, or seller and buyer in which parties engage in reciprocating but distinct practices, here different participants in circuits of withdrawal engage in the consummation or explosive rush of adrenaline, feeling and action. Scaled up, these might constitute "theaters" of war, but can we also think about the creation of other stages where social tension and conflict can—if not peacefully, then perhaps *erotically*—erupt?

Governing Pleasures, Caretaking, and the Commons

At the heart of this drama lie threatened pleasures: the youth camp, wedding, or school prom that was desired and anticipated but now, thanks to conservative Christian withdrawal, has become—if not thwarted—then more challenging and effortful to obtain. Sometimes it is conservative Christians' pleasures that are jeopardized, perhaps because, like the wedding florist or cake maker, they can no longer control the direction of their work or because, like the guesthouse owner, they cannot determine which bodies they may economically touch—who they will have to let into their homes and allow to lie in their beds. The corporeal integrity and, more particularly, organizational integrity on which conservative Christian pleasure depends gets depicted as damaged through having to incorporate dissonant bodies. Yet what is striking, if enduringly unremarked on, in this conflict is the dividing line between pleasure and governing. Pleasure lies in community belonging, creative expression, participation in rites and rituals, and vacationing.[53] It does not, it seems, lie (or at least lie *legitimately*) in organization, administration, and other governing processes.[54]

Yet in other contexts, it is the pleasures of governing that are eroticized: the motifs of domination and control deployed in BDSM; the registers of sexual pleasure associated with governmental forms of domination and cruelty. Mbembe (2006: 300) draws on Georges Bataille to characterize war in erotic terms as "a spectacular manifestation of absolute and sovereign power."[55] This erotic power is not usually read positively. Critical scholars mainly oppose the eroticization of governing, with its violence, surveillance, and degradations, even as they often valorize (or at least accept) the enrollment of domination and simulated cruelty within erotic life.[56] Yet the eroticization of governing does not have to invoke the satisfactions of domination.[57] Governing and expressions of political authority can take other pleasurable forms.[58] Mark Rifkin (2012) explores how native writers in the United States have drawn on the erotic to posit a different conception of sovereignty and political authority. His work draws on four writers, including Qwo-Li Driskill (2004) and his notion of a "Sovereign Erotics" to explore the erotic as a collective relationship of bodies to land, traditions, and histories, reaching beyond individual sexual pleasure and the normative marital household. This is a form of "sensuous engagement" and "shared experience of intimacy," a "connection [that] is lived not as a formal political identification . . . but as an erotics" (Rifkin 2012: 81). There is a resonance between this approach to erotic sovereignty and discourses of "commoning," a contemporary term for the work of commons making. This work has its pleasures, as I describe, but what does it have to do with conservative Christian withdrawal?

The drama of this book demonstrates performances of sovereignty ignited by an erotic energy, oriented to the pleasures of refusal, libidinal circuits of withdrawal, and risky modes of play as these take shape across highly sensitized liminal thresholds of normativity and legality, where disagreement is performed and sometimes fiercely duked out.[59] But the sensory pleasures of politics are not necessarily the same as the sensory pleasures of governing. (While the two concepts shape and fold into each other, I do not want to treat them as synonymous.) In exploring what this legal drama brings to thinking about the pleasures of governing, let us shift attention from state body making—where the gathered state is given form through, among other things, the attractions, repulsions, wants, needs, and desires expressed and manifested in withdrawal—to the broader state conception proposed in this book. As the shape and condition of public governing, the state identifies a terrain that includes organized state and non-state forms. It also includes practices, such as commoning, which seek to prefigure a different kind of collective self-governing.[60]

Litigating parties in this legal drama, unsurprisingly, did not characterize themselves (or others) as "commoning," a term used in different ways but loosely coalescing around the collaborative work of bringing spaces and things into common and shared identification and usage.[61] To the extent, however, that commoning can take an *institutional* form, we might identify varietals of it within this conflict. Some might find glimpses in conservative Christians' collective attempts to forge a normative world against the secular world in which they found themselves. But I am more interested here in those endeavors that sought to use withdrawal to produce common uses, access, and identities: from the refusal of law societies across Canada to recognize TWU's new law degree to the withdrawal of subsidies and support by American cities, school boards, state employees, and others from the Boy Scouts.[62] Describing these practices as commoning is contentious. Not only did they involve withdrawal or pulling back rather than provisioning; they also involved state resources, institutional hierarchies, and, particularly in the case of TWU's law school, the gatekeeping work of limiting access to a profession, with all the economic and cultural capital at stake.[63] At the same time, while these withdrawal practices remain some distance from the ideal of "returning uses and things to the commons," the drive to produce nondiscriminatory goods demonstrates how state activism, caretaking, and the expansion of public concern meet at the liminal threshold of a newly emergent hegemonic politics. This is a governance project validated through notions of common benefits and usage. It is also a governance project in which a loose network (at times only a discursive network) of diverse bodies comes together using institutional resources, including unexpected ones, to advance a gay-inclusive public agenda.

Commoning brings us ways of thinking about governing, but it also does something else. What it offers is an understanding and foregrounding of the relationship between horizontal, everyday governing (as creating and repurposing) and sensory pleasures. Leila Dawney and colleagues (2016: 15) describe how "commoning," as a verb, shifts attention from resource use "to the lived intertwining of body, material, experience, and love that in-scribes an *excess* into life." Jenny Pickerill (2016: 39) describes building an eco-community in similar terms, quoting one participant who character-ized it as built "with clay, mud and love." These are pleasures, for the most part, that do not reside in the making of a "decision" (something I have sought to decenter in thinking about the democratically embedded state in chapter 2). Instead, they reside in the flow of doing—a doing characterized as collaborative, caring, and pleasurable. I do not want to idealize com-moning. What also emerges in writing on particular sites and experiments are the struggles, difficulties, and tensions that ventures in collaborative production and re-use can generate. The legal drama surrounding conser-vative Christian withdrawal similarly reveals some of the conflictual condi-tions within which collaborative governance projects emerge and endure, along with the challenges in creating reconditioned public goods.[64] At the same time, cases such as *Barnes-Wallace v. Boy Scouts of America* emphasize the bodies-experiences-pleasures that *should have been created* and were not as a result of antigay discriminatory practices (being legally enabled).[65] In this case, parents challenged the Boy Scouts' leasing of public parkland because of the Scouts' explicit gay-excluding, theistic stance. Their actions disputed the commoning deemed to be taking place as it also identified the commoning that *might and could have happened* if earlier withdrawals (by the Scouts and by the city in favor of the Scouts) had not occurred. As such, the demand for public acts of pulling out, to challenge the withdrawal or refusal of others, invite us to develop more ambitious imaginaries of what should and could have been created and the part that state parts might play in the process.

Concluding Remarks

How might we reorient our understanding of the state through the erotic? This is the question posted in this chapter. Addressing the erotic dimen-sions of states and public governing demonstrates some of the drives, drivers, and stakes of political practice that are otherwise easy to overlook. The erotic provides a useful lens for thinking about the energy that *goes into* governmental politics and the energy that comes back out. It also stimu-lates questions about what states could be like: the place (and places) that pleasure, sensation, excitement, and desire might occupy, and also create, in progressive practices of governing. Exploring this terrain in this chapter has involved engaging with two sets of terms developed through the course of the book. The first concerns the distinction (and relationship) between the state as the condition and shape of public governing and states as gathered and embodied forms. While the latter can be read as a dimension of the former, it can also be seen as standing in the way of a looser account in which the state is merely society in its public governing dimension. This book has proposed turning toward a looser account while recognizing the contemporary importance of gathered states as sites of public responsibility. The erotic foregrounds the imaginary and material aspects of this dual account and of the relationship between them. Writing on the erotic often focuses on already existing bodies, causing the erotic to be understood in terms of the desires and sensations that particular bodies experience and create. But desire and erotic energy (attuned to contact) can also *produce* particular forms of embodiment. In the case of states and other governance formations, these bodies do not precede—in a stable, already determined sense—the erotic relations they express. As this chapter has explored, erotic relations may undercut and transgress the divisions that keep bodies and parts separate. They may also work to intensify and recuperate them, for instance through the prohibitions imposed on public bodies' excessive touch. While this may sustain separate bounded entities, it can also have a disembodying quality, disarticulating and dismembering bodies to generate bits and pieces of governance in looser and far more contingent relationship, as independence, separation, and controlled forms of connection become important provisions to secure.

The second set of terms for reimagining what it could mean to be a state highlights the activist, embedded, caretaking dimensions of state governing. While these can operate in tension with each other (Cooper 2017), they can also combine in less conflictual ways. Attempts to use governmental and regulatory powers to pursue emerging or newly hegemonic political agendas are routinely interpreted by opponents, and sometimes by the courts, as an excessive, irresponsibly libidinal display. Yet these same kinds of state activism often involve the assumption of responsibility, as the Nova Scotia Barristers' Society sought to do, taking care in who might be able, and seen as able, to enter the profession, a process that also took care of (and with) the society's own professional image.[66] State activism speaks to the embedded character of different public bodies as they express, in adjusted ways, particular social movements' agendas (see chapter 4). At the same time, because public bodies are embedded, because they condense—

rather than simply control—social life, relations within and among such bodies gives rise to conflict. How this happens, of course, varies. Ruskola (2010) uses the highly charged language of rape to explore the nonconsensual penetration of one nation-state by another. This book has focused on a different, more punctuated, and diffuse register of conflict in which the friction, entry, and attachment of governmental bodies—not primarily national bodies but City Councils, school boards, provinces, and professional regulatory bodies—emerges as more flexible, reciprocal, and protean.

It would be easy to dismiss the erotic life of everyday governance forms, setting it aside because it lacks the grand passions and crimes associated with nation-states. Yet while the erotic life explored in this chapter may have circled around minor acts of governmental politics, it nevertheless generated intense sensations (including through the self-stimulation of dissident bodies who—occupying uncomfortable, sometimes hostile spaces within other bodies—found their own had become highly charged). In this way, the erotic provides a register for *remaking* everyday political encounters as exciting, energetic, and vital, both practically and interpretively. The conventional dichotomy drawn between the erotic and the state assigns to public governing a heap of dull and dry qualities presumed, and so encoded, as naturally belonging to it. Yet the claim that states can be erotic also poses important questions about the kinds of erotic qualities (if any), when it comes to governing, that we might want.

One form of pleasurable stewardship already developing and being cultivated in (neo)liberal jurisdictions is that of commoning. Academic work often assumes that governmental, as opposed to grassroots, stewardship and care is paternalistic—that it is disciplinary, top-down, and patronizing. While this is often practically true, it tacitly assumes a bounded state vertically relating to society. Unsettling this formulation in terms of what states could come to mean, *in a project oriented to other kinds of states* in both a broad and narrow sense, allows us to explore how the development of public goods might demonstrate forms of state caretaking in which the state is not set apart from other social participants. The alliances and actions of secular public bodies, opposed to the withdrawal of goods and opportunities on behalf of their gay populations, do not necessarily demonstrate the creative, horizontal, ecologically committed tending of present and future that much grassroots commoning emphasizes. However, they do provide glimpses of how state and other public governance bodies might engage in the ongoing work of producing and sustaining common uses and spaces;

and how different kinds of organized bodies, including state ones, might make it possible for others to engage in commoning as well. This commoning is not erotic in the sexual sense—at least, not usually. But what it does highlight is a broader understanding of erotic governance in terms of the desires, pleasures, and sensations that come from assuming a shared responsibility for making more inclusive and just social worlds. In the final chapter, I consider what this means for thinking about the state: how the shape and condition of public governance, and the gathered states that help make it up, might be pleasurably reimagined and refashioned through mimetic forms of play.

SIX. **Feeling Like a Different Kind of State**

This book has centered on a paradox: that conservative religious action can stimulate progressive state thinking. The tendency, when looking for left-wing inspiration and ideas, is to search for them in sympathetic institutional projects, utopian texts, or grassroots activism. This book has searched for them someplace else. The legal drama that arose around conservative Christian refusal to participate in (neo)liberal regimes of gay equality does not have unique traction when it comes to reimagining left-ward what it could mean to be a state. Other legal dramas could also have provided grounds for this discussion; and as this book evolved, conservative Christian legal opposition to other progressive causes and constituencies, including movements around gender transitioning, grew increasingly pronounced. But what a drama over gay equality offers at this particular legal moment, in those jurisdictions where it has been most avidly staged, is a drama of status change, as the terms of the acceptable and unacceptable shift. The cases discussed in this book evidence this shift, as well as its precarity and moments of flux, as subjects claiming to be injured, marginalized, and excluded, and bodies worrying about undesired emissions and contamination repeatedly switch. Through these changing bodily relations, with their fusions, connections, divisions, and separations, we can think about the place of states and what the state could come to mean.

I have approached the state oriented to the desire for more just ways of living. At the same time, I wanted to avoid reconceiving the state in ways that tied it too securely to a specific political project. Seeking to claim the state as a productive concept for left politics, I did not want to replace current definitions, anchored in authority, control, and domination, with counterdefinitions that sutured the concept of the state exclusively to progressive, egalitarian forms of practice. Instead, this book has developed a looser, more flexible account that recognizes states can take diverse political forms. Combining the sociomaterial with the imaginary to form new conceptual lines, I have suggested we think *toward* a conception of the state as the shape and condition of public governance—a conception that makes room for very different kinds of states, both in this broader sense and in terms of the differently scaled gathered states that form. States, in both senses, can be authoritarian and unitary or diffuse and polycentric, with thin and thick connections between bodies and parts. But in exploring the possibilities for different kinds of state conceptual lines, four dimensions have guided my discussion: heterogeneity, plurality, play, and the erotic.

None of these dimensions should be romanticized. Heterogeneity, in the form of internal dissidence and refusal, may advance right-wing agendas as well as progressive ones. Diffusing state authority and power, by holding up its plural forms, may diminish the capacity of states to advance radical change. Play and the erotic may deny or trivialize political responsibility—masking and so intensifying inequalities and relations of domination in the process.[1] Nevertheless, the proposal of this book is that, in pursuit of a more hopeful approach to the state, these four dimensions are important. Taking them up as features of states as they are (as well as in relation to what states might come to mean and be) can prove disorienting as the bearings, way finders, and paths of more familiar critical politics become displaced. Yet one aim of this book has been to explore the terrain that reimagining the state can open up. Attending to internal heterogeneity and state-based practices of resistance draws attention to the agonistic politics and antihegemonic moves that take shape within, *and as part of*, public institutions. This avoids the "black-boxing" that comes from assuming that dissidence is exclusively located in "civil society" or just concerns moments of electoral democracy prior to a new government's formation. Foregrounding heterogeneity can also unsettle the conventional mold states are placed in and so pose questions about state presence within other spaces and practices—how states are carried and called into being in places that seem far removed from the everyday world of state bureaucracy. This move poses questions, in turn, about how such spaces and practices might inhere in the state, passively or actively. Yet, approaching state heterogeneity in ways that recast the contours of the state can seem to leave us with an overexpansive conception. Pluralizing the state unsettles assumptions about what such expansion entails, recognizing the possibility and presence of different kinds of states—micro- and local as well as national and regional. In its strong form, state pluralism also rejects the notion that there can be agreement in what it means to be a state (or a particular state) thanks to different perspectives and definitions. This disagreement may relate to states that exist; it may also relate to what states and statehood could become. "Better" state forms may be associated with places other than the nation-state. While local and micro-states have their share of histories of authoritarian or exploitative forms of rule, they have also proven important sources of innovation, care provision, and defiance.

Play and the erotic also invoke interesting questions about governing—about whether it would be desirable, and what would be needed, for public governing to be pleasurable, playful, sensual, and desire-enhancing, where these qualities work to support rather than undermine social justice. As discussed in chapter 4, gathered states use game techniques in their policy and planning decisions. But play, as I explore further shortly, can also be more open, democratic, and experimental. Studies of political activism suggest that play disarms; others have suggested that it can defuse overly shored-up investments and antagonisms. While my discussion of play's capacity to weaken people's attachments to their propertied beliefs warns against an overly celebratory view of play's emancipatory power, play does nevertheless provide a generative register of contact between bodies. This contact is important if we are to approach governing as something that can be properly expressive: animated and sensual rather than purely instrumental.

Exploring withdrawal highlights this. It reveals the sensations that pulling out generates, including the intensification of relations it precipitates. Dramas of withdrawal, such as the one over antigay posters on London buses discussed in chapter 5, prompt us to rethink our understandings of political waste; consider how micro-challenges, including to progressive hegemonies, may generate lively sparks; and appreciate that governing can involve pleasurable relations with a range of sociomaterial things, as well as other bodies.

Heterogeneity, plurality, play, and the erotic open up ways to think about gathered states and the evolving shape and condition of public governance. They signal thought paths for what both forms could entail in conditions where responsibility is tied to relations of accountability, responsiveness, and an obligation to act and take care. Yet approaching the state in this way poses not only the question, What does it mean to feel like a state but also the rejoinder, What could it mean to feel like a *different* state? I have played with the ambiguity and polysemy of the first question in several ways, exploring how states *feel* to themselves and others, such that one might say something touches and feels like a state. To the extent that "feeling" is a relationship of identification and knowing, however, as well as of contact, sensation, and heft, how do we know when something "feels" like a state? States are routinely expected to feel hard, impersonal, cruel, coercive, dominating, and humorless; to feel like an assemblage of institutions that relate to members in probing, scrutinizing, controlling, directing, authorizing ways, where the way they relate to others is a large part of what makes them recognizable as states. Feeling *like* a state, of course, does not necessarily mean one *is* a state (in terms of self-perception or the perception of others). It can instead invoke a relationship of resemblance such that when an authority is so described, the premise of the analogy is that the authority is *not* a state but yet feels *like* one (whether to itself or others), perhaps because it, too, has territory, bodies that govern (often coercively), and that legislate and adjudicate *over* people, things and spaces (entities it may also help create).

Considering how states, and state-like formations, feel is important for thinking about what it might mean to feel like a different kind of state—a question at the heart of the state's reimagining. This book has taken the standard state perspective as its interlocutor to open up the question of what it *could* mean to feel like a different sort of state. How might a micro-state, a state that is horizontally playful or one that seeks to advance social justice, care, and commoning, feel to itself and others? How might it touch; with what expression, purposes, and rationalities? And what might its touch feel like? If feeling like a state is also a relationship of desire—that a state is what one seeks and wants—what might feeling like, in the sense of desiring, a different kind of state entail?

Feeling the Way to a Different Kind of State

This book has been about the desire for other kinds of states, a desire given voice through the making of different interpretive cuts in the social fabric to bring other state shapes to life—even as the distance invoked by such a project means new state shapes may be more useful as orientations rather than detailed endpoints. Yet the cuts so far have assumed a largely virtual life. Reimagining the state in this book has been driven by, and anchored in, an intensely material conflict as the practicalities of life get withdrawn, conditionally provided, and fought over. But the lines of development to arise so far have largely taken a contemplative form, expressed through ideas and questions about what a different kind of state could mean. While some, such as Jacques Rancière (2009: 114), affirm the "material realit[y]" of ideas,[2] I am interested here in exploring the social character of their manifestation when expressed by a politics that moves beyond simply wishing or imagining that the state was otherwise. For when it comes to states, *actually transforming practices of governing* seems crucial. This is most obviously for the material effects on people's lives that come from experiencing other kinds of states. But it also comes from the power that new practices can have in revitalizing, stimulating, and challenging engagements with the state, something that takes place *within* (state) governing practices, as well as at an institutional distance.

Explicit attempts to remake states in ways that combine ideational and sociomaterial change are many. Particularly relevant here are those with a prefigurative cast, where states are enacted and manifested *as if* they were the state, or at least closer to the state, that is desired and sought.[3] Jacob Mundy's (2007) account of state prefiguration in camps established for the exiled Sahrawi people of the Western Sahara, in southwestern Algeria, is one example (see also Farah 2009).[4] According to Mundy (2007: 275), "The camps offered nationalist movements a chance to practise the forms of governance and social organisation they would establish following independence. Thus the camps became a microcosm, a prefigurative lived model, of what an independent Western Sahara would, and still could, look like."[5] Yet the difficulty in prefiguring the state can be witnessed from the fact that most initiatives involve small-scale projects, even as the states being prefigured tend to assume a national or regional shape. Chiara de Cesari (2012) explores this relationship of project to nation in her account of the "anticipatory representation" of the Palestinian state through arts initiatives, such as a pavilion at the Venice Biennale and the creation of a national museum. De Cesari (2012: 95) writes, "Appropriating the idiom of the pavilion was a performative statement of (the right to) nation-statehood; behaving 'as if' the Palestinian exhibition were a proper national pavilion was a way to evoke the future existence of the Palestinian state . . . , the performance or prefiguration of an institution that does not yet fully exist."[6]

De Cesari's (2012) account focuses on the representational and performative efforts of art and curatorial projects; the rest of this discussion explores the enactment of progressive kinds of states through mimetic forms of play.[7] Play has proved a touchstone for this book in several respects. Johan Huizinga ([1949] 1970) describes litigation as a core play form, and certainly combative interactions, from court hearings to the mischievous deceptions and defiant refusals that gave rise to litigation (as witnessed in the "wedding cake wars"), have suffused this discussion.[8] Recreational play, from parties and cakes to vacations, highlights how play can become a battleground in other respects as forces strategically withdraw the places and things that make others' leisure and pleasures possible. But play is also about inventiveness, contact, and immersion. As such, it can be deployed by governments, companies, and other organizations to create new products and policies, to manage and defuse conflict, and to develop and cultivate other norms. In this final discussion, I want to take up this relationship to revising what *is*, with its creation and development of alternative immersive worlds, to explore progressive attempts to imagine and fashion other kinds of state and public governing practices through play. What can imitating statehood-with-revisions (the kind of state play I want to address) contribute to a conversation about reorienting and reimagining what it could mean to be a state?

In his third-person account of his own approach to method, Jacques Rancière (2009: 114) describes paths as lines of journeying that are created rather than followed "to know where you are, to figure out the characteristics of the territory you are going through" (see also Etxabe 2018). Since this final discussion shifts its focus from reimagining what it could mean to be a state to considering what enactment of new state imaginings might entail, I want to bring in other sites where states and state institutions have been simulated through play. My aim is to think about how imagining states otherwise can take a practical (if not necessarily a densely material) form. I therefore engage a disparate group of state simulations, tying them to one another in ways that rarely, if ever, happens, as well as to the discussion of this book. My new interlocutors invoke withdrawal in various forms: detaching from the symbolic embrace of the state, from reliance on national state currencies, from institutional frameworks, and from state authorities and procedures. They also explore ways of combining the practice of the imagination with putting the imagination into practice.

Playing at being a state (state play for short) usually takes a conventional form.[9] Mock parliaments and other simulated governmental and institutional fora, such as the United Nations, provide a pedagogic arena in which children (and sometimes adults) playfully imitate simplified (often idealized or schematic) conceptions of legislative and other official deliberative processes to explore how they "work."[10] Other state role play moves beyond inducting people into state structures that already exist, to explore and rehearse other possibilities (e.g., McConnell 2016). Oriented to what states and their institutions *could* be like, these rehearsals or experiments help people explore and develop desires (and attachments) for other ways of governing, adjudicating and living. State play with revisions shares ground with other kinds of mimetic state play in the sense of being "producer-oriented." In other words, initiatives foreground the activities carried out by institutions and state actors rather than playfully exploring, and revising, users' relationship to state activity. At the same time, state play with revisions diverges from other kinds of state play in its critical, sometimes ironic relationship to existing state forms. It also provides an umbrella term for quite varied initiatives that diverge from each other in the extent and quality of their actualization, realization, humor, provocation, and copying. Some initiatives, for instance, resemble one-off ironic jokes; others seek to pose lasting challenges to state hegemony or enact new counterinstitutional forms. Indeed, as I discuss, many initiatives reject their characterization as simulating the state and as play. Thus, my use of both terms is contentious and based on very particular definitions of what it means to be both a state and play. I discuss this further shortly, but first let me set out the kind of examples I have in mind, they include:

1   Initiatives that loosely take up the language of statehood to encourage aspirational, "out-of-the-box" thinking, such as the Utopian Council Project, which asked people to imagine what they would write to a local council, meeting in 2066, about the changes they wished to see.[11]

2   Self-declared micro-nations, such as the People's Republic of Brighton and Hove founded in 2015, and Frestonia founded in 1977 from a small patch of West London.[12] In these two instances, residents, with some degree of playfulness and wit, declared their secession in protest at government policies as they embarked, with irony, on the symbolic business of establishing an independent state.[13]

3   The progressive simulation of institutional processes and procedures, such as the globe-spanning Feminist Judgments Project; and the one-off British initiative, originating in the London School of Economics, to crowdsource a new "People's Constitution."[14]

4   Institutional projects, from free universities and local currency networks to people's tribunals, that seek to actualize counterinstitutional processes and yet remain "play," as I use the term here, to the extent that a significant part of what gets actualized remains unrealized (a distinction I return to).[15]

Framing these different initiatives as state play underscores the ambitious possibilities they open up. Far from being what trails behind, play is that dimension of innovation that stretches ahead—the forward arc of a thrown ball rather than the tail of a comet (if with far less certainty about where it will land). The space beyond what is currently realizable is particularly valuable when it comes to states in their gathered form. Generally, in the global North, possibilities for doing states otherwise—for acting and feeling like a different kind of state—seem slim, especially (although not only) for subjects without significant political and economic power. Unlike other kinds of prefigurative practices—such as those in the field of sexual politics, which can be practically realized by grassroots subjects doing gender and sexuality differently (Cooper 2019)—states (local, regional, and national) appear as hardy, top-down structures, given shape by vertical institutional processes and elites. This book has explored different ways of challenging this assumption, including in the ways states are made and remade through everyday practice. Yet this seems a slow, largely emergent way of instituting change, reliant on the "drip effect" of reiterated alternative performances. In such conditions, state play may seem to provide a complementary, faster-paced register through which dissenting ideas about institutions and states can be explored, piloted, and experimented with—removed from official state processes (although they do not have to be) and with the potential to exceed play's "magic circle." While state play often takes a miniaturizing form (like the projects of "anticipatory representation" mentioned earlier, see de Cesari 2012), its readiness to extend into the realm of "what could be"—to stretch beyond what is currently realizable—frees it from certain constraints and limitations. Yet this point is complicated by the fact that many of the initiatives referred to earlier, such as local currency networks, do not recognize themselves as simulated role play or unrealizable imitation (also McConnell et al. 2012).[16] Discussing international people's tribunals,[17] Craig Borowiak (2008: 166) makes a similar point: "With their juridical form, most tribunals are not trying to merely mimic states in a mocking display of political theater. On the contrary, the tribunal form affords them an opportunity to substantively and publicly appeal to law and international norms." I want to return to this counterclaim shortly. However, the space of nonrealization, so often discounted, is important for thinking about the reach of political play.

In her discussion of university equality and diversity documents, Sara Ahmed (2012: 117) identifies texts that express a "commitment" to equality and diversity but fail to realize this commitment. Drawing on Judith Butler and John Austin, she describes these textual commitments as nonperformatives, where the failure "is not a failure of intent or even circumstance, *but is actually what the speech act is doing* . . . such that the names [of the effects] come to stand in for the effects." In the context of university documents expressing an institutional attachment to diversity and antiracism, nonperformatives appear problematic; not only may they displace practical action, they can also mask its failure to occur. But the nonperformative qualities demonstrated in this chapter's discussion identify something different. Building on chapter 4, where I explored play's mutating "as if" qualities, I want to foreground play's practical surplus. Instead of treating this surplus solely in terms of failure and disappointment, of play unable to actualize its own self-description (and what that self-description is intended to realize), we can approach this surplus as play's ambition and promise—the potential play carries for other things to happen beyond what is currently possible.

Play and the Democratic Everyday State

State democracy and the challenge of creating more participatory governing processes remain a core site of academic and policy activity.[18] According to Gianpaolo Baiocchi and Ernesto Ganuza (2017: 4), "The idea of participation today occupies an exceptional position in the pantheon of policy prescriptions . . . solving difficult problems and remedying the inherent flaws of democracy." Yet academic work, to date, tends to focus either on formal procedures and initiatives for citizens' inclusion, such as participatory budgeting, citizen juries, and consultative committees, or on the "less civic," more unruly forms that gathered states confront when they become targets of political lobbying, protests, and deliberate disregard by others.[19] With its focus on withdrawal, this book, by contrast, has foregrounded relations and processes that are less official, often tacit, sometimes transgressive, and that tend to downplay both deliberation and formal decision making.

Processes and relations of withdrawal, alongside resistance to it, challenge the corporeal boundaries of the state, taking up its resources and authority, and becoming part of its composition through insertions, attachments, fusions, exchanges, and translations. So conservative Christian forces used the power and opportunities that came from being part of states (as workers, politicians, and public service users) to say "no" and to communicate their aversion, exemplified by the antigay teachers who used the time, space, authority, and bodies their position made available to condemn nonmarital and homosexual sex. Then there were conservative Christian couples, such as Owen and Eunice Johns, who worked to insert affective discourses of "love" into highly formalized state procedures. There were gay couples who, on booking a guesthouse that turned out not to want them, arrived at the dwelling with the equality state "on their backs." There were the gathered states that took up institutionally modified versions of lesbian and gay politics, along with the community organizations that took up state policies to make contact (which was sometimes a fusing and sometimes a defiant sort of contact) with public bodies. And there were the broken-off attachments as liberal public bodies withdrew contracts, subsidies, and recognition from Christian bodies and Christian bodies withdrew support and recognition from gay ones in contexts where pressure to act, or the threat of such pressure, came from many sides. As this book has explored, bodily contact is not always welcome. Many antagonists in this legal drama acted out of an expressed fear (or, at least, made fear a legal argument) that labor, contact, and an inability to say "no" would leave a residue of their self on other bodies, even as other bodies' discharges would stick to them.

It does not, I think, make sense to think of these entangled relations in the conventional terms of participatory democracy. Not only are they informal, often fleeting, and easily overridden, but they reflect the unstable and mutating character of political governance formations. Rather than identifying such processes as community involvement in public decision making, they seem closer to Rancière's (2009: 120) account of democratic action inasmuch as they involve the "staging" of an alternative political sense in contexts where particular bodies or claims are treated as out of place. I have used the language of embodiment to capture these relations less because they are principally (or necessarily) relations between living human bodies than because idioms of corporeality speak to the reciprocating character of this entwining. Reciprocation does not mean equality, however, and the radically unequal power and force of different bodies (or formations) is crucial to acknowledge. At the same time, the informal, diverse ways that bodies shape one another identifies possibilities for more horizontal, embedded, participatory relations of governing that do not depend solely on designed or orchestrated forms that, while important, are not enough.[20]

If the language of entangled bodies—of human bodies, institutional bodies, and other bodies—can illuminate ways to intensify the everyday character of democratically embedded states, what can state play with revisions contribute? I want to consider two possibilities here. The first concerns the political agency of non-elite bodies in taking up, and so both claiming and forging, their right to remake the state. The second concerns the possibilities for public governance to take up and be shaped by new kinds of articulation. These go beyond the neoliberal networked forms that have been extensively discussed by others while contesting the top-down forms asserted, at different times in this legal drama, by both conservative Christian bodies and (neo)liberal states.

Playing with statehood and its institutions—acting as if the state's sacrosanct objects and practices can be taken up and revised by publics[21]—has a boldly democratic quality. Christian dissent demonstrates the declaratory (if conservative) take-up and authority of non-elite withdrawal, of what it means to say "I will not" when "I will not" is spoken from within the skin of state agency, such as when firefighters in Glasgow refused to hand out fire-safety leaflets at a Gay Pride event;[22] when a family doctor refused to treat the child of lesbian mothers;[23] and when a Christian teacher repudiated gay-equality norms, using his professional authority and access to teenagers in a classroom to tell them that gay ways of living were "disgusting" (see chapter 1).[24] But while these refusals helpfully illuminate how state power can be accessed and redeployed, they are not refusals I want to celebrate. Instead, I want to pursue some more progressive forms of state play that, sourcing their power from a variety of different places, demonstrate the declaratory vitality of a kind of democratic, everyday "yes." Here, creating new local currencies, fashioning a modern constitution through intense public engagement,[25] rewriting the law in feminist judgments, judging international corporate and state action through people's tribunals,[26] and declaring a community's secession to avoid corporate redevelopment collectively assert the readiness, willingness, and entitlement of people to undertake state work.

Processes of state making come most explicitly, if least seriously, to the fore in playful claims to secede. Forming a new micro-nation has something in common with the everyday democratic inventiveness of state free-running, in its "tinkering" with a structure to see how it works and in its readiness to clamber across the state's terrain (at least virtually) to forge something playfully new (see chapter 4). Founding a state, particularly when undertaken in opposition to government policy, wryly asserts a horizontal relationship to the polity that is left, even if counteractualization remains limited (marked by little more than new flags, passports, postage stamps, allocated ministerial offices, and a mapped border). The drive to become a republic "because we are unhappy," as with Frestonia or the People's Republic of Brighton and Hove, symbolically asserts a normative expectation that statehood and citizenship are contingent on the people's assent. This assent can be withdrawn or given to a new emergent state once members are no longer satisfied. As a depiction of states *as they are*, this formulation is obviously problematic. Statehood, as we experience it, does not depend on people's consent let alone their actively expressed willingness, and critics are right to challenge, as dangerously fictive, the claim that consent or a people's contract underpins, and is at the heart of, state form and authority even in liberal states (see Kinna 2019). But the mimetic assertion of statehood or institutional formation, discussed here, does something different. While it can be read as demanding that the liberal state live up to its imagined democratic core, it can also be read as an "anticipatory representation" of the shape and condition of "better" public governance, where state play not only contributes to its imagining but also forms part of any realized shape, since public governance needs space for experimental play, creative innovation, and the sensory pleasures of public goods.

State play can contribute to transformative politics in several respects, as I discuss further below. But I want to turn here to the question of articulation. What kinds of new articulations (the joins and cuts that hold states together and apart) can state play offer? And can play provide a space for fabricating linkages and connections that might give the state of public governance a new, progressive shape? State play typically involves a relatively fragmented realm of virtual institutions: a free university here, a local currency or feminist court there. Can state play suggest forms of connection beyond those that typically connect bodies engaged in public governance? Can it help to reimagine and refashion what governance articulations could be like? In contemporary (neo)liberal polities, contract, ownership, partnerships, grants, audits, accreditation, and law support and give shape to public governance networks. Partnerships, accreditation, and grants proved central to many of the episodes animating this legal drama, as state bodies pulled back and pulled out, removing subsidies, joint working arrangements, and delegated authority from withholding conservative Christians. But aside from debating the merits of these actions, how might we locate them within the diverse options for articulated forms of governance? Certainly, some of the governance forms deployed (and withdrawn) reflect the logics and techniques of neoliberal arrangements, with its greater reliance on "outsourcing" and contractual arrangements between state and other bodies. Others, though, reflect the state in its welfare form, providing grants, venues, and facilities to recognized or "approved" community projects (while the decision to withdraw and practices of doing so underscore the conditional character these arrangements can take).[27]

Can state play, then, provide a basis for exploring other ways of composing public governance's broader terrain—ways that are not just more horizontal but oriented around progressive values also? Individual state play initiatives certainly express other values. Local currency networks, for example, systematized reciprocity, neighborliness, and sometimes gifting in their endeavor to generate social economies. The establishment of micro-nations, such as Frestonia and the People's Republic of Brighton and Hove, denoted the importance of solidarity among those affected by (or concerned about) Conservative, market-oriented policies. But to the extent that individual state play initiatives express progressive values, can these values shape relations *between* institutional forms—between, for instance, micro-nations and local currency networks, or between a people's university and a crowdsourced constitution?[28] Posing this question may seem to set us off on an unhelpful path, with its implication that progressive governance requires, if not uniformity, then at least coordination and mutual coherence. I do not want to argue against the value of "weak ties" or dismiss out of hand the inevitability or even the value of mutually illegible (or unintelligible) governance entities (see chapter 3). At the same time, articulations between bodies have benefits, producing (at least to some degree) coordination, normalization, reciprocal support, relations of intelligibility, convergent procedures, and interlocking forms of power and authority. They can help to sustain new institutions, creating entities that are more durable, resourceful, and capable, with doings and meanings that remain irreducible to their individual parts; and they can provide an impetus for growth and development. But if there is value in stronger as well as weaker ties, what might stronger ones look and feel like, and what can play bring to their enactment?

Typically, progressive politics and progressive political imaginaries turn to meetings and federated (or loosely networked) structures to do much of the work of articulation. More recently, the Internet and other forms of information technology have garnered interest for the contribution they might make in supporting communication and coordination among bodies. What has received less attention is the capacity of counterinstitutional projects to contribute to developing new systems, where emerging logics and rationalities, alongside emergent desires and interests, may help create interconnected and durable processes. These processes will, of course, involve conflict, tension, and change. What is important, however, is whether new systems can benefit from the mutual recognition that nonhegemonic initiatives might reciprocally show. Play here is useful. Its "pretend" form facilitates creative experimentation, trying out connections that might suture free universities to local currency networks, for instance. Adopting a mimetic approach to the challenge of how to cultivate horizontal, everyday forms of public governance invokes the diffuse, multivalent character of power.[29] If systems work, in a sense, by generating power—creating elements able to produce specific effects (and so have force) thanks to their recognition by other elements—play offers a register for exploring forms of power outside the neoliberal handbook.

Developing such modes of recognition and power, though, is far from straightforward. Could a make-believe people's constitution authorize feminist judgments that, in turn, might deliberate on the provisions of this new constitution? Could a free university provide forms of learning recognized as a training path for feminist judges? Might newly seceded republics create and use local currencies? Yes, possibly. The difficulty, as these examples suggest, is that state play can end up replicating conventional modes of articulation based on authority, cultural capital, and markets. The more challenging process is to experiment in creating articulations based on quite different values[30]—those associated with commoning (chapter 5), for instance, with its emphasis on collaboration, ecology, friendship, neighborliness, and gifting. In this way state play can contribute not just to reinventing the institutions that make up public governance, but to teasing out new, interconnected shapes.

Experimenting with State Responsibility

Earlier in this book, I explored the question of what makes certain gathered entities states. While state definitions vary, along with the cuts and joins deemed to compose state bodies, one dimension I have stressed is that of responsibility. At a historic moment when neoliberal pressures relocate governmental responsibility with individuals and non-state providers, this book has deliberately foregrounded public responsibility, tying it back to what it means to be a state. At the heart of my account is the work gathered states undertake in holding, assuming, and (re)generating responsibility for diverse subjects, places, and things (including humans, animals, water, trees, and land), as well as for diverse activities, functions, and practices. While many bodies have responsibilities *allocated* to them, the account of state responsibility in this book emphasizes the importance also of the constant, reflexive reaching toward (as well as sometimes the rejection or abandonment of) new responsibilities.[31] Struggles over responsibility's allocation and practice are at the heart of the drama over conservative Christian withdrawal. They are there in the extension of human rights and antidiscrimination instruments to sexual orientation, and in the opposition to it; in conservative Christians' demands to be an exception as they assert the responsibilities demanded of them in other terms; and in the rationalized withdrawal and sanctions, made in the name of an inclusionary public responsibility, by liberal state bodies in response. Thus, this drama provides an interesting site through which to think about state and public responsibility—not simply in terms of the changing configuration of its exercise as a kind of weighty duty, but also in relation to the practices responsibility rationalizes, its circuits of movement as withdrawal by one provider precipitates (compensatory or "corrective") action by another, and in the relationship of state responsibility to institutional creativity, inventiveness, and sensation.

How can we advance understandings of what state responsibility could mean and entail? For the most part, liberal state action in this legal drama ties responsibility to inclusion in its drive to render lesbians and gays part of the "we"; and, so, part of the constituency whose welfare is of state concern. Yet as many radical critics have argued, this notion of responsibility is a limited one—constrained and mediated by nationality, class, ethnicity and religion, as only some kinds of lesbian and gay lives get constituted as legitimate objects of state concern and regard, and only in some kinds of limited ways. If this is so, does state play offer a format through which other registers of institutional responsibility might be experimentally explored? Can it provide a more flexible mode of engagement, where innovation is easier and where the costs of negative consequences may prove less?

In developing ideas about state responsibility, play can work in several ways. It can extend the spaces and groups to whom institutions are expected to pay concern. The development of people's tribunals foregrounded the responsibilities states and other powerful forces owe to people afar as well as near, challenging attempts to legally, temporally, and spatially curtail relations of actionable culpability. "Wild law" judgment writing sought to extend responsibility to nonhuman actors (Rogers 2017).[32] Bee Chen Goh, for instance, revisits the famous British tort case of *Donoghue v. Stevenson* from the neglected perspective of the snail to whom, as a "neighbor," a legal duty of care should be owed.[33] State play can also innovate in terms of identifying where responsibility lies. This is often backward-facing, locating culpability with bodies or a system that has insulated itself from taking responsibility.[34] By approaching gathered states as meta-responsible formations, the discussion in this book has focused on forward-oriented versions of institutional responsibility, in which responsibility is taken up and developed *because* bodies can make a difference but also *so* they can make a difference, while recognizing the contested often risky character of this role. Free universities and micro-nations can be read as projects that seek to institute forward-oriented collective subjects in the form of counterinstitutions that are ready and willing to act. Finally, state play can experiment with governmental mechanisms so that responsibility is assumed for social and ecological well-being in new ways. Local currencies might be one example of this. Here, a refashioned money system aimed to support and build local interdependence, forge good relations and contact between people, and, in some cases, support greater equality in how work and workers are valued. Similarly, free universities have experimented with forms of education that emphasize public goods and collaborative learning. "Against the growing marketization of education," universities can contribute to the good society in ways that do not involve commercial partnerships, competition, and the maintenance of unequal access to cultural capital.[35]

Yet while play may provide a good experimental register for exploring how states and institutions can advance transformative agendas, including through the assertion and assumption of new forms of responsibility, play struggles when it comes to actually *taking* responsibility, not least because of the difficulties it faces in realizing the provisioning it wishes to secure. Several writers have addressed the limited power or force of state imitations when key contextual elements that give state actions authority are missing. While the focus is often on the state's distinctive (if not exclusive) capacity to cause violence (e.g., Rogers 2008: 440–41), the state's distinctive (if not exclusive) capacity to resource is also at stake. In her discussion of wild law, Rogers (2017: 8, 12) distinguishes between "authoritative performances," such as by the courts; "extralegal performers," such as people's tribunals; and "pseudo-legal" performances, such as feminist and wild-law judgment writing projects. In the case of the crowdsourced constitution and Feminist Judgments Project, pseudo-legal forms may advocate greater equality in the distribution of resources through legal texts that cannot *enact* that equality. Other forms of play may *simulate* the public provision of housing and food yet lack the authority and capacity to bring homes and nourishment into being. These limitations came to the fore in the case of local exchange trading systems (LETS). While advocates presented LETS as grassroots currency networks that would enable people to meet their economic needs (and some of their desires), schemes struggled, at least in Britain, with their incapacity to actually fulfill members' demands for foodstuffs, domestic repairs, and other everyday goods.[36] In other words, LETS actualized new forms of currency. They just could not accomplish what currencies were supposed to accomplish in enabling economic exchange.

I have described LETS as a form of play because its ambitions outstretched what it could realize. But if play is no longer play when it realizes its ambitions, the potential for play to become something else is an important dimension of what state play can bring to developing public responsibility as part of the state's refashioning. Play may stimulate, revitalize, and experiment, but in its capacity to become something other than play, other performative consequences emerge (even as these performative consequences are part of what it means to no longer be play). How play becomes something else, however, can take quite different routes. One involves play intervening in, and being recognized by, existing social and political arrangements.[37] We could imagine fictive feminist judgments being cited by official judges in court (perhaps as something that is neither quite a precedent case not quite an academic article). We might imagine the crowd-sourced constitution produced through the London School of Economics being taken up in the development of a British constitution-making parliamentary bill, or free universities taking part in interuniversity committees and projects.[38] Such recognition might reflect the wider intelligibility of some forms of mimesis with revisions, including the intelligibility they are given when translated by existing state institutions.[39] However, recognition can also have undesirable consequences, as participants in British LETS found when local currency earnings were cast as potentially real money for taxation and benefit deduction purposes. Recognition may also function as a form of cooptation or attach to those aspects of state play that seem least threatening. Frestonia's postage stamps, for instance, were briefly recognized by the Royal Mail, allowing a few letters using them to be delivered abroad (some turned up in Denmark and the United States).[40] This kind of recognition, which can also be a deliberately playful *misrecognition* (artfully treating a simulation as real while "knowing" that it is not) can contribute to state experiments' enduring *unreality*. Indeed, when official institutions and actors join in the play, they may put an experiment's survival even *as play* in doubt. Witness the exchange between Horace Cutler, Conservative Party leader of the Greater London Council, and Frestonia. Cutler wrote, "All I can say is were you not to exist it would be necessary to invent you," to which Frestonia replied, "Since we do exist, why is it necessary to destroy us?"[41]

The ability of state governments to recognize and, by playfully recognizing, to trivialize and subdue state play with revisions suggests that we may need to look elsewhere to appreciate play's value in remaking states. Earlier, I suggested that state play might contribute to reimagining articulations between loosely connected public governance bodies and activities according to progressive rather than neoliberal principles. Forging connections among different initiatives can help the worlds that state play invokes to develop and deepen. In the legal drama of this book, conservative Christians sought to extend a rather different world. They used withdrawal—and the networks supporting and connecting different forms of withdrawal (through money, litigation, media, and bodies)—as one means of doing so. The recognition conservative Christian participants gave one another, in the face of external refusal to validate the truth value of their beliefs, was an important aspect of this process. Networked recognition has also been important to state play, particularly in contexts where others dismiss the activities' significance. Fiona McConnell and her colleagues (2012) discuss the federations that formed to represent the often ludic-seeming interests of micro-nations.[42] More progressive attempts to forge connections can be seen in the relation between people's tribunals and the development of People's Law grounded in the retrieving and retelling of histories of violence and liberation, and in the claimed entitlement of subordinate people to act, particularly against colonization (see Nayar 2001, 2007): "Peoples' law is about creating a different authority for judgement and action altogether. It is about standing up to . . . those laws of Power that inflict violations upon the people for Power's profit" (Nayar 2007: 12). Jayan Nayar's conception of power is different from mine. However, his work powerfully addresses the challenge of creating counterinstitutional constellations of practices and forces so that initiatives which might otherwise be written off as mere make-believe have the force to move from positing new stages to positing new worlds.

Precedents and Transitional Concepts

Immersion in new developing worlds can mean that what once seemed fictions start to become more thickly realizable. Yet when it comes to state play, the dispersed, ad hoc character of imaginative initiatives seems to thwart their accumulative effect. Or does it? Can the precedent value of common law cases provide a helpful analogy for thinking about what state play can do? I have not focused in this book on precedents—the take-up (and refashioning) of earlier decisions in the course of forging later ones (a technical process that is also, of course, not distinctive to this area of law)—choosing to focus instead on narratives about the state, as well as its subjects and their governance. Yet a striking feature of this legal drama is the way court decisions circulated not just within jurisdictions but also between them, as judgments in one country got taken up elsewhere. Extra-jurisdictional decisions are not binding; a legal decision in Canada cannot determine how to decide a case in Australia. But they do become part of the materials and resources of judgment. Thus, we might think of judgments as having both an actual and a virtual life: the former in the judicial process of coming to a legal decision, and what it is such a decision presumes to perform (even as its accomplishment may fail); the latter in the potential power of legal decisions, which is also a less knowable power, to shape or be drawn on in future cases. This is the life beyond its own facts that a common law judgment is able to have.

The virtual life of precedents is helpful for thinking about the state play discussed here—in what it is and what it can do. Some kinds of state play and some kinds of artifacts may be immediately actualized—a feminist judgment, a crowdsourced constitution, classes at a free university, a newly painted kitchen or set of darned socks purchased with local currency. Yet while darned socks may be bought with local money, few (other than the most enthusiastic advocates) would consider such trades to be *realizing* a new kind of money. In other cases, simulation itself may be limited. Micro-nations, for instance, declared their founding, but their nation-making activities, as I have said, rarely extended beyond the creation of state insignia and emblems (flags, anthems, passports, ministerial offices, borders, and postage stamps). If state play, then, remains unrealized, and on some occasions is scarcely actualized, if it remains unrecognized by mainstream authorities and fails to connect up with other play initiatives to produce its own normative world, how can it have more durable effects? Certainly, play should not be reduced to what it accomplishes. As discussed in chapter 5, the doing of governing is important for its own sake, and this applies especially, it would seem, when the doing is a mimetic, playful one. At the same time, the performativity of state play is not limited to what its actual life brings forth.

Like common law judgments, artifactual forms of state play may be picked up at any moment (indeed, a moment may be created from their pick-up). Echoing Rita Felski's (2015) postcritical account of literary texts' ongoing life as they get curated, translated, criticized, and built on at different times and places, the things of state play can also be enrolled in new networks to do new things. Conservative Christians know this. Their activism is attuned to their growing archive of legal conflicts, judgments, and acts of defiance.[43] For the left, a large and rich archive also exists from which to draw. Contemporary commoning practices, for instance, draw on histories of the commons. Discussing People's Law, Nayar (2007: 17) identifies a varied archive, including "Declarations and Charters, . . . Statements and Calls for Action, . . . Peoples' Tribunal Verdicts, vision statements, solidarity messages, poetry, folk songs." Local currency networks, free universities, people's tribunals, and micro-nations are all mimetic practices that have inspired take-up by others. In the 1990s, LETS spread rapidly across different jurisdictions as people became captivated by its potential. Two decades later, the Feminist Judgments Project also spread furiously— if mainly among academics—as one project led to another. Strikingly, in both cases the initiatives undergoing such explosive movement and growth stayed relatively isomorphic. Feminist judgment writing inspired other progressive rewriting practices, such as the wild law judgment project (see Rogers 2017), but its influence to date seems anchored in judgment writing (and, to a lesser degree, in statute writing as interest in what can be done with legal form evolves[44]). Time, however, may cause initiatives to reappear in quite different forms. Take Mordecai Noah's failed attempt in 1825 to establish Ararat, a Jewish statelet or "city of refuge" in rural New York (see Weinryb 1954).[45] Almost two centuries later, Ararat remerged, this time as a literary and visual form of play.[46] The later Ararat was cast as an imaginary sovereign nation-state, given shape and life through "parahistorical artifacts," including stamps, postcards, and dollar bills.[47] In other instances, changes in form have traveled in the reverse direction, as with the American intentional community Twin Oaks, whose establishment was inspired by B. F. Skinner's (1948) utopian novel *Walden II*, published two decades earlier (see also Kinkade 1974).

Left-wing practices, fantasies, and experiments can inspire and enthuse, be critiqued and abandoned. They can motivate other examples, get taken up decades later, be forgotten, and sometimes be retrieved in a new and different form. What, then, does this mean for the state, not simply in terms of progressive attempts to reimagine and remake it, but in how the left engages with the concept of the state more generally? This book has explored ways of thinking about the state driven by the challenge of disorienting forms of imagining and actualization, where what it means to be a state involves radically new cuts and joins. And while these articulations do not, alone, make states just, playful, democratically embedded, responsible, and sensual, the question posed by this book is what thinking *toward* such re-cut states might do. Yet for many left critics, including, but not only, anarchists, such an approach is deeply wrong-footed. As I discussed in the introduction, for them, recuperating the concept of the state invests in a political imaginary that artlessly discounts the violent, exploitative practices and forms that states as very real material structures produce. It also spectacularly fails to detach, emotionally and culturally, from a state-centered worldview. Critiques of state dominance, including for its hold over our political imagination, underlie several of the play forms I have discussed, from local currency networks to people's tribunals. Reflexively perceived as grassroots non-state initiatives, they "draw support from a conviction that law [or money] does not belong to governments alone" (Borowiak 2008: 166). Thus, these initiatives aim to contest the state's monopoly over currency systems, public forms of responsibility, and adjudication. From this perspective, remaining mired in the terms of statehood (however reimagined) falls for (and into) the state's seductive trap, where feeling like a different kind of state evokes a desire for a political object and attachment that sustains, legitimates, and expands the state's symbolic empire.

This book has paid attention to antistate left perspectives since they pose important challenges to progressive currents that rely on scaled-up states, and scaled-up state power, as the means of instituting change. At the same time, while this book has thought *with* this critique, confronting the questions it demands we ask to avoid simply treating the state as the natural answer, it is not a critique I have fully adopted. Instead I have held on to the state, albeit provisionally, in a way that recasts it as a "transitional concept."[48] On the left, approaching the state as a temporary object of attachment and comfort, that manages the fraught complexity of relations among people en route to more advanced modes of self-governance is not uncommon. From this perspective, which is not my perspective, however dirty and odorous the state as an entity (or concept) seems, and however much it is mutilated and rejected, it endures because humans are not yet ready to give up its possession and move on to better ways of living in common. This dream of moving on has echoes of the communist notion of the state withering away. As a thesis of real politics in postcapitalist societies, the "withering" state (see Engels [1878] 1934: 355) has acquired more than a century's worth of scorn (given the failure of postrevolutionary states to in any way approach it).[49] Yet approaching the state as a "transitional concept" does not mean signing up to Lenin's ([1917] 2014) envisaged future (see also Levine 1985). My suggestion is *not* that states are temporary or transitional "objects" in *staging* human development; that they represent a necessary or useful step in the movement from a relationship with God (or some other omnipotent ruler) toward human self-government. Rather, we might use the idea of a "transitional concept" to think about the state's temporary conceptual value.[50]

Radical antistate critiques demand that we shed, and suggest that we are ready to shed, the state as a security blanket. But states, at least conceptually, continue to provide a useful *proxy* in (neo)liberal regions for thinking about public governance formations and for exploring the potential— which remains an unrealized potential—for such formations, and the gathered states that help make them up, to advance a shared responsibility for the collective well-being of humans, other life-forms, and wider ecologies. The conceptual usefulness of the state is, of course, temporally and spatially specific. States are not necessarily the concepts always and everywhere nearest to hand, or those that people should invariably reach toward when searching for fruitful ways of reorienting or disorienting governmental thinking. Other concepts may prove better in imagining and enacting more just, socially organized forms of life. At the same time, this book argues, the state should not be too quickly discounted; for it offers valuable conceptual terrain in thinking about how we organize living together. This is not to justify and rationalize statehood (or even stateness) across an infinitely extended future. This book has focused on gathered states in thinking toward the state as the shape and condition of public governance. But this thinking toward is anchored in the present; it is not a demand on the future. For now, we may want to give states a place—practicing and experimenting with what feeling like a different kind of state could entail through diverse mediums, including play. What follows after of course remains unknown.

INTRODUCTION

1. Country Mill Farms et al. v. City of East Lansing, Opinion and Order, no. 1:17-cv-487, filed 15 September 2017.

2. *Country Mill Farms et al.*, 5.

3. *Country Mill Farms et al.*, 5.

4. *Country Mill Farms et al.*, 9.

5. This book focuses on "public" governance formations, raising of course questions about the status and definition of ostensibly nonpublic forms, such as intimate or personal kinds of governance, which public governance also helps to define and structure. The distinction between public and personal governance is necessarily fuzzy, provisional and contested. In this book, my interest is in governance forms that (should) engage people, politically, as members of publics, take responsibility for "public things" (Honig 2017), and build more collectively responsible worlds.

6. I use "(neo)liberal" rather than the more common "neoliberal" to emphasize that while certain state practices, systems, and discourses are neoliberal, in the (deliberately narrow) sense of being organized to imitate and support abstract market paradigms and advance commercial interests, other state qualities speak to more traditional liberal conceptions of political and social liberty, justice, and formal equality. These latter are tied in to the history of economic liberalism and the development of postindustrial societies. However, they have a contemporary salience that is not entirely aligned with market rationalities. My analysis in this book seeks to reimagine the state from the geopolitical spaces of the (neo)liberal global North. This is not the same as seeking to reimagine the (neo)liberal state, but rather is a recognition of the ways in which location and context (this book was written in London between 2013 and 2018) structure thinking in both conscious and less conscious ways.

While the legal drama of this book is constituted by, and entangled in, the contemporary legal politics of common law jurisdictions in the global North, it draws on interdisciplinary scholarship across (and addressing) a range of geopolitical spaces to support alternative ways of thinking about what it could mean to be a state.

7. This question has been sidelined or "black-boxed" in much contemporary critical scholarship. The influence, over more than two decades, of work on governance and governmentality has been to foreground the "how" of governing rather than the "what," with the "what" seen as overly reifying. The trouble, however, when leaving the "what" behind is that it becomes hard to reimagine what states *could* be or become.

8. Or, to the extent states draw (figuratively) on human or other animal forms of embodiment, we might draw on critical work that reimagines what this entails. I explore this further in chapter 5.

9. In some utopian fiction there is no state at all. In *News from Nowhere*, William Morris ([1890] 2003) depicts a society where government and state have been abolished. When the narrator asks, "How do you manage with politics?" Hammond, his interlocutor, replies, "I am glad that it is of *me* that you ask that question. . . . Indeed, I believe I am the only man in England who would know what you mean. . . . I will answer your question briefly by saying that we are very well off as to politics—because we have none . . . a man no more needs an elaborate system of government, with its army, navy, and police, to force him to give way to the will of the majority of his *equals*, than he wants a similar machinery to make him understand that his head and a stone wall cannot occupy the same space at the same moment" (Morris [1890] 2003: 73, 65; see also Buzard 1990). Other utopian novels, however, assume that state-like governments remain. Thus, their accounts present different models of government involving a wide variety of scales, from the planetary and global to the national and local. Utopian fiction can stimulate the imagination even as it also demonstrates the limits of what is thinkable in particular times and places (see Jameson 1982). One striking illustration of the anachronistic character of past/passed state utopias is H. G. Wells's *A Modern Utopia* ([1905] 2005).

10. On critical utopias, see Moylan 1986.

11. I have explored this further in relation to the new urban socialism in Britain of the 1980s (see Cooper 2017).

12. For Wright (2010: 6), visions are important contributors to social change, but "vague utopian fantasies may lead us astray, encouraging us to embark on trips that have no real destinations at all, or, worse still, which lead us toward some unforeseen abyss." What are needed, he suggests, are proposals that are viable given the current conditions of postindustrial states (even if not all will prove *realizable* thanks to contemporary social and political constraints). Several writers, including Levitas (2013: 148), have criticized Wright for developing a utopian framework that sticks too closely to, and so is limited by, current realities.

13. For helpful and interesting accounts on rethinking the state through experiments in governing, see Fung and Wright 2003; Hancox 2013; Mundy 2007. Experimenting through mimetic forms of play is explored further in chapter 6.

14. This book does not focus on the structural character of drama in social life. Its concern is, rather, with the expressive, evolving, dynamic character of legal conflict,

read here as a particular organizing moment within the wider contours of a "social drama" (see Turner 1980, 1982) involving conservative Christianity, gay-equality activism, and liberal states. Describing this conflict as a drama is not, in any way, to diminish it as an "over-show" of heightened emotion or to reduce it to a performance composed and staged solely for its audience. At the same time, heightened feeling and the conflict's staged character, particularly in the courts, are important parts of its legal enactment.

15. Use of the term "conservative Christian" (or "Christian right") has been questioned on the grounds that ideological positions configure differently in the different jurisdictions of this book. For instance, in Britain conservative stances on sexuality and the family may not correspond with conservative positions on economic issues (see, e.g., Walton et al. 2013). My use of the term "conservative Christian" refers to positions taken on gay equality and gender/sexual politics more generally, rather than necessarily equating to a conservative stance on other issues. I also do not discuss *pro*-gay or gay-equality Christian politics.

16. As such, it builds on the conceptual methodology I develop in Cooper 2014.

17. There is an extensive literature on this legal drama (see, e.g., Koppelman 2016; MacDougall and Short 2010; Major 2017; Malik 2011; Malloy 2017; Massaro 2010; Stychin 2009a, 2009b; Velte 2018; Wintemute 2014). The intensely uneven geopolitical character of this drama is, of course, not because political opposition to gay equality is limited to these few countries or even because litigation that addresses issues of gay sexuality is so limited. The drama explored in this book involves *withdrawal* as a calculated response to gay equality's formal legal advancement, where it can be *legally* rationalized on religious grounds. It therefore is limited to those jurisdictions in which legal protection exists for both sexual orientation and religious beliefs.

18. Ladele v. London Borough of Islington, 2009 EWCA Civ 1357.

19. Indeed, the prominence given to antigay politics may be displaced in coming years by a growing focus among conservative Christians with gender fluidity, transitioning, flexible gender categories, nonbinary identities, and governmental attempts to accommodate these sociopolitical changes. One case being litigated as this book went to press involved the Colorado Masterpiece Cakeshop, whose litigated refusal to make a wedding cake for a same-sex couple (see chapter 4) was followed by a refusal, in 2017, to make a cake that was pink inside and blue outside for a customer's birthday to celebrate her coming out as trans, on the grounds the shop owners believed sex was "immutable" and "God-given"; see Masterpiece Cakeshop v. Elenis verified complaint, USDC Colorado, Case 1:18-cv-02074, para. 199; discussed also by John Culhane, "The Cake Controversy That Just Won't Go Away," *Politico Magazine*, 16 August 2018, accessed 16 August 2018, https://www.politico.com/magazine/story/2018/08/16/masterpiece-cakeshop -controversy-219365. For a related story, see the case of the British printer who in 2017 would not print business cards for a consultant in transgender diversity, citing loyalty to fellow Christians struggling against contemporary diversity politics: Frank Cranmer, "Gender, Religious Belief and Discrimination in Service Provision," *Law and Religion U.K.*, 21 October 2017, accessed 2 July 2018, http://www.lawandreligionuk.com /2017/10/21/gender-religious-belief-and-discrimination-in-service-provision.

20. This book focuses on a relatively narrow, if dense, set of legal cases, all concerning opposition to "gay" equality, as an entry point for thinking about the state. My argument is not that these cases are more significant in advancing and expressing conservative Christian agenda than others or that they are the only set of cases to provide a productive ground for reimagining the state. Rather, this book is intended to sit in conversation with accounts of the reimagined state drawing on and from other (re)sources.

21. Talk of "moments" rather than eras or stages avoids the assumption that gay equality developments, in the face of conservative religious opposition, have a universal trajectory (or path dependency), with different countries going through the same process and stages even as the timing of their starting point may differ. Contemporary sexuality politics reveals how the standard trajectory of progress can be compressed, reversed, or mixed in domestically distinctive ways. For a useful troubling of the notion of shared geopolitical narratives of linear progress, see Mizielińska 2011; Mizielińska and Kulpa 2011.

22. Quoted for instance in Tara John, "The Six Moments That Defined David Cameron's Leadership of the British Government," *Time*, 13 July 2016, accessed 2 July 2018, http://time.com/4403622/david-cameron-leadership-legacy.

23. Judith Butler (2008: 3) describes how the Netherlands used photographs of two men kissing to test potential new migrants' liberal sensibilities. Israel has been similarly criticized for "pink washing" (see Franke 2012; Gross 2014; Puar 2011).

24. On Romania, see Stychin 2003: 134–35. On the politicization of homophobia since the European Union accession, see Graff 2010.

25. Although as Stychin (2003: 122) discusses in the Romanian context, some of the pressure came from domestic nongovernmental organizations, routed through international organizations as a way of pressing for internal reform.

26. For a thoughtful and perceptive account of the struggle over same-sex marriage in Hawai'i, see Goldberg-Hiller 2002.

27. Archbishop Bartolomeu Anania, quoted in Roxana Dascalu, "We Want to Join Europe, not Sodom—Romania," 12 December 2000, accessed 2 July 2018, https://www.iol.co.za/news/world/we-want-to-join-europe-not-sodom-romania-44242.

28. On the ties between domestic opposition to LGBT rights in the global North and opposition elsewhere, see Browne and Nash 2014; see also Buss and Herman 2003.

29. For further discussion on this point, and the associated perception that Christianity has become improperly marginalized, see Herman 1997; Kettell 2017; McIvor 2018.

30. In her work on the U.S. Christian right, Didi Herman (1997: 62, 64) explores their late twentieth-century depiction of gay sexuality as a "plague" or "tidal wave" that had to be resisted if children were not to "drown" and civilization was not to collapse. During this third moment, conservative Christians identified the harm that they felt the recognition of gay relationships would cause as lying in the *simulation* and claimed equivalence with heterosexual marital arrangements rather than in gay relationships' difference from normative heterosexual sex. For earlier depictions of hypersexual gay masculinity, see Herman 1997: 80–82.

31. For critical discussion of the discursive shift from family values to religious freedom in the U.S. context, see Williams 2018.

32. Adam Dinham and Vivien Lowndes (2008) usefully explore this in the British context, addressing faith networks' involvement in urban governance through taking up activities previously performed by government. Yet in a context where religious bodies and values are foregrounded as relevant to secular governance activities, from "civic renewal" to running schools, there may be even more impetus on liberal states to "de-radicalize" religion, using law (alongside other techniques) to differentiate between mainstream faith practice and less comfortable varieties.

33. For recent exploration of some of the complex legal and moral issues that religious-based exceptions raise, see Vallier and Weber 2018.

34. See also Christian Concern's response, 7 December 2015, accessed 2 July 2018, https://www.christianconcern.com/press-release/response-to-the-woolf-institutes -commission-on-religion-and-belief-in-british-public-l.

35. The politics of sexuality has been a source of much dissent in *internal* Christian politics, including in the Anglican/Episcopalian church, where it also functioned as a way of articulating and enacting other divisions. For discussion of internal Christian disagreements over gay sexuality, see also Hunt 2014; Sachs 2009.

36. For discussion of conservative Christian "public interest" law firms and litigation organizations in the United States, see Hollis-Brusky and Wilson 2017.

37. Developing a normative concept from social practice can risk carrying or encoding the commonsense assumptions of the social practice. This is a critique made of some context-based normative theory that extracts and abstracts from the ground in which it is anchored (or embedded). On nonideal (and ideal) theory, see Hamlin and Stemplowska 2012; Valentini 2012. My aim, however, is not to identify the best kind of state, to develop principles for more effective governing, or even to determine what better governing means for participants. Rather, I am interested in purposively interpreting this legal drama—a drama that foregrounds noncompliance and refusal—in ways that generate traction for reimagining the state. The state is not a normative concept in the ways concepts such as justice, equality, and democracy are conventionally understood. Thus, this book offers a postnormative conception of the state, enrolling conceptions of the state within a transformative progressive politics without either limiting the state to a narrowly prescriptive definition or determining, more practically, what the state ought to be or become.

38. For detailed discussion of liberal perspectives on conscientious objection, see Nehushtan 2016.

39. On protest camps as a deliberately signaled withdrawal from the "system," that is sometimes accompanied by newly declared (grassroots) states or republics (see Frenzel 2014). I explore this further in chapter 6.

40. For a helpful discussion of withdrawal in this context, see Simpson 2014.

41. I have explored some of the challenges in thinking about ostensibly benign forms of state touch further elsewhere (see Cooper 2014: chap. 3).

42. See, e.g., Herman 1994; Smith 1999. Both address these themes in relation to the legal character of gay politics in Canada. See also Stychin 1998a.

43. An important and extensive literature on the left has debated the value and limits of human rights and antidiscrimination provisions (see, e.g., Bumiller 1992; Fudge and Glasbeek 1992; Goldberg-Hiller 2002; Herman 1993, 1994; McNeilly 2018).

44. This includes legislative debates and media (including social media) stories, as well as accounts from litigation advocacy groups. In cases to do with "compelled speech," where conservative Christians refuse to express the pro-gay perspectives required of them by their work, litigation documents and supplementary texts provide a space through which not simply refusal and silence but the *desired* speech of litigants and supporters can be expressed.

45. For discussion of these issues, see for instance Baron and Epstein 1997; Ewick and Silbey 1995. As a social drama, the withdrawal of goods and benefits by conservative Christians and liberal public bodies is knotted into a complex series of struggles that stretch through time and space. However, this complexity is whittled down, bounded, and contained in the course of its production as a legal drama. Since the disputes at the heart of the book acquire their specific form through litigation, law becomes a key determinant of how withdrawal comes to be authoritatively framed. In other words, the complex entanglement of economic, political, social, and philosophical issues, bleeding across different places and times, become delineated, pruned, and framed to produce the legally salient act or series of acts involving withdrawal. This cutting is given effect politically, as well as judicially, since activist and media attention mobilize in relation to litigation and the events litigation references, which are sometimes treated as detached, discrete episodes and sometimes as part of a wave of events or protests.

46. For discussion of "stock narratives," see Chesler and Sneddon 2017; see also Herman 2011.

47. For instance, Roger Parloff suggests conservative Christian documentation surrounding the litigation over wedding cakes frequently described bakers as "cake artists" to emphasize the (legally important) expressive dimension of their work: see Roger Parloff, "Christian Bakers, Gay Weddings, and a Question for the Supreme Court," *New Yorker*, 6 March 2017, accessed 2 July 2018, https://www.newyorker.com/news/news-desk/christian-bakers-gay-weddings-and-a-question-for-the-supreme-court; see also chapter 4.

48. Because these texts are framed by secular law, they do not foreground Christian specificity. In other words, while they are about religious rights as taken up and articulated by Christians, the specificity of Christian spiritual imaginaries, understandings, and texts are downplayed beyond their broadest brush-stroke representations. While these cases are brought by Christians for reasons discussed earlier, many of the legal claims and court judgments could apply equally well to other religions.

49. For discussion of this narrative, see Jessop (2010).

50. See for instance contemporary work on the patriarchal and racist state (e.g., Bracey 2015; Kantola 2006), extending and complicating earlier writing on the capitalist state. A critical account of antistatism is also addressed in work on "state phobia" (see Foucault 2008: 187–88). Foucault's exploration of state phobia is discussed further in Dean and Villadsen 2016; Dhawan 2019.

51. Hay (2014: 477) writes, "The key to resolving 'the difficulty of studying the state' . . . is not the abandonment of the concept of the state . . . but, instead, the recognition that the state is in fact a conceptual abstraction which belongs—like patriarchy and the class structure—to the realm of the 'as if real' and not to the real." Colin

Hay's work on the state is helpful and interesting. However, by distinguishing a certain set of abstract "composite" concepts and locating them within a space of the quasi-real, in contrast to the seemingly unproblematic reality of other, apparently less abstract concepts, Hay's approach presumes what needs demonstrating—namely, that some concepts (would motherhood or Parliament count?) are somehow *really* "real." The approach I adopt here avoids distinguishing between more and less abstract concepts. It approaches concepts (and my focus is nontechnical concepts) as taking shape in the oscillation between imagining and actualization (two dimensions that also fold practically into each other), while recognizing that forms of actualization (or manifestation) will vary depending on the concept (see Cooper 2014: chap. 2).

52. For an interesting discussion of this point in relation to Arctic states, see Medby 2018.

53. In a detailed and nuanced account of decentered regulation, Julia Black (2001: 145) suggests that "hierarchy will always lurk behind heterarchy."

54. For an account of states' complex and contradictory relationships, domestically and internationally, to capitalism and how this varies according to different state projects and capacities, see Jessop 2016.

55. Jessop (2010) explores how states also seek to manage capitalism's rhythms and mobility.

56. For further discussion of this point, see Cooper 2017; Cumbers 2015; Newman 2012a.

57. For useful discussion, see Angel 2017; Angel and Loftus 2017; Jessop 2016; Lake 2002; Lefebvre 2009; Martin and Pierce 2013; Poulantzas 1980; Van den Berg 2003.

58. See Jessop (1990; 2016: chap. 3) on the strategic and structural selectivity of the state, and on the state as a social relation, for some of the complexities of how this occurs.

59. For one discussion that emphasizes the place of the local state and local institutions in developing anticapitalist initiatives, see Cumbers et al. 2016.

60. For discussion of this point, see Geels and Smit 2000; Tutton 2017.

61. For a parallel discussion of prefigurative theory as a way to emphasize "those elements of [the world] worth promoting," see Davies 2017: 17. For further discussion, see chapter 6.

62. While I take a different approach, my account is indebted to work on "essentially contested concepts" (Gallie 1955). See also Collier et al. 2006; Dryzek 2016; Haugaard 2010.

63. For discussion of ideal and nonideal (more context-dependent) approaches in political theory, see Hamlin and Stemplowska 2012; Valentini 2012.

64. In this sense, I also diverge from Mieke Bal (2002: 11), whose very interesting book on "travelling concepts" focuses on concepts which "hover . . . between ordinary word and theoretical tool."

65. We also, of course, politically inhabit the present in what we imagine states—materially and culturally—could come to be; for discussion of this point in relation to health prognosis, see Bhandar 2009. For a detailed exploration of the relationship between prognosis and time, see Grabham 2017.

66. On the need to reimagine the present to encourage and help produce other futures, see Gibson-Graham 1996. For a strongly formulated argument on the performative character of social-science scholarship, see Law and Urry 2004.

ONE. **Legal Dramas of Refusal**

Epigraph: Vanessa Willock v. Elane Photography, LLC, HRD no. 06-12-20-0685, 2008, para. 20 (New Mexico Human Rights Commission, decision and final order); see also Elane Photography, LLC v. Willock, 309 P.3d 53 (NM 2013).

1. Focusing on withdrawal rather than discrimination shifts attention from differential treatment based on social characteristics—how one person or grouping is treated compared with another—to the relationship between the one withdrawing and the one withdrawn from vis-à-vis the things (tangible or otherwise) that are withdrawn.

2. See, e.g., Cobaw Community Health Services v. Christian Youth Camps Ltd. and Another, 2010 VCAT 1613, para. 339–40.

3. In some instances, it is potential customers or service users who turn away: see, e.g., Barnes-Wallace v. City of San Diego, 530 F.3d 776 (9th Cir. 2008). Here, parents would not let their sons use facilities given by the city to the Boy Scouts of America because of the organization's discriminatory policies.

4. See, e.g., Kirk Session of Sandown Free Presbyterian Church, re Application for Judicial Review, QBD, 2011 NIQB 26, para. 61. The Advertising Standards Authority concluded that while the church could advertise its "opposition to sodomy or the Gay Pride March," the advertising in question was legitimately rejected because of its "strident and offensive language." This was overturned in court on Article 10 (freedom of expression) grounds. For a quite different judgment, see R on the Application of Core Issues Trust v. Transport for London and Another, 2014 EWCA Civ 34, discussed in chapter 5.

5. In some cases, acts of withdrawal were pitted against each other; in other cases, as with Catholic adoption agencies and their relationship to the Catholic Church, charities demanded the right to withdraw to stop withdrawal by their Catholic funders: see, e.g., Catholic Care (Diocese of Leeds) v. Charity Commission for England and Wales, 2012 UKUT 395 (TCC), paras. 29–30.

6. Rumsfeld v. Forum for Academic and Institutional Rights, Inc., 547 U.S. 47 (2006).

7. Autonomy may also be asserted by individuals or groups refusing to defer to the authority of another body. For discussion of such refusal in relation to anarchist left politics, see Klausen and Martel 2011.

8. Writing about Tibetan refugees, McGranahan (2016: 338) discusses how their attachment to Tibetan citizenship also led them to *refuse* citizenship offers from both India and Nepal. She writes, "Refusing citizenship constitutes one means of asserting a right to sovereignty, of producing a state history and a subject-body, and thus of generating desired political effects at the level of the individual and the collective."

9. For further discussion in relation to inoperativity and the possibility of opening up to new uses, see Agamben 2014; Honig 2015.

10. Aihwa Ong (2007: 5) uses the language of exception in relation to neoliberalism in East and Southeast Asia to explore "extraordinary departure[s] in policy that can be deployed to include as well as to exclude." Later, resonating with my discussion here, she writes, "positive kinds of exception . . . create opportunities, usually for a minority, who enjoy political accommodations and conditions not granted to the rest of the population" (Ong 2007: 101).

11. NeJaime and Siegel (2015: 2520) describe these as "complicity-based conscience claims" to differentiate them from other religious-based requests for accommodation, such as in relation to religious dress, holy days, or prayer times. On religiously based claims to conscientious objection, see also Eisgruber and Sager 1994; Sepper 2014a. Kelly (2018) provides a helpful account of conservative Christian claims to conscience in relation to the twentieth-century development of freedom of conscience principles.

12. See, e.g., McClintock v. Department of Constitutional Affairs, 2008 IRLR 29.

13. For discussion of Canadian cases, see MacDougall and Short 2010.

14. See also Ghiotto v. City of San Diego, no. D055029 (Ct App. Cal. 2010), in which firefighters claimed that unlawful sexual harassment took place during a gay parade.

15. See, e.g., Ward v. Polite, 667 F.3d 727 (2012), in which a graduate student was expelled from a counseling program after requesting that a gay client be referred to other counseling students because of her own religious objections to homosexuality.

16. R (Johns) v. Derby City Council, 2011 EWHC 375 (Admin).

17. Similar issues have arisen in relation to professional education. In Keeton v. Anderson-Wiley, 664 F.3d 865 (11th Cir. 2011), Keeton unsuccessfully sought an injunction on free speech and free exercise of religion grounds against being dismissed from a school counseling training program because she refused to participate in a remedial plan to address failings in her "ability to be a multiculturally competent counsellor" in relation to LGBTQ issues.

18. Aaron Eades, "Man Refuses to Watch Training Video, Hires Lawyer," *Illinois Homepage.net*, 8 September 2016; accessed 24 July 2018, https://www.wcia.com/news /local-news/man-refuses-to-watch-training-video-hires-lawyer/545540650.

19. Kelowna v. O'Byrne (1999) 19 BCTC 132 (SC).

20. Hudler v. City of London (1997) 31 CHHR D/500 (Ont. Bd. of Inquiry), paras. 21, 27.

21. Chamberlain v. Surrey School District No. 36, 2002 SCC 86.

22. A. W. et al. v. Davis School District, case no. 1:2012cv00242 (District of Utah 2013).

23. Parents, Families, and Friends of Lesbians and Gays, Inc., v. Camdenton R-III School District, 853 F.Supp.2d 888 (2012).

24. In the United States, states attempted, with varying degrees of success, to protect the refusal to provide goods and services to lesbians and gay men on religious grounds through the introduction of state-based Religious Freedom Restoration bills and related legislation. For a useful summary of laws introduced across the states, see Marissa Lang, "The Definitive List of States Considering Anti-LGBT Legislation," SFGate, 22 April 2016, accessed 24 July 2018, https://www.sfgate.com/nation/article/Definitive -list-of-states-considering-anti-LGBT-7304253.php. Demonstrating the dynamic and reciprocating character of withdrawal, the deliberation and passage of these bills to

legitimate withdrawal on religious grounds precipitated a series of academic, cultural, and commercial boycotts opposing any attempt to deny or "water down" gay rights protections. For a nice example, see the Arizona pizzeria that posted, "We reserve the right to refuse service to Arizona legislators" in its restaurant window in response to a state bill which, it was feared, would permit firms to discriminate against gay people on grounds of religious beliefs: Rocco DiGrazia, "Why I Put That Sign in My Pizzeria Window," CNN, 27 February 2014, accessed 24 July 2018, https://edition.cnn.com /2014/02/26/opinion/rocco-pizzeria-arizona/index.html. See also E. Collins, "PayPal Pulls North Carolina Center over New LGBT Law," *Politico*, 5 April 2016, accessed 24 July 2018, https://www.politico.com/story/2016/04/paypal-north-carolina-LGBT -charlotte-center-221568.

25. For discussion of the guesthouse cases, see Forman 2012.

26. See, e.g., Brush and Nib Studio v. City of Phoenix, CV 2016-052251 (Arizona Superior Ct. 2016) affirmed in Brush & Nib v. Phoenix, 1 CA-CV 16-0602 (Arizona Court of Appeal 2018); Masterpiece Cakeshop Ltd. v. Colorado Civil Rights Commission, 584 U.S. (2018).

27. Lexington-Fayette Urban County Human Rights Commission v. Hands On Originals, case no. 2015-CA-000745-MR.

28. Other challenges have involved preemptive lawsuits prior to any claim of discrimination. In *Brush and Nib Studio v. City of Phoenix*, the plaintiffs brought a pre-enforcement civil rights lawsuit arguing that Phoenix's city code, which made discrimination in places of public accommodation unlawful, violated, among other things, the Arizona constitution.

29. Eadie and Thomas v. Riverbend Bed and Breakfast and Others (No. 2), 2012 BCHRT 247, paras. 51–53.

30. See, e.g., Pemberton v. Inwood, 2015 ET 2600962/2014.

31. Boy Scouts of America v. Dale, 530 U.S. 640 (2000). Later in this chapter, I explore the litigation that arose as public providers withdrew benefits from the Boy Scouts; others also withdrew, including a number of Eagle Scouts who returned their Scout badges as a form of insider "divestment" (Houdek 2017). In July 2015, the BSA formally rescinded its national ban on gay leaders: Todd Leopold, "Boy Scouts Change Policy on Gay Leaders," CNN, 28 July 2015, accessed 24 July 2018, https://edition.cnn .com/2015/07/27/us/boy-scouts-gay-leaders-feat/index.html.

32. See Ontario Human Rights Commission v. Christian Horizons, 2010 ONSC 2105.

33. Heintz v. Christian Horizons, 2008 HRTO 22, para. 179.

34. On U.S. legislative efforts to regulate discrimination toward gay employees and service users while allowing for religious-based exemptions, see Thompson 2015.

35. *Heintz v. Christian Horizons*, para. 26. On the territorial character of banishment as a contemporary governmental strategy, see Beckett and Herbert 2010, which explores banishment in relation to antisocial policies that target poor people. For discussion of the concept of "social flesh," see Beasley and Bacchi 2012.

36. Country Mill Farms v. City of East Lansing, case 1:17-cv-487, 2017 (opinion and order granting motion for preliminary injunction).

37. I explore the activist state further in Cooper 1994, 1999, 2017; also Cooper and Herman 2019.

38. See Christian Legal Society Chapter v. Martinez, 130 S. Ct. 2971 (2010); see also Massaro 2010.

39. For a small-scale example of symbolically punitive withdrawal, see the story about a high-school principal in Ventura, California, who refused to sell donated meals from Chick-fil-A because of the company's political stance on same-sex marriage: see "California's Ventura High School Scraps Chick-fil-A from Fundraiser, Citing Chain's Gay Marriage Stance," *Huffington Post*, 12 September 2014, accessed 4 July 2018, http:// www.huffingtonpost.com/2014/09/12/ventura-high-school-chick-fil-a_n_5812884.html.

40. Boy Scouts of America v. Wyman, 213 F. Supp. 2d 159 (D. Conn. 2002); Cradle of Liberty Council v. City of Philadelphia, 851 F. Supp. 2d 936 (2012); Evans v. City of Berkeley, 127 Cal. Rptr. 2d 696 (2002); Boy Scouts of America v. Till, 136 F. Supp. 2d 1295 (S.D. Fla. 2001). For an analysis of the BSA as a "quasi-religious" body, see Reuveni 2006.

41. See, e.g., Cochran v. City of Atlanta, 150 F. Supp.3d 1305 (2015), where a fire chief's position was terminated for a book written outside of work that, among other things, described homosexuality as contrary to God's will. In other cases, registration on university programs, fostering of children (e.g., *Johns*) or the freedom to engage in physically close forms of counterprotest such as at Gay Pride marches (see Marcavage v. City of Philadelphia, 778 F. Supp. 2d 556, 2011) have been withdrawn.

42. In Savage v. Gee, 716 F. Supp. 2d 709 (S.D. Ohio 2010), a university librarian proposed a book for assignment to incoming university students perceived as homophobic by colleagues, which led to action against him and a claim for constructive dismissal. For an example outside of work, see also Page v. NHS Trust Development Authority ET Case No: 2302433/2016, para. 11; here a non-executive NHS director was suspended for giving media interviews on his views about same-sex couples and heterosexual families. For a useful discussion of the implications in British law of penalizing off-duty staff for antigay acts and statements, see Mantouvalou (2008).

43. For example, Haye v. London Borough of Lewisham (2010) ET 2301852/09.

44. For example, Smith v. Trafford Housing Trust [2012] EWHC 3221; for another case of antigay remarks posted on a Facebook page, see Caroline Wilson, "School Chaplain Axed after Gay Disorder Claim," 7 January 2014, accessed 4 July 2018, http://www .heraldscotland.com/news/home-news/school-chaplain-axed-after-gay-disorder-claim .23100558. A related case arose in relation to a social work student who was expelled after posting comments supporting a conservative biblical approach to marriage on his Facebook page: "Christian Student to Seek Further Action after Expulsion from University Course," *Christian Concern*, 8 April 2016, accessed 4 July 2018, http://www .christianconcern.com/our-concerns/freedom-of-speech/christian-student-to-seek -further-action-after-expulsion-from-univers. In Chief of the Defence Force v. Gaynor (2017 FCAFC 41, para. 11), a major in the Australian Army Reserve disseminated antigay and anti-trans remarks, including as posts on his personal web page and through Twitter.

45. For example, see Mbuyi v. Newpark Childcare Ltd. [2015] ET 3300656/2014.

46. The London teacher Robert Haye was banned from teaching as a result of antigay comments made in the classroom; the ban was upheld by the High Court: see "Anti-Gay Deptford Teacher Robert Haye's Ban Upheld," BBC News, 12 April 2013, accessed 4 July 2018, https://www.bbc.co.uk/news/uk-england-london-22120706.

47. Apelogun-Gabriels v. L. B. Lambeth, 2006 ET case no. 2301976/05.

48. Rainbow Committee of Terrace v. City of Terrace, 2002 BCHRT 26, para. 39.

49. Trinity Western University v. Nova Scotia Barristers' Society, 2015 NSSC 25, para. 94.

50. For further discussion on state governing through the withdrawal and denial of its government, see Rose 2014.

51. *Heintz v. Christian Horizons*, paras. 251, 261.

52. Reaney v. Hereford Diocesan Board of Finance, ET 1602844/2006, para. 90.

53. *Heintz v. Christian Horizons*, para. 85.

54. In seeking to change its charitable objects to come within an exemption allowing it to legally exclude same-sex parents from its adoption services, "The Charity argues that the discrimination proposed is proportionate to the achievement of the legitimate aim it identifies because the discrimination would take the form of the denial of services which would not be available to same sex couples from the Charity, *but would be available to them via other voluntary adoption agencies and local authorities*": *Catholic Care (Diocese of Leeds) v. Charity Commission for England and Wales*, para. 15, emphasis added.

55. Here, homosexuals (along with some other queer figures) function as quasi-sacred figures in that their thwarting appears to be an essential performative dimension of contemporary conservative Christian practice.

56. At the heart of much queer analysis is a distinction between those whose lives are deemed precarious and often unlivable due to acutely unequal racialized, classed, and gendered relations, such as queer sex workers and poor, nonwhite trans people (particularly those with uncertain immigration status), and the homonormative, patriotic lifestyle of middle-class white gays: see Duggan 2002; Puar 2006; Richardson 2004.

57. For a legal example of this process of stigma contestation, see *Page v. NHS Trust Development Authority*, para. 59: "The Claimant and his representative said a number of times during hearing words to the effect of 'but what about the rights of Christians?'. However, that rather misses the point. There has been no suggestion as far as the tribunal is aware that there was, or has ever been, any issue with Christians suffering disproportionately from mental health problems [compared with the LGBT community] or any difficulty for Christians engaging with and/or accessing the mental health services provided by the Trust."

58. Many of those experiencing discrimination and abandonment also, of course, do not litigate. For an analysis of the complex conditions and character of taking up a legal subject position of victimhood, see Bumiller (1992).

59. Lord Bishop of Winchester, in United Kingdom, *Hansard Parliamentary Debates*, House of Lords, 21 March 2007, col. 1319. See also *R (Johns) v. Derby City Council*, para. 33: "Mr. Diamond's skeleton argument [on behalf of the Johns] opens with these words, 'This case raises profound issues on the question of religious freedom and whether Christians (or Jews and Muslims) can partake in the grant of "benefits" by

the State, or whether they have a second class status' . . . . He submits that the State 'should not use its coercive powers to de-legitimise Christian belief'. He asserts that what he calls the modern British State is 'ill suited to serve as an ethical authority' and complains that it 'is seeking to force Christian believers "into the closet" . . . that 'the denial of State benefits to those who believe homosexuality is a "sin" must be premised on the basis that such beliefs are contrary to established public policy".' For further discussion of the court's rejection of the Johns' legal claim, see chapter 2.

60. Quoted in "Christian Couple Lose Foster Ruling over Views on Homosexuality," *The Telegraph*, 28 February 2011, accessed 9 November 2018, https://www.telegraph .co.uk/news/religion/8352017/Christian-couple-lose-foster-ruling-over-views-on -homosexuality.html.

61. See McFarlane v. Relate Avon Ltd. [2010] EWCA Civ 880, para. 16. George Carey, former Archbishop of Canterbury, said in his witness statement: "It is, of course, but a short step from the dismissal of a sincere Christian from employment to a 'religious bar' to any employment by Christians. If Christian views on sexual ethics can be described as '*discriminatory*', such views cannot be '*worthy of* respect in a democratic society'. An employer could dismiss a Christian, refuse to employ a Christian and actively undermine Christian beliefs. I believe that further Judicial decisions are likely to end up at this point and this is why I believe it is necessary to intervene now." These arguments were given short shrift by Lord Justice Laws. However, Strhan's (2015) empirical research provides insights into feelings of shame and uncertainty among British evangelicals caught between their desire to share their faith and acute awareness of the secular norms operating within work and public spaces.

62. Although usually associated with the left, the right can also act prefiguratively (to the extent the concept foregrounds the practice of enacting hoped-for aspirations in the present rather than acting in specifically progressive ways). See chapter 6 for further discussion.

63. For helpful accounts of prefigurative politics, see Boggs 1977; Maeckelbergh 2011; Yates 2015.

64. Lord Carey (intervener), written submission, *McFarlane* and *United Kingdom* ECHR application no. 36516/10.

65. *Eadie and Thomas v. Riverbend Bed and Breakfast and Others*, paras. 58, 61, 64, 130.

66. *Masterpiece Cakeshop Ltd. v. Colorado Civil Rights Commission*, 1A.

67. Yet the "necessity" here is not simply to be exempt from pro-gay dimensions of antidiscrimination and human rights law; it is also the necessity to make decisions *countering* gay rights. Given the apparent significance of homosexuality for contemporary conservative Christian practice, lesbian and gay equality must be countered through decisive acts of refusal as a way of activating and incarnating God's will (see also Norton 2011).

68. *McFarlane v. Relate Avon Ltd.*, para. 21.

69. Ladele v. London Borough of Islington, 2008 UKEAT 0453_08_1912, para. 73.

70. This approach, however, was doubted by the European Court of Human Rights in Eweida and Ors v. United Kingdom, 2013 ECHR 37.

71. See Lord Justice Laws in *McFarlane v. Relate Avon Ltd.*, para. 21.

72. Chiang v. Vancouver Board of Education and Others, 2009 BCHRT 319, para. 109.

73. *Keeton v. Anderson-Wiley*, 875.

74. Withdrawal and refusal, as practices of "conscientious objection," emphasize both the corporeality and personhood of the provider, that they have not lost themselves in "the depersonalised, fragmented, mechanical actions of the productive process" (Bennett 2010: 108); nor are they simply a conduit or tool of their employer.

75. In Christian Legal Society Chapter v. Martinez, 561 U.S. 661 (2010), the Supreme Court addressed the difficulties in separating status from practices and beliefs in terms of what constituted illegitimate discrimination. For further discussion of these difficulties, see Business Leaders in Christ v. the University of Iowa et al., case no. 3:17-cv-00080-SMR-SBJ (2018). In this case, a gay-identified student inquired about serving as vice-president of the university's Christian society, Business Leaders in Christ. He was told he was not eligible for a leadership position. However, on the facts, as described by the court, it was unclear whether the rejection was due to his (emerging) sexual identity or his disagreement with the society's biblical position on homosexuality.

76. See, e.g., Lee v. Ashers Baking Company Ltd & Ors (Northern Ireland) [2018] UKSC 49; for a critique of this judgment as too narrow in its interpretation of equality law, see Yossi Nehushtan and Stella Coyle, "Ashers Baking (Part 1): The Supreme Court's Betrayal of Liberalism and Equality," *U.K. Const. L. Blog*, 5 November 2018, accessed 5 November 2018, https://ukconstitutionallaw.org/.

77. See, e.g., Barronelle Stutzman, "Why a Friend Is Suing Me: The Arlene's Flowers Story," *Seattle Times*, 9 November 2015, accessed 5 July 2018, https://www.seattletimes .com/opinion/why-a-good-friend-is-suing-me-the-arlenes-flowers-story. What counts as speech in this context varies. In *Rumsfeld*, the court held that "accommodating the military's message does not affect the law school's speech, because the schools are not speaking when they host interviews and recruiting receptions": *Rumsfeld v. Forum for Academic and Institutional Rights*, 64.

78. Telescope Media Group et al. v. Lindsey et al., Civil no. 16-4094 (District of Minnesota, 2017), 6.

79. *Telescope Media Group et al. v. Lindsey et al.*

80. *Telescope Media Group et al. v. Lindsey et al.*

81. Lexington-Fayette Urban County Human Rights Commission and Aaron Barker for Gay and Lesbian Services Organization v. Hands on Originals (Kentucky Court of Appeal, NO. 2015-CA-000745-MR), 16: "While the shirts merely bore a screen-printed design with the words 'Lexington Pride Festival 2012,' the number '5,' and a series of rainbow-colored circles, the symbolism of this design, the festival the design promoted, and the GLSO's desire to sell these shirts to everyone clearly imparted a *message*."

82. Heather Clark, "State Human Rights Commission Appeal Seeks to Force Christian Business to Print 'Gay Pride' T-shirts," *Christian News*, 2 November 2015, accessed 5 July 2018, http://christiannews.net/2015/11/02/state-human-rights-commission -appeal-seeks-to-force-christian-business-to-print-gay-pride-t-shirts.

83. Yet this position of creator-ownership is further complicated by an additional layer of belonging. While conservative Christians suggested that they retained an important connection to the things that they made, they also argued that what they

were being asked to make was colored and shaped by the recipients, such that a wedding cake for a gay couple was in fact a gay wedding cake. As Justice Neil Gorsuch stated, "It was the kind of cake, not the kind of customer that mattered": *Masterpiece Cakeshop Ltd. v. Colorado Civil Rights Commission*, 4. For a contrasting argument, see Justice Ruth Bader Ginsburg in *Masterpiece Cakeshop Ltd. v. Colorado Civil Rights Commission*.

84. For further discussion in a U.S. context, see Cruz 1994; Sepper 2014b; Wessels 1989. However, see also Amy Lynn Photography Studio et al. v. City of Madison et al., case no. 17CV0555, declaratory judgment 30701 (2017), which held that a photography studio was not a public place of accommodation since it lacked a "physical storefront open to the public" (the studio was run out of the photographer's apartment) and thus could not be subject to Wisconsin's public accommodations law. This meant the photographer could explicitly declare she would decline work that promoted same-sex marriage (and abortion).

85. *Eadie and Thomas v. Riverbend Bed and Breakfast and Others*, para. 165.

86. See the Australian case *Cobaw Community Health Services v. Christian Youth Camps Ltd. and Another*, para. 242.

87. Opposition to a liberal division of normative spheres comes also from critical sexuality scholars. The critical law and sexuality scholar Carl Stychin (2009a: 733) writes, "Ironically, supporters of sexuality equality at times fall back on the public-private, belief-conduct distinctions as the justification for curtailing religious freedom—relegating those of faith to the closet from which they themselves have emerged." The language of the closet, interestingly, was also taken up by some conservative Christian advocates in arguing for their right to withdraw. Bob Diamond, acting on behalf of the Johns in their foster care case, described the British state as "seeking to force Christian believers '*into the closet*'": *R (Johns) v. Derby City Council*, para. 33 (emphasis in original).

88. One direction this has taken relates to employers' withdrawal of certain benefits from employees on grounds of the employers' conservative religious stance. See the discussion surrounding Burwell v. Hobby Lobby Stores, Inc., 134 S. Ct. 2751 (2014), an American case that allowed a company to exclude contraceptive services from its employees' health plan on grounds of the company's beliefs (NeJaime and Siegel 2014; Sepper 2014b; Nadel 2017).

89. *Brush and Nib Studio v. City of Phoenix*, Complaint, para. 11.

90. *Brush and Nib Studio v. City of Phoenix*, Complaint, para. 270–71, emphasis added.

91. Cassandra Jardine quotes the turned-down foster parent Eunice Johns as saying, "Our Christianity isn't something we can just take on and off": Cassandra Jardine, "Our Christianity Is Our Lifestyle—We Can't Take It On and Off," *The Telegraph*, 1 March 2011, accessed 5 July 2018, https://www.telegraph.co.uk/news/religion/8355786 /Our-Christianity-is-our-lifestyle-we-cant-take-it-on-and-off.html. This is discussed further in chapter 2.

92. On whether a Catholic university can refuse to recognize gay student organizations that clash with its norms and values, see the dissent in Gay Rights Coalition v. Georgetown University, 496 A.2d 567 (1985).

93. *Heintz v. Christian Horizons*, para. 10.

94. In one Canadian case, a student, Marc Hall, was forbidden by his principal (with backing from the school board) to bring his boyfriend to the school prom as his date. The principal declared that interaction at a prom between romantic partners was a form of sexual activity, and if permission was granted, it would be seen as endorsement and condonation contrary to the Catholic Church's teachings: Hall v. Powers, 59 O.R. (3d) 423. See also Grace and Wells 2005.

95. Critics of this stance argue that doing one's job does not connote approval or endorsement, although refusal or withdrawal clearly does send a message (see Mac-Dougall and Short 2010). A difficulty with this disagreement is that both sides act as if there is a certain answer: provision either does or does not endorse.

96. *Vanessa Willock v. Elane Photography, llc*, para. 23, emphasis added.

97. *Willock* differs from the public sector employment cases because it concerns the right to discriminate as a commercial provider rather than the right to accommodation by a state employer. Being self-employed, Willock has the right, within liberal property discourse, to claim an attachment to her work as an artist, although this may not give her a legal right to discriminate within the marketplace. For a sharp judicial rebuff, see *Brush and Nib Studio v. City of Phoenix*, ruling denying plaintiffs' motion for preliminary injunction (16 September 2016), 13. Here, the court rejected the notion that making a wedding card was tantamount to endorsing a same-sex wedding: "There is nothing about the creative process itself, such as a flower or vine or the choice of a particular font or color, that conveys any pledge, endorsement, celebration, or other substantive mandated message by Plaintiffs in regard to same-sex marriage."

98. For discussion of the cultural politics of stickiness, see Ahmed 2004.

99. See, e.g., Christian Legal Society v. Martinez, 561 U.S. 661.

100. *R on the Application of Core Issues Trust v. Transport for London and Another*.

101. See also Ross v. New Brunswick School District No. 15, 1996 1 scr 825, para. 44: "Teachers do not necessarily check their teaching hats at the school yard gate and may be perceived to be wearing their teaching hats even off duty."

102. I should stress that I am not suggesting conservative Christians routinely adopted progressive perspectives on workers' rights. However, here conservative Christian litigants countered the full alienation of their labor with arguments based on "conscientious objection" and religious rights. For an account of a more conservative approach to employment within the context of an evangelical job-readiness program, see Purser and Hennigan 2017.

TWO. **Retrieving Dissident State Parts**

Epigraph: Mitchell 1991: 93.

1. United Kingdom, *Hansard Parliamentary Debates*, House of Lords, 21 March 2007, col. 1309.

2. Lord Carey (intervener), written submission, *McFarlane and United Kingdom*, echr, application no. 36516/10, para. 22.

3. United Kingdom, *Hansard Parliamentary Debates*, House of Lords, 21 March 2007, col. 1319.

4. More attention has been paid to the many ways liberal states undermine or fail to support gay equality. In the British context, much of this work has focused on local government and other public sector organizations (see, e.g., Colgan and Wright 2011; Cooper 1994, 2006; Richardson and Monro 2012).

5. United Kingdom, *Hansard Parliamentary Debates*, House of Commons, 26 February 2013, col. 226, emphasis added.

6. Referring to "society" in this way does not assume it is a distinct bounded entity.

7. I am thinking particularly of Passoth and Rowland 2010. See also Carroll 2009.

8. Here, I part company with Martin Müller (2012: 380, emphasis added), who writes that we need to see organizations "as socio-material networks—arrangements of human and material elements that *work together toward a shared mission*." Despite Actor-Network Theory's orientation toward heterogeneity, the suggestion that we follow the connections to determine which forces and things contribute to *state* outcomes, including of institutional reproduction, seems to presume that we have already decided what makes actions or outcomes *state* ones. But how should such a characterization be made? Is stateness determined by a set of qualities or characteristics predefined as state ones? By a relationship to a sociomaterial entity *already* identified as the state (even if elements of its extended networks could be defined otherwise)? Does what counts as the state depend on particular histories and genealogies assumed to be state genealogies, or does it depend on the pursuit of particular functions or activities assumed to be state ones? These questions are explored further in chapter 3.

9. For a more progressive account of the relationship between social work and faith-based social action, see Shaw 2018.

10. For a useful discussion of public sector middle managers' policy ambivalence, drawing on accounts of the "ghostly," see Pors 2016. This is a staffing tier that controls and is controlled, that resists and is resisted.

11. However, Maynard-Moody and Musheno (2000: 341) are uncomfortable describing this localized and particularized process, which often lacks consistency and coherence, as "policy-making."

12. For a quite different account of frontline workers, see the discussion of immigration officers, who view their work as protecting the state and treat people as cases (i.e., as "a series of issues materialised in a set of documents bundled together"), in Fuglerud 2004: 36. Colin Hoag's (2010) account of immigration officials, in South Africa, also diverges from Maynard-Moody and Musheno's account, in characterizing street-level officials as far more attuned to system maintenance, to avoiding abuse, and as often feeling out-maneuvered by clients or their legal advisers.

13. See Bernardo Zacka's (2017: 14) interesting account of street-level practice. Recognizing the discretion that is often exercised at the front line, Zacka advocates supporting "bureaucrats to retain adequate moral dispositions."

14. Sometimes more autonomous work by public sector staff is encouraged and enabled by government structures, particularly local ones. On other occasions, it is

seen as an effect of the changing character of governance or as something that is seized (rather than given).

15. Alison Mountz (2004), for example, advocates paying attention to the constitutive bodies of individuals who make up the state (and other organizations) to expose what gets obscured by the smooth black-box narratives of powerful organizations.

16. See the narrative of events in London Borough of Islington v. Ladele [2012], UKEAT 0453_08_1912.

17. For an interesting discussion of this point in relation to the very different context of female mayors in Yucatán and their performance of minority ethnic and gendered interests and identities, see Loyola-Hernández 2018.

18. Her account also suggests a different conception of policy-making diffusion to that of the street-level bureaucracy literature, since "it looks beyond the bureaucracy to forms of work—formal and informal, paid and unpaid—that connect new governing logics to social and political action" (Newman 2014: 140).

19. Not all gay and lesbian council officials supported the municipal sexuality agenda. See also Richardson and Monro 2012.

20. I explore this further in Cooper 1994.

21. R on the Application of Core Issues Trust v. Transport for London and Another [2014], EWHC 2628 (Admin).

22. *R on the Application of Core Issues Trust v. Transport for London and Another.*

23. *R on the Application of Core Issues Trust v. Transport for London and Another*, para. 44, italics removed.

24. On some of the challenges of "insider activism" experienced by gay public sector staff in Brighton, see Browne and Bakshi 2013. For discussion of conservative Christian accusations of gay special interests in the North American context, see Goldberg-Hiller and Milner 2003; Herman 1997.

25. At the same time, MacDougall and Short (2010: 153) resist the claim that being compelled to provide services, such as marriage, "injects" gay equality norms into the reluctant service provider. For contrasting positions on the wider issues, see Benson 2007; Trotter 2007.

26. Daniel Boucher (2010: 52), writing from a Christian perspective, argues for the importance of bringing religious, and particularly Christian, values and organizations into government activities. Otherwise, Christians face disadvantage when "others are able to take their projects (and therein values, since no projects are values free) into the process of government."

27. Eunice Johns, commenting on her inability to leave her conservative Christian sexual ethics behind when making an application to become a foster parent, quoted in Cassandra Jardine, "Our Christianity Is Our Lifestyle—We Can't Take It On and Off," *The Telegraph*, 1 March 2011, accessed 5 July 2018, https://www.telegraph.co.uk/news /religion/8355786/Our-Christianity-is-our-lifestyle-we-cant-take-it-on-and-off.html. See also the discussion of this point in chapter 1.

28. R (Johns) v. Derby City Council, 2011 EWHC 375 (Admin).

29. This case sits alongside others in which conservative Christian marriage registrars and therapists argue that they lack the right kind of thick self for the work. Thus,

they should be exempt from providing a service to gay individuals or same-sex couples since they cannot (authentically) provide the affirmation or celebration that the work properly requires.

30. *R (Johns) v. Derby City Council*, para. 10.

31. "Christian Foster Carers Campaign for Re-Instatement by Derby Council," *Christian Concern*, 6 April 2011, accessed 6 July 2018, http://www.christianconcern.com/our-concerns/sexual-orientation/christian-foster-carers-campaign-for-re-instatement-by-derby-council.

32. Interestingly, Nicola Reynolds (2015) describes British Christians' deployment of values, such as love, as a way to convey Christianity within secular policy contexts and public debate in contrast with articulating explicitly religious ideas that might undermine the speakers' credibility. Thus, she presents "love" as a bridging rather than dividing (or provoking) term.

33. The place and presence of emotion within state bodies has generated growing discussion (see, e.g., Albrow 1992; Hunter 2015; Jupp et al. 2016; Newman 2012b). I return to this in discussing the erotic state in chapter 5.

34. *R (Johns) v. Derby City Council*.

35. On "police" as a mode of "partitioning" or ordering in which there is no "void" or "supplement," see also Rancière 2010: 44.

36. However, Rancière (1999: 29) states explicitly that policing does not refer to "state apparatus" if the state is understood as a "'cold monster' imposing its rigid order on the life of society."

37. In the case of the Johns, the husband's remark that he would "gently turn [foster children] around" if they showed signs of a gay orientation was taken up by Derby City Council as a concern: *R (Johns) v. Derby City Council*, para. 7.

38. David Hodge's (2002) work on the "oppression" of evangelical Christians in social work demonstrates how conservative Christians have constructed a police order in which their religious views and presence are unwelcome, largely excluded, and presented as backward. Hodge describes how secular liberal control leaves evangelicals voiceless, defined as fundamentalist by the new "dominant ideology" and, as such, outside the terms of legitimate discourse. At the same time, in the jurisdictions discussed in this book, explicit discrimination against religious people is also unlawful. The complexity here is that the discrimination claimed relates not directly to religious subjects but to their antigay beliefs.

39. On this more general point, see Rancière 2010: 39.

40. See the case of Richard Page, whose term as a non-executive director of the National Health Service (NHS) was not renewed because of his views on same-sex parents: Page v. NHS Trust Development Authority, ET case no: 2302433/2016. See also "Christian 'Driven from Public Service' after Saying That Children Ideally Need Mother and Father," *Christian Concern*, 22 November 2016, accessed 6 July 2018, http://www.christianconcern.com/our-concerns/adoption/christian-driven-from-public-service-after-saying-that-children-ideally-need-m; and "Christian Couple Blocked from Adopting because of Their Belief That Children Need Mum and Dad," *Christian Concern*, 9 November 2016, accessed 6 July 2018, http://christianconcern.com/our

-concerns/adoption/foster-parents-prevented-from-adoption-because-they-believe-a
-child-should-hav.

41. I discuss this register of state presence further in Cooper 2016a.

42. See for instance Samuel Schueth's (2012) discussion of the state's changing relationship to "fiscal illegalisms" within early twenty-first-century Georgia.

43. This is something I have explored in relation to dissent and noncompliance by locally elected state officials in the 1980s in response to the Thatcher government's attack on local government; and by educators in response to the institutionalization of Christian-based prayer and religious education in British schools in the late 1980s and early 1990s (see Cooper 1996, 1998).

44. See Caroline Gammell, "Care Home for Elderly Christians in Gay Row," *The Telegraph*, 28 December 2008, accessed 6 July 2018, https://www.telegraph.co.uk/news/religion/3999004/Care-home-for-elderly-Christians-in-gay-row.html. See also Baskerville 2011. Funding was subsequently restored after legal action on grounds of religious discrimination commenced: see David Harrison, "Christian Care Home Victorious in Gay Dispute," *The Telegraph*, 7 February 2009, accessed 6 July 2018, https://www.telegraph.co.uk/news/health/news/4548761/Christian-care-home-victorious-in-gay-dispute.html.

45. The Equality Act (Sexual Orientation) Regulations 2007 were subsequently incorporated into the Equality Act 2010. The quote is from United Kingdom, *Hansard Parliamentary Debates*, House of Lords, 21 March 2007, col. 1303.

46. Writing in the different context of Turkey and "the physicality of the political" there, Yael Navaro-Yashin (2002: 181) remarks, "A political culture . . . is embodied, to the point when the state is carried in the bodies, habits, and . . . reactions of its subjects." Jeff Garmany (2009: 729) makes a similar point: "Governance is maintained by self-disciplining individuals who enact the state in their daily routines and discourses, producing it through practice as a constituted, socially constructed reality."

47. In other instances, it is public bodies that fear they are "sticking" to the anti-gay action carried out by their staff and thus becoming part of a network of action conducted beyond the workplace. For further discussion, see chapter 1.

48. For a striking account of populist depictions of the grotesque state in the postcolonial context, see Mbembe 1992.

49. For a sharply worded expression of this, see the District Court's decision in Fulton et al. v. City of Philadelphia et al., 2:2018cv02075, 51: "css [Catholic Social Services] is performing governmental work, including the dissemination of governmental messages in entering a contract for foster care services. . . . css's work under the Services Contract is, thus, an extension of [the] dhs's [Department of Human Services] own work and css's speech . . . constitutes governmental speech."

50. The Christian heritage (and ongoing) character of the British state was routinely asserted by those opposed to extending equality provisions to sexual orientation, and who supported British acts of conservative Christian withdrawal and refusal. Debating the sexual orientation equality regulations, the Archbishop of York commented, "I fear that we are in danger of losing the formative Christian inheritance and foundation of this great nation, a foundation upon which our laws, society and culture have

been built, but which is in danger of being undermined": United Kingdom, *Hansard Parliamentary Debates*, 21 March 2007, col. 1309. Bishop Michael Nazir-Ali similarly remarked, "Everything from the Coronation Oath onward suggests that there is an inextricable link between the Judaeo-Christian tradition of the Bible and the institutions, the values and the virtues of British society. If this judgment is allowed to stand [referring to the *McFarlane* case where a counselor unsuccessfully claimed unfair dismissal after losing his job with a relationship counseling organization because he would not provide psychosexual counseling for same-sex couples], the aggressive secularists will have had their way": Michael Nazir-Ali, "The Legal Threat to Our Spiritual Tradition," *The Telegraph*, 30 April 2010, accessed 6 July 2018, http://www.telegraph.co.uk/news/religion/7655457/The-legal-threat-to-our-spiritual-tradition.html.

51. There is an extensive literature on historical and contemporary relations between state bodies and Christian organizations, including on the extent to which Christian organizations became enrolled in state projects or were able to influence and reshape them. Paula Maurutto (2004) provides an interesting account of the complex relations between the Roman Catholic church and the local and regional state in Toronto, Canada, between 1850 and 1950. Contemporary accounts, relating to the jurisdictions of this book, also address the particular role and visibility of religious-based service organizations as a result of public bodies' withdrawal from provision and the growth in postsecular politics (see, e.g., Adkins et al. 2010; Williams et al. 2012).

52. In their work on secular governance assemblages in London and southeastern England as "part private, part public, with bits and pieces of institutional authority, legal rights and territorial infrastructure," John Allen and Allan Cochrane (2010: 1078) use Saskia Sassen's work to explore new kinds of governance instability: "The emergent assemblage, which is neither national nor global, represents an unstable power formation in the making . . . unstable not only because different economic, political and legal elements may co-exist in novel arrangements, but also because such elements may operate according to different temporal rhythms and institutional pace which come together in both enabling and contested ways."

53. For useful accounts of the entanglement and coexistence of state and informal regulatory orders, see Raeymaekers 2012; Reyntjens 2014.

54. For a skeptical picture of the power and autonomous capacity of network governance beyond the state in the field of community safety, see Crawford 2006.

55. For a helpful discussion on ways of thinking about responsibility that go beyond neoliberal forms, see Trnka and Trundle 2014. Devolving responsibility for welfare to individuals themselves has also been criticized, in other contexts, for relying on, and consolidating, a differentiation between subjects deemed capable of acting responsibly and therefore allowed to self-regulate and those deemed irresponsible and so subject to coercive regulation by the police, criminal law, and public health. For discussion of this governmental approach in the context of people living with AIDS, see Kinsman 1996.

56. Gathered states entail, at least in part, a self-authorized responsibility and accountability to people living at a geopolitical distance where the governing-at-a-distance presence of particular states in their lives also enrolls them (passively or actively) within those states. For discussion of this point oriented to the ways in which

place and its associated responsibilities are constructed in conditions of social inter-connectedness, see Gatens and Lloyd 1999; Keenan 2015; Massey 2006.

57. For a more nuanced and complex reading of the socially networked character of culpability-based responsibility, see Young 2006.

58. In the litigation relating to Trinity Western University's law school, the university argued that their creation of additional law school spaces would free up spaces in other law schools for LGBT students. For discussion of this point, see Major 2017. See also chapter 3.

59. See, e.g., Michael W. McConnell (for the petitioner), oral argument before the Supreme Court, 19 April 2010, in Christian Legal Society Chapter v. Martinez, 561 U.S. 661 (2010). Characterization as "private" can exempt bodies from equality provisions that apply only to governmental bodies: see Trinity Western University v. Nova Scotia Barristers' Society, 2015 NSSC 25, para. 10. The university's depiction of itself as a private body was challenged by provincial law societies that claimed its educational function was public and secular: see Supreme Court decisions that found in favor of the law societies, namely, Law Society of British Columbia v. Trinity Western University, 2018 SCC 32; Trinity Western University v. Law Society of Upper Canada, 2018 SCC 33. See also Major 2017.

60. This argument was also made by the court in relation to Catholic Care in declaring that the charity's view "that the traditional family should be promoted is not entitled to the same degree of weight as if it had been adopted by the national authorities": "The Roman Catholic Church is not a national body authorised by the democratic political process to establish public rules or laws binding the whole country. . . . It is a private institution distinct from the state, representing only the views of its adherents and incapable of setting general standards of public policy": Catholic Care (Diocese of Leeds) v. Charity Commission for England and Wales, 2012 UKUT 395 (TCC), paras. 46–47.

61. *Catholic Care (Diocese of Leeds) v. Charity Commission for England and Wales.*

THREE. **Pluralizing a Concept**

Epigraphs: Albert 2014: 527; Brunkhorst 2012: 178.

1. Trinity Western University v. British Columbia College of Teachers, 2001 SCC 31. For discussion of TWU litigation, see also Smith 2004.

2. *Trinity Western University*, para. 5.

3. *Trinity Western University*, para. 4.

4. See Law Society of British Columbia v. Trinity Western University, 2018 SCC 32; Trinity Western University v. Law Society of Upper Canada, 2018 SCC 33. See also Feinstein and Hamill 2018; Major 2017. Shortly after the Supreme Court judgments, TWU announced that students would not be required to sign the Community Covenant; Matt Robinson et al., "Trinity Western University's Community Covenant No Longer Mandatory," *Vancouver Sun* 15 August 2018, accessed 15 November 2018, https://vancouversun.com/news/local-news/trinity-western-universitys-community -covenant-no-longer-mandatory.

5. Questions of state scale are not straightforward. They are complicated by, among other things, the overlapping reach of different kinds of states, as when local states engage in international relations and international policy development, as well as by the scale-making (and not just scale-expressing) activities of different state bodies.

6. For instance, Thomas Pogge (1992: 58) writes, "Neighborhood, town, county, province, state, region, and world at large. People should be politically at home in all of them, without converging upon any one of them as the lodestar of their political identity."

7. Chamberlain v. Surrey School District No. 36, 2002 SCC 86; see also Smith 2004.

8. In April 1997, "The Board adopted a resolution stating that resources from gay and lesbian groups were not approved for use in the Surrey School District. . . . After this resolution was passed, certain resources, including library books, posters and pamphlets, were removed from schools within the district": *Chamberlain v. Surrey School District No. 36*, paras. 45–46.

9. *Chamberlain v. Surrey School District No. 36*, para. 27, emphasis added. Elsewhere, the court remarked, "The Board is a political body . . . on which the legislature has conferred a circumscribed role in approving books. However, the deference that might be warranted by these factors, standing alone, is undercut by clear commitment of the legislature and the Minister to promoting tolerance and respect for diversity" [para. 14].

10. Justice Gonthier, *Chamberlain v. Surrey School District No. 36*, para. 155.

11. *Chamberlain v. Surrey School District No. 36*, para. 102.

12. *Chamberlain v. Surrey School District No. 36*, para. 154.

13. Proposed class action complaint, Weber v. Davis School District, 2013, case no. 1:12-CV-242-EJF, para. 76, https://www.aclu.org/files/assets/02-complaint.pdf.

14. *Weber v. Davis School District*, para. 70; see also paras. 60–67.

15. See the American Civil Liberties Union web page relating to this case: "*Weber v. Davis School District* (2013)," 12 January 2013, accessed 11 July 2018, http://www.acluutah.org/legal-work/resolved-cases/item/331-weber-v-davis-school-district-2013.

16. Smith and Chymyshyn v. Knights of Columbus and Others, 2005 BCHRT 544.

17. *Smith and Chymyshyn*, para. 55. According to the director of Catholic information for the Knights of Columbus, "If the Knights had allowed the Hall to be used by the complainants for the celebration of their marriage, it would have resulted in a serious rupture between the Catholic Church and the Knights. In the Charter, Constitution and Laws of the Knights, a Knight forfeits his membership if he does not remain in union with the 'Holy See'": *Smith and Chymyshyn*, para. 13.

18. *Smith and Chymyshyn*, para. 71.

19. *Smith and Chymyshyn*, paras. 92, 134.

20. Bernstein et al. v. Ocean Grove Camp Meeting Association, OAL DKT no. CRT6145-09, 12 January 2012.

21. For further details, see the respondent's brief in support of a motion for a summary decision, in *Bernstein et al.*

22. *Bernstein et al.*, 3.

23. "Finding of Probable Cause," Bernstein et al. v. Ocean Grove Camp Meeting Association, DCR DKT no. PN34XB-03008, 4, 29 December 2008, https://www.nj.gov/oag/newsreleases08/pr20081229a-Bernstein-v-OGCMA.pdf.

24. "Finding of Probable Cause," *Bernstein et al.*, 9–10.

25. Bernstein et al. v. Ocean Grove Camp Meeting Association (OAL DKT. NO. CRT 6145-09).

26. Lack of registration meant the student society was denied the use of the Hastings Law School logo, email address, certain means of publicizing events, and funds, although it was not prohibited from meeting on campus. See Christian Legal Society Chapter v. Martinez, 561 U.S. 661 (2010).

27. *Christian Legal Society Chapter v. Martinez*. See also Business Leaders in Christ v. the University of Iowa et al., case no. 3:17-cv-00080-SMR-SBJ.

28. Cardinal Cormac Murphy-O'Connor to Prime Minister Tony Blair, letter, BBC *News*, 22 January 2007, accessed 11 July 2018, http://news.bbc.co.uk/1/hi/uk_politics /6290073.stm.

29. Murphy-O'Connor to Blair.

30. See also "Apostolic Letter Issued 'Motu Proprio' of the Supreme Pontiff Benedict XVI on the Service of Charity, 11 November 2012, accessed 11 July 2018, http://w2 .vatican.va/content/benedict-xvi/en/motu_proprio/documents/hf_ben-xvi_motu -proprio_20121111_caritas.html. A different case exemplifying this kind of pressure was Ambridge Event Center v. Holy Rosary Church of Portland, Oregon, complaint, 18CV20835. In this case, a company running an event center in property owned by the Catholic Church received a notice of termination as a result of its decision to associate with the LGBTQ community and hire a gay employee, which was deemed in breach of the "Morality Clause" in its contract.

31. For similar events in the United States, see Rutledge 2008.

32. See, e.g., Catholic Care (Diocese of Leeds) v. Charity Commission for England and Wales [2012] UKUT 395 (TCC). For discussion of the law relating to this case, see Morris et al. 2016.

33. "Bishop of Lancaster Writes on Break with Catholic Adoption Society," *Independent Catholic News*, 22 December 2008, accessed 11 July 2018, https://www .indcatholicnews.com/news.php?viewStory=770%202/5.

34. "Bishop of Lancaster Writes on Break with Catholic Adoption Society." Caritas Social Action Network (a Catholic agency) permitted the adoption society to join, ignoring their "legal" expulsion from the diocese: see William Oddie, "How Many Catholic Adoption Societies Have Actually Closed Down; and How Many Are Now Quietly Handing Children over to Gay Adoptive Parents?" *Catholic Herald*, 4 July 2013, accessed 11 July 2018, http://www.catholicherald.co.uk/commentandblogs/2013/07/04 /how-many-catholic-adoption-societies-have-actually-closed-down-and-how-many-are -now-quietly-handing-children-over-to-gay-adoptive-parents.

35. See "Bishop of Lancaster Writes on Break with Catholic Adoption Society."

36. For an interesting account of diverse conceptions of the state, including pluralist perspectives, in the context of late nineteenth-century Britain, see Meadowcroft 1995.

37. For a useful account of early twentieth-century English political pluralism (and its subsequent decline), see Runciman 1997. For other pluralist state accounts, see Hirst 1997; Laski 1919; Morefield 2005; Pogge 1992.

38. At the same time, conventional pluralist accounts can end up reifying the pluralist state—whether as a historically emergent political form, as an ideal, or in terms of its essential features. What is important to the pluralist account developed in this chapter is its conceptual, rather than normative or empirical, character. As I discuss later, this recognizes that there is no detached Archimedean position from which to know particular states (or the conceptual state); states can be imagined in diverse ways depending on how the social is "cut," and different "conceptual lines" express (and construct) different political or epistemological understandings and consequences. For further discussion, see the introduction.

39. Filip Reyntjens (2016) helpfully puts legal pluralism into conversation with work on pluralist state forms.

40. This does not mean, however, that different authorities, or the sources of their legitimacy and power, are unconnected (e.g., in relation to the conditions that generated them or in relation to their content and form). It means simply that a single authoritative system or representation of agreed on authorized authority does not exist.

41. Paul Schiff Berman (2007: 1166) writes, "There is no external position from which one could make a definitive statement as to who is authorized to make decisions in any given case. Rather, a statement of authority is itself inevitably open to contest."

42. Indeed, the architectural allocation of rights, responsibilities, and power may beg the question of whether this is pluralism at all or simply the functional and orderly distribution inherent to any complex entity.

43. *Chamberlain v. Surrey School District No. 36*, para. 28, emphasis added.

44. In his dissenting judgment, Justice Gonthier remarked, "The curriculum established by the Minister clearly contemplates that even provincially approved resources may be considered inappropriate for use in certain local communities, and that parental concerns about such 'sensitive issues' constitute a valid and proper consideration in the exercise of the teacher's discretion to use such materials": *Chamberlain v. Surrey School District No. 36*, para. 148.

45. The court also diverged on how to imagine "parents." According to the majority, "The Board gave no consideration to the needs of children of same-sex parented families and instead based its decision on the views of a particular group who were opposed to any depiction of same-sex relationships in K–1 school materials": *Chamberlain v. Surrey School District No. 36*, para. 60. By contrast, treating gays and parents as two separate, nonoverlapping groups, Justice Gonthier declared, in his dissent, that there was "a need to respect both the right of homosexual persons to be free from discrimination and parental rights to make the decisions they deem necessary to ensure the well-being and moral education of their children": *Chamberlain v. Surrey School District No. 36*, para. 79.

46. See also Christian Lund (2006), who discusses the range of institutions and organizations attempting to exercise public authority in Africa and the challenges this poses for conceptualizing the state.

47. For development of a related argument in the Angolan and Congo context, see Sidaway 2003. For an account of "multiple and overlapping sovereignties" at the Myanmar-Thailand border, see Grundy-Warr and Yin 2002: 98–99.

48. See, e.g., the Aboriginal Provisional Government's website at http://www.apg.org.au. For further discussion, see Day 2001.

49. Trinity Western University v. Law Society of Upper Canada, 2015 ONSC 4250.

50. For a useful discussion of the differences between a liberal pluralist approach and one that seeks to universalize liberal values in the context of the TWU litigation, see Bateman 2015.

51. See *Trinity Western University v. Law Society of Upper Canada*, 2018, para. 19; also *Law Society of British Columbia v. Trinity Western University*, paras. 96, 98.

52. For religious responses to the decision to make TWU's Community Covenant nonobligatory for students following defeat in the Supreme Court, see also Deborah Gyapong, "TWU's Dropping of Community Covenant Raises Concerns," *The B.C. Catholic* 22 August 2018, accessed 15 November 2018, https://bccatholic.ca/content/twu-s-dropping-of-community-covenant-raises-concerns.

53. For a close parsing of the distinction between nation-state law and other legal and normative orders, see Tamanaha 1993. For a different and more conciliatory approach, see Tamanaha 2000.

54. For further discussion on statehood as a "relative concept," see Clapham 1998.

55. On the Tibetan government in exile, which claimed many state-like functions even as it lacked control over territory, see McConnell 2016.

56. In *Smith and Chymyshyn*, para. 9, the description of the Knights of Columbus does not use the language of nation or statehood; however, it describes an international society with more than 1.6 million adult male members, a constitution, rules and laws, a Supreme Council, and nearly twelve thousand subordinate councils—in other words, what is described is legally recognizable, at least in some respects, as a government-like structure.

57. For further discussion in relation to legal pluralism, see Melissaris 2004; Tamanaha 2000.

58. Nation-states are also the normative subjects of international law. For an interesting discussion of "incomplete and deficient" subjects (non-state subjects in international law) in the early twentieth century, see Wheatley 2017: 758.

59. I explore left-wing urban authorities further in Cooper 2017. For interesting attempts to rethink the place of "regressive" state features, such as coercion and borders, in reimagining the state for progressive politics, see Clarke 2019; Gill 2019.

60. For instance, Skinner (1989: 91–92, 99, 110) describes how earlier discourse on the state used the term to refer to the "state or standing of rulers," the "condition of a realm or commonwealth," "prevailing regimes," and the "condition of a city."

61. Adopting a dual conception of statehood opens up other ways of reading claims of statelessness, where forms of public governance (i.e., governance that affects relations among publics and that should generate forms of public accountability) take place, so that states in a broader sense exist, even though a stable official political structure, recognized by other states, may not be present. See, e.g., the discussion of governance in southern Somalia in Bakonyi 2013.

62. For a useful review of different approaches, see Blatter 2001: 183–86.

63. For interesting parallel discussion on multiple visions of "sovereigntyscapes," see Nairn (1998) quoted by Sidaway 2003. For discussion of *Martinez* in the U.S. context, see Massaro 2010.

64. See Trinity Western University v. Nova Scotia Barristers' Society, 2015 NSSC 25, para. 32.

65. See *Christian Legal Society Chapter v. Martinez*. For further discussion on the diverse ways of framing the relationship of law school and student society, see Massaro 2010. See also McClain 2011.

66. *Christian Legal Society Chapter v. Martinez*.

67. *Christian Legal Society Chapter v. Martinez*. See also Christian Legal Society v. Walker, 453 F.3d 853, para. 14, describing the CLS chapter as a "private speaker" and not a "mouthpiece . . . for the university."

68. *Catholic Care (Diocese of Leeds) v. Charity Commission for England and Wales*, para. 26.

69. *Catholic Care (Diocese of Leeds) v. Charity Commission for England and Wales*, paras. 60, 66. See also the discussion on multiple "state bordering practices" in Parker and Adler-Nissen 2012.

70. For further discussion on the relationship between legal imaginaries of social bodies, such as parades, and whether lesbian and gay exclusion is legally justified, see Stychin 1998b. For a useful discussion on "enacting the social" albeit focused on the performativity of social science scholarship, see Law and Urry 2004.

71. See, e.g., *Christian Legal Society v. Walker*. But see also the dissenting judgment on the problem of the CLS forcing an "affiliation" between itself and the university as "a state institution": *Christian Legal Society v. Walker*, para. 76.

72. *Smith and Chymyshyn*, para. 78.

73. Boy Scouts of America v. Dale, 530 U.S. 640 (2000).

74. See, e.g., the respondent's brief in *Bernstein et al. v. Ocean Grove Camp Meeting Association* (no. CRT6145-09), which emphasized the integral religious character of the land and pavilion owned by the association, as well as its noncommercial approach to charges for hosting a wedding, in order to emphasize that the pavilion, and weddings held in it, were part of its ministry. This narrative was legally rejected.

75. On the ongoing processes by which state institutions are re-formed in conditions of growing (or contracting) stateness, see Lund 2006.

76. Ryan Felton, "Deputies of Kentucky Clerk Jailed over Gay Marriage Stance Will Issue Licenses," *The Guardian*, 4 September 2015, accessed 12 July 2018, https://www.theguardian.com/us-news/2015/sep/03/kentucky-clerk-contempt-of-court-marriage-licenses.

77. See Hall and Another v. Bull and Another [2011] EW Misc 2 (CC), para. 13. We might also read antidiscrimination litigants in this legal drama as "police" officers (in Rancière's use of the term [see chapter 2]), given the legal scrutiny of conservative Christian actions to ensure compliance with antidiscrimination and human rights law.

78. Seeing the state can also be politically guided by the ceremonial and emblematic ways that states present themselves to be seen (see Roy 2006). For an interesting discussion of visual representation in social theory, see Toscano 2012.

79. Allen Feldman (2006) also explores this governmental register of vision in relation to political violence, including by the British state in Northern Ireland.

80. Nicholas Simcik-Arese (2018) develops some of these ideas in relation to residential governance in Egypt to explore "seeing like a city-state."

81. Not explicitly explored in this book, although forming a striking parallel, is the place of smell (as a sensory idiom) in knowing the state. The notion that states or certain forms of state action have a "bad" smell is a common figure of speech. See, e.g., the reference to the "smell of cronyism" in Cradle of Liberty Council v. City of Philadelphia, 851 F. Supp. 2d 936 (2012), 954 (discussed in chapter 4). For a critical feminist account of sight for privileging boundaries, separation, and autonomous subjects in contrast to touch, "a sensation that both frustrates detachment and compromises objectivity by reason of its reversible nature," see Shildrick 2001: 393.

82. For a sociolegal account of nuisance law, see also Cooper 2002.

83. For a striking account of the relationship between sense and sensation in political life, see Panagia 2009.

84. See also Sara Ahmed (2006), who evocatively discusses the place and experience of tables in relation to queer and other phenomenologies.

85. For a powerful discussion of the coercive sexual character of the Turkish state, discussed in more detail in chapter 5, see Zengin 2016.

86. See also the guesthouse case Bull and Bull v. Hall and Preddy, 2013 UKSC 73, paras. 9–10, in which the online booking form noted that "a deep regard for marriage" meant the guesthouse gave double beds only to heterosexual married couples. However, because the booking was made by phone, the customer, Mr. Preddy, "did not see this clause."

87. *Smith and Chymyshyn*, para. 83

88. *Smith and Chymyshyn*, para. 83.

89. See also the findings, determination, and order in Bernstein et al. v. Ocean Grove Camp Meeting Association (no. CRT6145-09), 7, on the lack of any indication that the pavilion was part of a Christian "wedding ministry" in the association's website publicity.

90. For other contexts of tactile knowing, see Lammer 2007; Pink et al. 2014. Here, therapeutic work also involves feeling the resistance and reactions that touch generates.

91. This does not assume that critique and change are opposing polarities, since each enfolds the other. However, to the extent that thinking toward critique and toward change are oriented to different immediate tasks and concerns, they may depend on, and generate, different conceptual lines when it comes to the state. I explore this further in Cooper 2014, 2015.

92. But see David Nugent (2010) on how the Peruvian dictatorship's criminalization of the Popular American Revolutionary Alliance forced it underground so that it was no longer "visible." Yet as a consequence of the alliance's invisibility, Nugent suggests, government fantasies constituted it as more state-like than the state.

93. In imagining other entities as states (or state-like), my focus is the (neo)liberal, common law jurisdictions of this book. In other contexts and places, adopting an expansive approach to what counts as a state may prove counterproductive (see, e.g., Meagher 2012; cf. Sidaway 2003).

FOUR. **State Play and Possessive Beliefs**

1. One exception is Nicole Renee Baptiste (2009), who explores the relationship between work-place fun and well-being in relation to local authority senior managers.

2. For exceptions, see David Runciman (1997), who also discusses Ernest Barker's early twentieth-century writing on the state as a dramatic stage. More recent work in this area includes Shirin Rai's (2015) discussion of the performance and "staging" of politics in Parliament.

3. See, e.g., Hoehne (2009) on the geopolitical mimesis of statehood in Northern Somalia.

4. For a more sympathetic approach to the relationship between the arts/play and state making, see Cesari 2012. She explores how arts institutions and museums were enrolled in an attempt to prefigure (and bring about) the Palestinian nation-state through its "anticipatory representation," discussed further in chapter 6.

5. In other words, the courts expressed a particular paradigm of beliefs as interior and separate from practical action, although, importantly, beliefs were interpreted as informing and guiding action. For further discussion, see Cooper and Herman 2013. The interrelationship and impossibility of severing beliefs from action is something conservative Christian litigants also emphasized, paralleling similar claims by lesbian and gay equality litigants and advocates, who argued that discrimination against same-sex practices also constituted a discrimination against who they were (see chapter 1).

6. For evangelical Christians, this includes beliefs as "lived commitment" (see, e.g., Bielo 2012; Street 2010). For critical discussion of the tendency to universalize an emphasis on propositional beliefs associated with Protestant Christianity, see, e.g., Asad 1983; Montemaggi 2017; Ruel 1982.

7. See, e.g., Page v. NHS Trust Development Authority, ET case no: 2302433/2016, para. 11.1.

8. Masterpiece Cakeshop Ltd. v. Colorado Civil Rights Commission, 584 U.S. (2018).

9. According to Margaret Davies (1999: 329), "Forms of oppression which accumulate around the myth of property do not rest merely in formal legal relationships, but also in the way that property rhetoric is extended and used to structure the realm of the social." As a form of social discourse and thinking, property was idiomatically deployed in this litigation with a range of legal, social, and political consequences.

10. At the same time, litigants and legal judgments also sometimes referred to social actors as "belonging" to their beliefs and statuses. Thus, the Human Rights Commission in *Hands on Originals* somewhat awkwardly described Gay Pride as a process in which gay people expressed pride in "self-identification of being within that classification of person": Lexington-Fayette Urban County Human Rights Commission et al. v. Hands On Originals No. 2015-CA-000745-MR, 7.

For one account of the psychological character of ownership and attachment when it comes to beliefs, see De Dreu and van Knippenberg 2005.

11. For an interesting critique of possessive individualism in relation to the western Pacific, see Sykes 2007. On how the self can get experienced as *public* property in

certain circumstances, see also Shoshana 2012. For a challenging account of how the relationship between property and personhood may be moving away from the possessive self in certain economies, see Lisa Adkins 2005. Her account also addresses the relationship between gender and property in the self. For other explorations of this relationship, see, e.g., Cooper and Renz 2016; Davies 1999; Naffine 1998.

12. Macpherson's work has also been critiqued for its reading of core liberal texts (see, e.g., Breakey 2014).

13. See, e.g., the discussion of the early eighteenth-century feminist commentator Mary Astell in Perry 1990. For a discussion of the racialized relationship between property and people in the context of the "slave's two bodies"—"natural" and "legal"—see Ghachem 2003.

14. Petchesky (1995) argues that a more collectivist, noncommodified, pre-Lockean understanding of self-ownership became lost in this narrative.

15. From an investment perspective, conservative Christians sought not simply to protect property in their beliefs but also to engage in riskier investment practices, deploying their property to acquire further value (in terms of extending the reach, prominence, and authority of their religious estate). In Britain, this social practice was not one the courts in antidiscrimination cases largely supported, despite recognizing, and occasionally protecting, religious beliefs about gay sexuality as being the legitimate property of conservative Christians.

16. The inequality of capital that different identity beliefs historically have possessed is part of a wider capitalization of social identity or status. Cheryl Harris (1993) and others have explored how "whiteness" functions as property, underscoring the very unevenly acquired and distributed social and economic value that recognition as white affords certain subjects (see also Grabham 2009; Keenan 2010).

17. This is noteworthy, given the legally established church in Britain and thus the existence of legal provisions (albeit limited) that continue to treat Christianity (and particularly the Church of England) as special or distinct.

18. See Equality Act 2010, s. 12; this identifies the "protected characteristic" of "sexual orientation," which means, in ways that presume an increasingly anachronistic binary, being sexually oriented to "persons" of the "same," "opposite," or "either" sex.

19. It may seem far from coincidental that, at a time when conventional property forms appear to be growing increasingly unequal in their distribution, neo(liberal) states have turned their attention to more equally distributing identity property—a process that can be read as converting radical liberation projects into propertied entitlements, as I discuss.

20. See Lord Neuberger's rejection of the notion that the registrar's views on marriage constituted a "core" aspect of Christianity, Ladele v. London Borough of Islington [2009] EWCA 1357, para. 52.

21. Lucy Vickers (2010: 295) argues that courts should not determine whether particular beliefs are "core or peripheral" to a religion.

22. See, e.g., the British cases of Smith v. Trafford Housing Trust [2012] EWHC 3221; Haye v. London Borough of Lewisham, 2010 ET 2301852/2009; Mbuyi v. Newpark Childcare Ltd., 2015 ET 3300656/2014.

23. For instance, does property in religious beliefs provide a right to "comment on an American news website about Kim Davis," the U.S. county clerk who was imprisoned for refusing to process licenses for same-sex marriages? See R (Ngole) v. University of Sheffield [2017] EWHC 2669, para. 63.

24. This discussion takes up Judith Butler and Athena Athanasiou's (2013) suggestion that dispossession might involve unsettling the assumption that we are atomistic, self-sufficient individuals while recognizing, as they do, the relationship between dispossession and the loss of shelter, food, legal protection, and livelihood. On destructive forms of dispossession, see also Bhandar and Bhandar 2016.

25. From this perspective, beliefs are protected *because* they contribute to subjects' makeup, and it is the well-being and freedom of subjects that are key. Beliefs' substance and content are secondary (or irrelevant). See, e.g., Trinity Western University v. Nova Scotia Barristers' Society, 2015 NSSC 25, para. 24.

26. In *The Erotics of Sovereignty*, Mark Rifkin (2012: 50) makes similar claims, critiquing possessive individualism's application to Native identity. He argues that treating "Indianness as an internal property of discrete bodies . . . from which they cannot be alienated . . . [provides a way of reacting] to the 'sovereign violence' of U.S. projects of detribalization while unwittingly constituting Native sovereignty through their terms."

27. Moral, political, and religious beliefs are also mechanisms of contact (albeit an often fraught contact) rather than the separate siloes that a propertied conception suggests. Yet property law itself is also about contact and encounters, even as it provides a discourse of separation and detachment. For further discussion of the relationship between boundaries and contact, see chapter 5.

28. For further discussion in the context of Native American claims, see Coombe 1998; Keeshig-Tobias 1997; Young and Brunk 2012.

29. This does not mean that all those participating engage voluntarily. To the extent that they become objects of play, their active consent or intentional participation may be doubted. Recognition is also important to remaining a play subject. Huizinga ([1949] 1970) ties this to winning—where what is won is excelling before others and being honored for it. However, recognition can also simply be that one is an agentic subject capable of playing.

30. In this way creativity is tied to play's unscripted—or, at least, not fully scripted—character as play subjects interact and improvise, drawing on what is available and near to hand (see chapter 6). Play's capacity to create new ideas, designs, or practices is one reason it has been calculatedly and instrumentally deployed by companies, as I discuss later. But it also speaks to play's wider social and cultural value. Play may be seen as autotelic (at least to some degree), but anthropologists, sociologists, and philosophers treat play as highly functional—in building and consolidating social relationships; developing capacities for cognitive, creative, and ethical thinking and action; helping people to live ecologically well; and giving voice to those feelings and thoughts that a society (or subject) submerges. For an interesting, related account of the way "public [play] things," including television characters such as *Sesame Street*'s Big Bird, hold and mobilize political attachments and desires, see Honig 2017.

31. This is explored further in Nachmanovitch 2009: 1.

32. One political issue this raises concerns the contexts and conditions in which play does or does not occur, as well as the contexts and conditions that asymmetrically structure who different state officials "play with," and how.

33. This concern is evident in Cynthia Weber's (2010) critique of the notion of gamification techniques being applied to citizenship in the U.K. Her discussion draws on the Design Council's "Touching the State" Project, in which "the more you do for the State, the more loyalty points you accrue. Points could be awarded for voting, providing a community service or even holidaying in the UK. They could then be used in a variety of ways including going towards lowering your Council Tax or your National Insurance contributions. And with only a few thousand points you could even claim a Knighthood" (Design Council 2004: 66, quoted in Weber 2010: 2).

34. Benjamin Shepard (2012: 270) makes a similar point in relation to grassroots activist play when he states, "Ludic play is not as well tailored for many heavy issues such as police brutality."

35. This suggests that participation *as a player* cannot be driven by necessity (see Edwards 2013; also Huizinga [1949] 1970). Where people are state clients, the asymmetry of the relation and the need—often urgent and desperate—for state resources puts the capacity of state officials and applicants to play together, in any way, as horizontal subjects firmly in doubt, even as playing with state bodies strategically or transgressively, in such conditions, may prove politically valuable.

36. See Ronnie Polaneczky, "Store Dresses Down Bride for Being a Lesbian," *The Inquirer* (Philadelphia), 18 August 2011, accessed 15 July 2018, http://www.philly .com/philly/hp/news_update/20110818_Ronnie_Polaneczky__Store_dresses_down _bride_for_being_a_lesbian.html. Conservative Christian play has also been a way to express and strengthen religious values, see, e.g., Boy Scouts of America v. Dale, 530 U.S. 640 (2000). In this case, collective play was recognized as an important norm-generating activity that organizations should be able to protect and control, including by excluding players who they identified as expressing a "message" antithetical to their own.

37. See Brush and Nib Studio v. City of Phoenix, CV 2016-052251 (Arizona Superior Ct. 2016), complaint, para. 15: "The artist's internal space . . . is too valuable, too sacrosanct to open to government reprogramming and compulsion." This complaint associates the right to creative expression with obedience to God; both are represented as driving artists' commercial undertakings. However, while creative expression and religious obedience are linked to an inner self and oriented to the same outcome—namely, refusing gay people a particular service or product—in other respects the two are quite different. Arguing for the right to create, if understood as a right to play, suggests that outcomes are not determined in advance. It suggests that creative expression is dynamic and emergent; and that to flourish, action must not be coerced or speech compelled. However, the right to comply with religious law suggests something different, grounded in the stability and knowability of the stance taken. It is not that the florist needs the freedom to follow her artistic orientation wherever it will lead her. Rather, she must not be compelled by equality law to leave God's clear path.

38. See Lee v. McArthur and Others, 2016 NICA 39.

39. This is the wording quoted in media news stories. The bakery refused to ice the message, claiming they were too busy and lacked expertise given the complexity of the icing (including its use of color, capital letters, and number of words); the complaint against the baker was dismissed: Gordon Deegan, "Dublin Bakery's Refusal of Anti-Gay Marriage Cake 'Not Discrimination,'" *Irish Times*, 24 July 2017, accessed 15 July 2018, https://www.irishtimes.com/news/ireland/irish-news/dublin-bakery-s-refusal-of-anti -gay-marriage-cake-not-discrimination-1.3165211.

40. "The man said he placed the order both to test and 'balance out' the Ashers case. 'Why should the law favour people of a gay orientation and not deal with me the same way?' he asked the hearing, adding: 'What's good for the goose is good for the gander.'" Deegan, "Dublin Bakery's Refusal of Anti-Gay Marriage Cake 'Not Discrimination.'"

41. Here, actors are also made into objects as they get "toyed with," subjected to a "play" strategically arrived at in advance (see Kane 2005: 54).

42. Patrick Strudwick, "Conversion Therapy: She Tried to Make Me 'Pray Away the Gay," *The Guardian*, 27 May 2011, accessed 15 July 2018, http://www.theguardian.com /world/2011/may/27/gay-conversion-therapy-patrick-strudwick.

43. Mullins v. Masterpiece Cakeshop, Inc., 2015 COA 115. This judgment was over-turned by the Supreme Court. Paralleling this case were three complaints made by William Jack, also in Colorado, whose request for two Bible-shaped cakes with figures and biblical messages opposing homosexuality was rejected by three bakeries. His complaints were dismissed by the Colorado Civil Rights Division: see Jack v. Gateaux, Ltd., charge no. P20140071X; Jack v. Le Bakery Sensual, Inc., charge no. P20140070X; Jack v. Azucar Bakery, charge no. P20140069X.

44. See Affidavit of Stephanie Schmalz, para. 12, 3 January 2013, accessed 18 November 2018, http://static.aclu-co.org/wp-content/uploads/files/Affidavit%20of%20Stepha-nie%20Schmalz.pdf. For a similar episode in which reporters approached two cake makers who had turned away lesbian couples and requested cakes for other occasions, frowned on by Christians, in order to see what they would do, see Martin Cizmar, "The Cake Wars: Who among Us Is Righteous Enough to Eat of the Sacred Buttercream Bible-Beating Oregon Bakers Have Denied Gays?" *Willamette Week*, 28 May 2013, ac-cessed 15 July 2018, http://www.wweek.com/uncategorized/2013/05/29/the-cake-wars.

45. Whether contact can overcome conservative religious believers' negative at-titudes toward gay people is unclear. Some research suggests that heterosexuals can participate in and experience positive (or at least benign) encounters with gay people while sustaining negative religious beliefs on gay sexualities; positive encounters do not necessarily negate negative beliefs as may be hoped (see Andersson et al. 2011; Valentine 2008; Valentine and Waite 2012).

46. For further discussion, see Gordon et al. 2017; Lerner 2014; Mahnič 2014; and Salen and Zimmerman 2004.

47. Innes and Booher (1999) also discuss play's contribution to managing tension and uncomfortable inequalities of power between participants, through drama, emo-tion, storytelling, and humor. For an interesting discussion on the place and uses of humor in organizational life, see Barsoux 1996.

48. Katarzyna Balug and Maria Vidart-Delgado (2015: 1037) suggest that collaborative play, as a way to engage with urban development, offers a structure for "shedding old perceptions and embracing different possibilities of being."

49. While Augusto Boal's ([1974] 2000) influential "forum theater" focused on understanding and contesting relations of oppression and inequalities of power (see also Boal 2005), organizations and companies have drawn on related drama techniques to explore and preempt conflict and other managerial challenges (see, e.g., Clark and Mangham 2004; Meisiek 2002).

50. For a management perspective, including on the use of role playing to help employees understand minority sexualities, see Dickens et al. (2009: 39).

51. Iris Marion Young (1997: 353, emphasis added) remarked, "The purpose of theorizing moral respect as involving people putting themselves in one another's places is to give an account of how we can understand one another, so that we can take one another's perspective into account when making moral judgments. But *I have argued that we cannot put ourselves in one another's places.*"

52. See Keeton v. Anderson-Wiley, 664 F.3d 865 (11th Cir. 2011). See also Nick Duffy, "Christian Employee Who Refused to Watch LGBT Training Video Will Sue for 'Discrimination,'" *Pink News*, 9 September 2016, accessed 15 July 2018, https://www.pinknews.co.uk/2016/09/09/christian-employee-who-refused-to-watch-lgbt-training-video-will-sue-for-discrimination.

53. For an empirical account of student learning through role playing, see Druckman and Ebner 2008, which suggests that students learn more from participating in the *design* of simulations/role playing than from participating in their enactment, especially when it comes to understanding the relationship between concepts.

54. There are exceptions in some of the jurisdictions of this book, particularly (at time of writing) in the United States. At both the federal and state level, some statutes, legal judgments, and other state texts stress the importance of religious faith and religious freedom, and have sought to institutionalize greater legal protection for people, companies, and organizations that refuse to provide gay people with goods on religious grounds. While the formal affirmation of religion in the United States is not new, legal protection seems to come in waves. The recent wave has been given confidence and support by the public actions of the Trump administration: see, e.g., Office of the Attorney General, "Federal Law Protections for Religious Liberty," memorandum, 6 October 2017; see also chapter 1.

55. See, e.g., Catholic Care (Diocese of Leeds) v. Charity Commission for England and Wales [2012] UKUT 395, para. 47, emphasis added, in which the court declared, "The interest of promoting the traditional family on which the Charity relies has not been endorsed by the national authorities. . . . *I think that the view of the Charity that the traditional family should be promoted is not entitled to be given the same degree of weight as if it had been adopted by the national authorities.*"

56. For judicial concern about state officials showing hostility toward religion or suggesting that governments can assess offensiveness when it comes to distinguishing between wedding cakes for gay marriages and those iced with messages opposing gay marriage, see the Supreme Court decision in *Masterpiece Cakeshop Ltd. v. Colorado Civil Rights Commission.*

57. For instance, in the British employment decision in *Page v. NHS Trust Development Authority*, para. 48, the tribunal suggested that in relation to the belief that "'homosexual activity' is wrong[,] . . . the tribunal may well have concluded that this was not a belief that was worthy of respect in a democratic society." However, they distinguished this from the "belief relied on by the claimant" that "it is in the best interests of a child to have a mother and a father. That, the tribunal has concluded, is a belief that falls within the definition of philosophical belief for the purposes of EqA s10 [the Equality Act 2010]."

58. For further discussion, see Malabou and Butler 2011.

59. I explore this further in Cooper 2013.

60. This includes those occasions in which activists become state workers (see Newman 2012a; Richardson and Monro 2012). At the same time, activists can also incline toward the separate and distinct character of gathered states when they emphasize the importance of institutions, bureaucracies, and state law, rather than just civil society, taking up gay equality.

61. Taking up these simplified frames to ease the process of state translation contrasts with the processes discussed by James Scott (2009), who describes how highland peoples in Asia deliberately made themselves unattractive and difficult for states to govern and incorporate.

62. For an interesting discussion of this mode of governing in the Israel/Palestine context, see Joronen 2017: 1003, which describes how imposed delay and technical justification, "recognizing and performing rights without implementing them," became a means of denying, without overtly refusing, Palestinian rights.

63. McClintock v. Department of Constitutional Affairs, 2008 IRLR 29, para. 24.

64. *McClintock v. Department of Constitutional Affairs*, para. 20.

65. For further discussion of workplace play, see Fleming and Sturdy 2009; Sørensen and Spoelstra 2012; Spraggon and Bodolica 2014. Research also explores how companies use play to motivate, enroll, and control workers, particularly in highly routinized sectors (see, e.g., Costea et al. 2007).

66. Elizabeth Pears, "Tottenham Teacher Suspended after Gay Rights Row," *Tottenham and Wood Green Independent*, 29 April 2009, accessed 15 July 2018, http://www.thetottenhamindependent.co.uk/news/4329788.display. See also "Christian Teacher Suspended for Complaining over Gay Rights Presentation," *Pink News*, 27 April 2009, accessed 15 July 2018, https://www.pinknews.co.uk/2009/04/27/christian-teacher-suspended-for-complaining-over-gay-rights-presentation.

67. "Christian Teacher Suspended for Complaining over Gay Rights Presentation."

68. "Christian Teacher Suspended for Complaining over Gay Rights Presentation."

69. In one case in which the New Brunswick Human Rights Commission ordered a mayor to make a proclamation, he "did so at a city council meeting . . . but only after turning off his microphone": see "Fredericton Mayor Infuriates City Gays," *CBC News*, 10 February 1999, accessed 15 July 2018, https://www.cbc.ca/news/canada/fredericton-mayor-infuriates-city-gays-1.166914.

70. See, e.g, Okanagan Rainbow Coalition v. City of Kelowna, 2000 BCHRT 21.

71. Writers depict free-running and parkour as closely related but different practices, with free-running often described as more commercial and sports-oriented compared

to the more philosophically/ethically oriented parkour. Although my interpretation of gay activism is closer to parkour, for ease I use the term "state free-running."

72. On how spaces can become playgrounds, including through digital/web-based games which involve searching for things in particular places, see Klausen 2014. Most explicitly in parkour, participants try to "seize local city spaces from private, commercial interests," refusing to accept (even as they experience) the city as "artificial, cold, fragmented and impersonal" (Atkinson 2009: 180); see also O'Grady 2012.

73. Hudler v. City of London (1997) 31 CHHR D/500 (Ont. Bd. of Inquiry).

74. *Hudler v. City of London*, para. 21.

75. *Hudler v. City of London*, para. 23.

76. *Hudler v. City of London*, paras. 24–25.

77. While, in free-running, infrastructural bodies are often stationary and free-runners are in movement, the sport can also involve mobile parts of urban spaces. This same range exists in free-running states, as the movement of activists meets the relatively stationary and mobile parts of state bodies, with their procedures, policies, responsibilities, powers, and staff.

78. Oli Mould (2009: 743), for instance, suggests that the aim of parkour (or free-running) is to "use the . . . space in new and alternative ways, but never to disrupt, change, or damage."

79. Thus, we might compare institutionalized gay rights' commitments with other contemporary sexual projects or philias. In the case of pedophilia, scatophilia, and zoophilia, for example, enacted desires might generate contact with state bodies but, in a context in which desires are not recognized as acceptable, this may prove a repressive and punitive contact rather than an enabling one. Other philias, the erotic desire to touch velvet garments, for instance, might fail to support state contact altogether.

80. On free-running as a form of place making "that revers[es] the qualities of the setting," see also Daskalaki et al. (2008: 60).

81. Cradle of Liberty Council v. City of Philadelphia, 851 F. Supp. 2d 936 (2012).

82. *Cradle of Liberty Council*, 950.

83. *Cradle of Liberty Council*, 951, emphasis added.

84. *Cradle of Liberty Council*, 951.

85. See "Author Archives: Michiel de Lange," Hackable City, accessed 15 July 2018, http://thehackablecity.nl/author/michiel-de-lange.

FIVE. **The Erotic Life of States**

Epigraphs: Grosz 1995: 294; Secor 2007: 48.

1. In some cases, other bodies "stand in for" the state, including soldiers and those "missing in action" who are also depicted as dying for it (see, e.g., Hawley 2005).

2. Useful works for thinking about the application of these ideas to the state include Gray 2000; Haraway 1991; Hayles 1999. Just as the language of personhood is applied to states, so certain terms drawn from discussion of states or political communities,

such as "autonomy" and "invasion," are also applied to people. On this point, see the discussion in Ruskola (2010: 1531), which draws on Tuck (1999: 226).

3. There is, however, some interesting discussion of "queer states" (see, e.g., Otto 2007) in relation to entities such as the Vatican and a growing field of queer International Relations (see Weber 2016; Wilcox 2014).

4. For work on state emotions and emotional governance, see Hunter 2015; Jupp et al. 2017; Lea 2012; Stoler 2004.

5. Mbembe's (1992) account focuses on Togo and Cameroon. For further discussion, see Anderson 2010.

6. For instance, the anticommunist Orange Alternative in Poland, in the late 1980s, undertook a number of satirical political actions (see, e.g., Misztal 1992; Szymanski-Düll 2015).

7. For an interesting and different account, that focuses on the significance for political rule of same-sex trials, where "same-sex desire [was] perceived as affecting the good exercise of public powers," see Zanghellini 2015: 2.

8. A significant contemporary literature also exists on the deployment of sexual violence by soldiers and peacekeepers. On soldiers' racialized deployment of scopic and restraint-based techniques of humiliation at the Iraqi Abu Ghraib prison, see Puar 2004; Richter-Montpetit 2007; Weiss 2009.

9. For further discussion of the use of "savior" discourses in relation to lesbian and gay asylum claims and liberal states, see Keenan 2015.

10. Yet the notion that (neo)liberal states otherwise treat gay and straight sexualities equally is doubtful. While it varies between jurisdictions, a raft of state policies and practices continue to reproduce heteronormative social relations and cultures, ordering and assigning licit and illicit forms of sexual expression in ways that marginalize some while normalizing others. Liberal states may step back from regulating sex through the direct regulation of gay sexualized subjects, but other modes of sexual regulation and ordering endure (e.g., see Clucas 2012).

11. I explore the conceptual methods and challenges of doing so further in Cooper 2019.

12. On the performative enactment of multivalent gendered and sexualized coding in relation to states, see Weber 1998.

13. Reaney v. Hereford Diocesan Board of Finance, ET 1602844/2006.

14. I discuss municipal state ambivalence about sexuality further in Cooper 2006.

15. One instance of this arose in a series of cases in which conservative Christians' refusal was legally framed as a refusal to engage in speech that conflicted with their "religious and moral convictions." This required them to foreground their religious expressive identity through, and in relation to, the expressive commissions they refused to undertake: see, e.g., Respondent Hands on Originals' Verified Statement of Position, in Baker v. Hands On Originals, HRC 03-12-3135, 4.

16. The council initially offered her a temporary option of undertaking only those registrations that involved a signing process rather than an actual ceremony, but Ladele rejected the offer: Ladele v. London Borough of Islington [2008] UKEAT 0453_08_1912, paras. 7–9.

17. *Ladele v. London Borough of Islington*, para. 10.

18. *Ladele v. London Borough of Islington*; Ladele v. London Borough of Islington [2009] EWCA Civ 1357; Eweida and Ors v. United Kingdom [2013] ECHR 37.

19. See Trinity Western University v. Nova Scotia Barristers' Society 2015 NSSC 25; Trinity Western University v. Law Society of British Columbia, 2015 BCSC 2326; Trinity Western University v. Law Society of British Columbia, 2016 BCCA 423; Trinity Western University v. Law Society of Upper Canada, 2015 ONSC 4250; Trinity Western University v. Law Society of Upper Canada, 2016 ONCA 518.

20. Law Society of British Columbia v. Trinity Western University, 2018 SCC 32; Trinity Western University v. Law Society of Upper Canada, 2018 SCC 33.

21. Core Issues Trust v. Transport for London and Another [2013] EWHC 651 (Admin); R on the Application of Core Issues Trust v. Transport for London and Another [2014] EWCA Civ 34; R on the Application of Core Issues Trust v. Transport for London and Another [2014] EWHC 2628 (Admin).

22. See *R on the Application of Core Issues Trust v. Transport for London and Another* (2014, Admin), para. 4.

23. This phrase is from Wooley v. Maynard, 430 U.S. 705 (1977), 715. While its sentiment was expressed by the British courts, the phrase itself was not used there. On the additional problems caused by "advertisements [that] do not remain in one place," see *Core Issues Trust v. Transport for London*, para. 129

24. See *Core Issues Trust v. Transport for London*, paras. 53–58, subsequently readdressed as new emails came to light, in *R on the Application of Core Issues Trust v. Transport for London and Another* (2014), paras. 37–38, and *R on the Application of Core Issues Trust v. Transport for London and Another* (2014, Admin), para. 8. See also Fulton et al. v. City of Philadelphia et al., 2:18-cv-02075, 35; in which the court had to consider a similar claim—namely, that a Catholic foster care agency, which discriminated on grounds of sexual orientation, had experienced "impermissible hostility at the hands of the mayor" when new foster care referrals were withheld.

25. I discuss state activism further in Cooper 1994, 2017, Cooper and Herman 2019.

26. *Trinity Western University v. Law Society of British Columbia* (2016), para. 150. On the Law Society exceeding its powers by acting like a court rather than the tribunal it was characterized as being, see *Trinity Western University v. Law Society of British Columbia* (2016), para. 90.

27. *Trinity Western University v. Nova Scotia Barristers' Society*, para. 13, emphasis added.

28. See *Trinity Western University v. Nova Scotia Barristers' Society*, paras. 12–13, 235, emphasis added.

29. *Core Issues Trust v. Transport for London*, para. 35; see also *R on the Application of Core Issues Trust v. Transport for London and Another* (2014); *R on the Application of Core Issues Trust v. Transport for London and Another* (2014, Admin).

30. In the case, the court scrutinized in detail whether the convergence between the mayor and Transport for London over the decision to withdraw was the result of shared opinions or the effects of mayoral "instruction," *R on the Application of Core Issues Trust v. Transport for London and Another* (2014, Admin).

31. Judicial accounts of events here offered precise, minutely specific times for emails, some phone calls, and press statements to trace the exact order of events, along with their "breakneck" speed.

32. On the mayor's instruction to "pull" the ex-gay advertisements from London buses, see *R on the Application of Core Issues Trust v. Transport for London and Another* (2014, Admin), para. 62.

33. Perceptions of waste also arise in relation to activist state caretaking, which, in seeking to build capacity among disadvantaged constituencies through the creative use of governmental powers, is sometimes denounced by conservative opponents for engaging in the "overproduction" of government. At the same time, discrimination can be described as generating feelings of waste—for example, the rejected Church of England youth worker who described how "the bishop had made him feel a waste of space": see *Reaney v. Hereford Diocesan Board of Finance*, para. 42.

34. For further discussion on the cultural politics of sticking, see Ahmed 2004.

35. Writing on libidinal economies, Bennett (2010: 100) explores the associations between contamination, decay, and desire: "Fear that the ruling classes would be contaminated—in their morals, their health, and their racial stock—by contact with the 'prostitute class' extended to a fear of contamination by easy money."

36. *Ladele v. London Borough of Islington* (2008), para. 10.

37. *Ladele v. London Borough of Islington* (2008), para. 117.

38. *Ladele v. London Borough of Islington* (2008), para. 100. In the quite different context of regulating meat hygiene, Elizabeth Dunn (2007: 41) takes up the state's "ability to act as sewer" to explore state promises "to remove what was corrupt and contaminating." If readiness to eliminate damaging and contagious products is a significant legitimating rationale for state action, as Dunn suggests, public liberal bodies can be seen here as engaged in an analogous task of rechanneling and removing religious antigay waste.

39. This is the other side of the democratic principle, discussed in chapter 2, that what a state inheres in inheres in the state, a reciprocal relationship that can also sometimes be read through the bilateral language of touch.

40. In other cases, the courts rejected the depictions presented by the withdrawing party of what contact would produce. In *Christian Legal Society v. Walker* 453 F. 3d 853 (2006), para. 14, the court held that receiving public benefits did not make the student organization a mouthpiece of the university. Funding did not mean fusion or the spreading of "state-endorsed messages;" therefore the university could not claim it would be seen as endorsing what the club said.

41. *R on the Application of Core Issues Trust v. Transport for London and Another* (2014, Admin), para. 45.

42. *Core Issues Trust v. Transport for London*, para. 129.

43. This theme emerges even more prominently in Tim Dean's (2009) striking account of HIV's circulation during bare-backing, which he discusses as a form of kinship-making that joins together the bodies through which the "gift" of the virus passes.

44. When it comes to the state, a primary staged focus for this kind of desire is patriotic. Through the symbols, discourses, and requirements of patriotism, public and

individual bodies entwine, even as relations of patriotism conjure up a great deal of order and hierarchy. How might we, by contrast, then think about bodily attachments involving states that combine an erotic openness with horizontal, or more egalitarian and reciprocating, relations?

45. Courts also focused on questions of proper and improper adhesion in relation to fears that conservative Christians would fail to adhere to the law or would adhere to another authority instead. As Justice Elias remarked in *Ladele*, treating religious beliefs as a "solvent" would dissolve "all inconsistent legal obligations owed to the employer": *Ladele v. London Borough of Islington* (2008), para. 73; see also *Core Issues Trust v. Transport for London*, para. 36.

46. See the discussion in *Trinity Western University v. Nova Scotia Barristers' Society*, para. 212.

47. Those unwillingly touched were not, for the most part, state bodies but the human and organizational bearers of same-sex relations. In such cases, state bodies may function as the walled channels through which withdrawal must happen if conservative Christians are not to endorse gay adopters, families, or marrying couples. Liberal state bodies, on these occasions, have been depicted in terms resonant of *vagina dentata*, grasping and snaring conservative Christians as they try to pull out (see Braun and Wilkinson 2001; Creed 1993; Gear 2001; Raitt 1980; Ussher 2006).

48. The language of consent for some, and power for others, provides important frameworks for discussions of state entry, allowing writers to differentiate, in different ways, between incoming goods, capital, and people. For a critique of Jacques Derrida's work on hospitality for not distinguishing between welcoming people and welcoming inflows of foreign capital, see Cheah 2013.

49. There is, however, a growing body of work on the diplomatic and foreign policy agendas of local states, such as municipal government (see, e.g., Aldecoa and Keating 1999; Ewen and Hebbert 2007; Hobbs 1994; Hocking 1986; Jackson 2018).

50. Matt Stevens, "Kentucky Must Pay $224,000 after Dispute over Same-Sex Marriage Licenses," *New York Times*, 21 July 2017, accessed 16 July 2018, https://www .nytimes.com/2017/07/21/us/kentucky-taxpayers-gay-marriage.html.

51. Courts also engage in this type of reasoning: see, e.g., *Boy Scouts of America v. Till*, 136 F. Supp. 2d 1295 (S.D. Fla. 2001), 1309.

52. As the *Transport for London* case demonstrates, an erotic imaginary foregrounds and intensifies micro-sensation as minute changes of pressure and touch are disproportionately felt in conditions of highly sensitized attention. For further discussion on touch, see chapter 3.

53. In court, some forms of pleasure are cast as licit (or entitled) while others are not. For instance, wedding cake makers may be entitled to enjoy their craft but have no right to expect pleasure from the wedding they are supplying, a pleasure that belongs in rather exclusively propertied ways to the marrying couple and their guests. Although for a rather different approach, see the Supreme Court decision in Masterpiece Cakeshop v. Colorado Civil Rights Commission, 584 U.S. (2018).

54. Conservative Christians, perhaps, proved more willing to express micro-feelings of pleasure in guiding and governing the behavior of others. In *Reaney v. Hereford*

Diocesan Board of Finance, para. 31, for instance, the bishop claimed he would "rejoice" if the young man applying to be a youth worker had ended a same-sex romantic relationship *in order to* take up celibacy.

55. For other accounts of the "sexiness" of war and the desires associated with militarism, including soldiers' pleasure and loathing toward military and state hierarchy, approached as "analogous to a quasi-consensual 24/7 BDSM relationship with the state," see Crane-Seeber 2016: 43. For a critique of this account, see Catto 2017.

56. Critical scholars are also uncomfortable with the notion of pleasure being taken in being governed, whether because it reflects false consciousness, constitutes a mode of governmentality that bypasses rational decision making, or is too resonant of fascist state attachments (see, e.g., Neocleous 2005).

57. Litigation may function as a source of erotic pleasure for some, with its arousals, uncertain victories, and new alliances and opponents. Certainly, the pleasures from goods or membership that withdrawal denies or suspends may be rerouted into the excitement of legal drama. However, law's pleasures (like its play) tend to remain tacit and illicit, and they are not the pleasures I focus on here.

58. The gamification of public participation in policy decision-making is one example of this. Here, too, pleasure is associated with the process rather than purely with its outcomes.

59. On dangerous sports or "edgework," see Ferrell 2001; Lyng 2005a, 2005b; Newmahr 2011; Thompson 1971.

60. Bringing the state into a discussion of commoning is contentious given the term's common alignment with grassroots, sometimes anarchist, typically horizontally engaged, and often antistate—or, at least, non-state—initiatives (see Angel 2017; Cumbers 2015; Kalb 2017; Meyer and Hudon 2017). The commons historically has been associated with forms of ownership that are collective, shared, and sometimes open rather than with state ownership, although J. K. Gibson-Graham and colleagues (2016) argue for a process-based approach to commoning that does not depend on a particular form of ownership. The pluralist state account in this book means the concept of the state reaches *toward* the broad field of public governance and includes gathered states (involving different scales and forms, including micro ones). As a consequence, thinking about state participation in commoning is helpful. It suggests ways in which state bodies might be embedded in more horizontal forms of governance; illuminates state support (often at the municipal level) for commons projects, such as local currency networks or new democratic forms of devolved public ownership (Cumbers et al. 2016); draws attention to how state resources and opportunities are taken up in grassroots networks of action (see also Cooper 2016a); and helps identify the contribution of usage to governing: "When we speak of those who 'produce' the space we are not simply referring to those who undertake activities normally designated as work, but rather all those who take part in the space in different ways or forms" (Bresnihan and Byrne 2015: 46–47).

61. Approaches to commoning vary among different users. Some focus on activities and uses; others focus on the kinds of subjectivity created or the (organized) relations people have with others, including through decommodification and the collectivization

of social reproduction. On different approaches to the commons, see Fournier 2013. For one feminist reading of the commons and what it might entail, see Federici 2012.

62. In the decision in *Barnes-Wallace v. Boy Scouts of America*, 275 F. Supp. 2d 1259 (S.D. Cal. 2003), 1263, the District Court remarked, "At issue here is the City of San Diego's long-term lease of prized public parklands to the Boy Scouts. After *Dale*, it is clear that the Boy Scouts of America's strongly held private, discriminatory beliefs are at odds with values requiring tolerance and inclusion in the public realm, and lawsuits like this one are the predictable fallout from the Boy Scouts' victory before the Supreme Court."

63. See *Law Society of British Columbia v. Trinity Western University*, para. 29.

64. See, e.g., *Boy Scouts of America v. Till*, 1297–98, emphasis added, in which the court remarked, in relation to litigants' diverging perspectives on homosexuality (as "private sexual orientation" and as "immoral conduct"): "At issue are the efforts of public educators, parents, and the members of a private expressive association *to prepare young people for participation as citizens and to teach the values upon which our society rests.*"

If one public good is a belief in the equality of gay sexuality, with gay sexual desires retrieved, reconditioned, and made part of the liberal political commons, one challenge is how to sustain the political vitality of sexual beliefs so that they do not reemerge as property—siloized, depoliticized, and cut off from wider meanings. For further discussion of the propertied approach to beliefs that emerged through human rights and antidiscrimination law frameworks, and critically addressing play's capacity to unsettle such tendencies, see chapter 4.

65. *Barnes-Wallace v. Boy Scouts of America.*

66. By contrast, conservative forms of state-based activism involved the take-up of responsibility through redirecting public provision away from "wrongly" sexualized human bodies, as the marriage registrar Lillian Ladele, along with many other conservative Christians, sought to accomplish.

SIX. Feeling Like a Different Kind of State

1. As discussed in chapter 5, control, observation, and deployment of sex can prove a terrifying governmental power. Game techniques can also be used to generate public "buy-in" rather than to creatively develop new policy forms (see chapter 4). Moreover, calling for officials to be more playful with service users may seem to trivialize official power while underestimating the profound effects of resource constraints and unequal authority on the ability to play horizontally. For detailed discussion on the use of game techniques in policy decision-making, see Lerner 2014. For a critical exploration of "civic gamification," see Vanolo 2018.

2. I explore this further in Cooper 2014: chap. 2.

3. For further discussion of prefigurative politics, see Boggs 1977; Maeckelbergh 2011; Swain 2019; Yates 2015. I discuss prefiguring the state in more detail in Cooper 2017.

4. On other prefigurative state projects, see Fiona McConnell's (2016) account of the rehearsal of the Tibetan Government-in-Exile, which she describes as modeling (to some degree at least) a nonviolent, environmentally responsible form of statehood.

5. However, Mundy (2007: 294) later states, "It would be a mistake to assume that the political, economic and social structures in the camps will be grafted on to an independent Western Sahara without modification. The camps are too much of a controlled experiment to hope that an independent Western Sahara would apply them writ large."

6. Prefiguring the state is not always small-scale or unsuccessful. It is also not necessarily a left-wing endeavor. Late twentieth-century neoliberal state prefiguring in the global North treated the state as a formation whose primary (and, for some, exclusive) function was to support capitalist markets, including through institutional mimesis. Drawing on a range of legal powers at their disposal, conservatives not only reassembled the form of the state; they also drew on and advanced neoliberal state imaginaries of what it properly meant to be a state.

7. This discussion builds on earlier analyses (see Cooper 2016b, 2016c).

8. For discussion of the relationship between law and play, see Rogers 2008.

9. States may also be described as playing or pretending when they lack significant authority or external recognition. On Northern Cyprus as a political "make-believe" space, see Navaro-Yashin 2012.

10. See, e.g., the interesting discussion on the Model United Nations in Dittmer 2013. Some children's parliaments, by contrast, are intended to give children a "real" political voice and public presence (see, e.g., Kallio and Häkli 2011). But this is not my focus here. For a good overview of digital games used for "civic learning purposes," see Thiel et al. 2016.

11. See "Utopia Fair," *My Future York* website, 15 August 2016, accessed 18 July 2018, http://myfutureyork.org/category/utopia-fair.

12. See Bibi van der Zee, "The People's Republic of Brighton and Hove: Britain's Latest Breakaway Nation," *The Guardian*, 12 May 2015, accessed 18 July 2018, http://www.theguardian.com/uk-news/shortcuts/2015/may/12/britains-latest-breakaway-nation-peoples-republic-brighton-hove. The Facebook page for the People's Republic of Brighton and Hove, at https://www.facebook.com/pages/The-Peoples-Republic-of-Brighton-Hove/1613213145559715, had 21,274 "likes" and 20,345 "followers" as of 18 July 2018. Frestonia was described as being approximately eight acres in size, with a population of about 120: see "Application to the United Nations," Republic of Frestonia website, accessed 18 July 2018, http://www.frestonia.org/application-to-the-united-nations.

13. Frestonia declared independence on 30 October 1977 as a protest against attempts by the Greater London Council (GLC) to displace its residents in order to redevelop the site. Frestonia applied to the United Nations for membership with "autonomous nation status," informing that body that if the GLC invaded and forced evictions, "There will exist a crisis with international ramifications, and the necessity may arise for Frestonia to require the U.N. to send a token peace-keeping force," see "Application to the United Nations"; see also Dave Walker, "Frestonia: The Past Is Another Country," Royal Borough of Kensington and Chelsea website, 23 April 2015, accessed 18 July 2018, https://rbkclocalstudies.wordpress.com/2015/04/23/frestonia-the

-past-is-another-country. For further discussion of micro-nations, see McConnell et al. 2012; Routledge 1997.

14. There is a rapidly growing literature as more jurisdictions and fields of law take up the challenge of producing new feminist (or other social justice) decisions on past cases (see e.g., Douglas et al. 2014; Enright et al. 2017; Hunter et al. 2010; Rackley 2012). This initiative was inspired and preceded by the Women's Court of Canada (see Majury 2006). See also "The People's Constitution," London School of Economics and Political Science website, accessed 18 July 2018, http://blogs.lse.ac.uk/constitutionuk /http://blogs.lse.ac.uk/constitutionuk/2015/06/15/the-peoples-constitution.

15. See, e.g., the website of Free University Brighton, accessed 18 July 2018, http:// freeuniversitybrighton.org. For useful discussion of alternative currencies and what they seek to realize, see Lee et al. 2004; Meyer and Hudon 2017; North 2007, 2014; Seyfang 2001. There is a sizable literature on people's tribunals, including Borowiak 2008; Boyle and Kobayashi 2015; Byrnes and Simm 2018; Maloney 2016; Nayar 2001; Simm and Byrnes 2014.

16. Many local currency networks recognize they are outside the parameters of mainstream money but do not perceive their activities as play on the grounds that the language of play demeans and trivializes; that it suggests what they do is of no consequence and has no consequence. Rather, they see themselves as producing money *reimagined*. From this perspective, local currencies are real when they can do what they intended: support exchanges of goods and services, build an economy, enhance community, reallocate value, and so on. By contrast, for skeptics, local currencies are not deemed real money because they are not fungible, accumulable, investible, exchangeable, and so on. In some respects, this failed imitative status may have a protective dimension as I discuss later.

17. The first Russell Tribunal was held in 1967 to inquire into and judge American military action in Vietnam. Subsequently, ad hoc people's tribunals, and the Permanent People's Tribunal (established in 1979 and based in Rome) took shape as civil society tribunals within a wider, global geopolitical environment, which they sought to affect (see Simm and Byrnes 2014). For further discussion of people's (or citizens') tribunals, see also Maloney 2016; Nayar 2001.

18. For interesting accounts of participatory innovations and some of the dilemmas that state-led participatory designs raise, see Baiocchi and Ganuza 2017; Fung and Wright 2003; Lerner 2014.

19. For a useful discussion of these themes in a Latin American context, see Alvarez et al. 2017.

20. For further discussion of the politics, challenges, and value of "governing out of order," see Cooper 1998.

21. In many cases, this is likely to involve the activities (and sometimes the formation) of counterpublics. For further discussion of counterpublics, see Fraser 1990; Squires 2002; Warner 2002. I explore the relationship of counterpublics to other kinds of transformative publics further in Cooper 2016a.

22. The firefighters received written warnings, a requirement to undergo diversity training, and one was demoted: see "Firefighters Disciplined over Gay Pride Snub," *The*

Guardian, 31 August 2006, accessed 18 July 2018, https://www.theguardian.com/world
/2006/aug/31/gayrights.uk. But see also "Christian Fireman Given Damages over Gay
Pride March Row," *The Telegraph*, 21 January 2009, accessed 18 July 2018, http://www
.telegraph.co.uk/news/uknews/4304735/Christian-fireman-given-damages-over-gay
-pride-march-row.html, which describes the subsequent settlement in favor of the
demoted firefighter after he brought an Employment Tribunal case.

23. Ed Mazza, "Pediatrician Refuses to Care for Baby with Lesbian Mothers in
Michigan," *Huffington Post*, 19 February 2015, accessed 18 July 2018, http://www
.huffingtonpost.com/2015/02/18/pediatrician-refuses-lesbian-mothers_n_6710128.html.

24. See "Anti-Gay Deptford Teacher Robert Haye's Ban Upheld," BBC *News*, 12
April 2013, accessed 18 July 2018, http://www.bbc.co.uk/news/uk-england-london
-22120706.

25. Rather than waiting for the government or parliament to initiate the process,
academics took up the task themselves, developing an impressively extensive and
varied program of public engagement that led to a "proper-looking" constitutional text.
Yet this new constitutional text, with its proposed abolition of the monarchy and dises-
tablished church, could not bring into force the political and institutional settlement it
expressed. While it could do the process, it could not do what the process was intended
to accomplish. This "failure," however, needs to be placed alongside those official
participative constitution-making processes that also failed to legally realize new constitutions, see discussion on the "crowdsourced" Iceland constitution (e.g., Landemore
2015). Iceland's constitution was not seen by participants as play, but to the extent
it remained unrealized, might it now be usefully regarded as a form of experimental
play? Certainly, such a description can be attached to ambitious, "failed" projects, but
this would suggest that play is nothing more than a failed performative. As discussed
in detail in chapter 4, play also has other elements, including players' willing participation, creative action, plasticity, pleasure (in some form), and open-endedness.

26. See The Judgment of the Tokyo Women's Tribunal, quoted in Simm and Byrnes
(2014: 110, emphasis added): "This is a Peoples' Tribunal, a Tribunal conceived and established by the voices of global civil society. The authority for this Tribunal comes not
from a state or intergovernmental organization but from the peoples of the Asia-Pacific
region, and *indeed, the peoples of the world to whom Japan owes a duty under international
law* to render account."

27. And, of course, what constitutes "approved" projects changes, a factor precipi-
tating some of the litigation discussed in this book, as mainstream, widely accepted
organizations, the Boy Scouts being a prominent example, lost state approval and, as a
consequence, state subsidies from adopting an antigay stance.

28. This question raises two different issues. First, how might counterinstitutional
initiatives link up so that progressive values are expressed? Second, can progressive
values become embedded in the character of new articulations?

29. As discussed in chapter 1, a key dimension of this drama was its reliance on,
and foregrounding of, the power attached to (and exercised by) laboring bodies; state
recognition; public sector access and opportunities; community membership; the
withdrawal of goods; and the control of venues, promotions, training, and attendance.

30. If values can become systemic values, they may make hardier, if still evolving and mutating, relations possible among different public governance bodies.

31. In conditions where responsibility can take reactionary as well as progressive forms, sometimes social justice claims may demand others relinquish their assumption of responsibility; see Noxolo et al., 2012; Raghuram et al., 2009.

32. For initial development of the concept of wild law, see Cullinan 2003.

33. For the judgment and commentary, see Goh and Round 2017.

34. See Independent People's Tribunal on the World Bank in India, *Findings of the Jury* (2007), 11 September 2008, 23, accessed 21 November 2018, http://www .worldbanktribunal.org/WB_Tribunal_Jury_Findings.pdf. The tribunal drew attention to "an economic system that has benefited these stakeholders [international financial institutions and the private sector agendas of powerful nations] disproportionately, almost invariably at the cost of the poor." See also Simm and Byrnes 2014.

35. See, e.g., the Free University Brighton website, accessed 18 July 2018, http:// freeuniversitybrighton.org/about.

36. For an account of the decline of British LETS in the early twenty-first century, see Aldridge and Patterson 2002; Cooper 2014: chap. 6; Evans 2009.

37. Rogers (2008: 44) develops a similar line of argument in relation to the state's take-up of roles, objects, and performances developed in theater.

38. Indeed, the attempt by some LETS innovators to create exchange mechanisms between national and local currencies was an attempt to do exactly this (see Cooper 2014: chap. 6).

39. The question of how play appears in wider social worlds has been addressed in relation to regulating cyber-worlds such as *Second Life*. If wealth accrues or crimes take place in *Second Life*, when, if ever, should they be recognized in "first life"? What should they be recognized as being? And should first life courts be used to adjudicate in *Second Life* property struggles or only when these property conflicts also exist as first life ones? These questions have been subjected to considerable academic debate (see, e.g., Kerr 2008; Mayer-Schoenberger and Crowley 2006; Stoup 2008).

40. Other mail was impounded: see "Frestonian Postage Stamps," Republic of Frestonia website, accessed 18 July 2018, http://www.frestonia.org/frestonian-postage-stamps.

41. "Response from Horace Cutler, Leader of the GLC," Republic of Frestonia website, accessed 18 July 2018, http://www.frestonia.org/response-from-horace-cutler -leader-of-the-glc.

42. See, e.g., "What Is the LOSS?" League of Secessionist States website, accessed 18 July 2018, http://www.reuniao.org/loss/engl.htm. See also "Official News Site," Grand Unified Micronational website, accessed 18 July 2018, https://gumnews.wordpress .com.

43. On the international conservative Christian networks and looser connections that have been forged (and grown) to oppose lesbian and gay equality, see Browne and Nash 2014; Buss and Herman 2003.

44. Wild law writing, for instance, "abandoned" the principle of feminist judgment writing projects that decisions should stay within the parameters of the legal frameworks operating at the time of the original decision (see Rogers 2017: 5).

45. The state was named after Mount Ararat, where Noah's Ark was imagined to have come to rest.

46. See, e.g., *Mapping Ararat*, a twenty-first-century project, funded by a Canadian research council, and described as offering "the user/participant the tools to imagine an alternative historical outcome for Noah's Ararat and to navigate through an imaginary Jewish homeland": *Mapping Ararat: An Imaginary Jewish Homelands Project*, accessed 19 July 2018, http://www.mappingararat.com/project. See also Kaplan 2013.

47. See "Ararat Vernacular Culture," *Mapping Ararat: An Imaginary Jewish Homelands Project*, accessed 19 July 2018, http://www.mappingararat.com/ararat-vernacular -culture. See also Kaplan 2013: 256–61.

48. Approaching the state as a transitional concept draws on Donald Winnicott's (1953) discussion of transitional objects, as well as discussions by others who have taken up the idea in social analysis (see, e.g., Hamber 2009). See also Julia Kristeva's (1993: 41) account of the nation as a "transitional object" within a series of increasingly scaled-up attachments. For further critical discussion, see Bonnie Honig (1997: 126), who draws on "transitional objects" to think about the "transition to a future democratic cosmopolitanism."

49. For further discussion of the state "withering away," see Adamiak 1970; Bloom 1946; Valiavicharska 2010.

50. This is the state as a name and idea, on the one hand, and a sociomaterial formation, on the other, two dimensions of the concept of the state that are co-constituted, and in dynamic interrelation.

Abrams, Philip. 1988. "Notes on the Difficulty of Studying the State (1977)." *Journal of Historical Sociology* 1 (1): 58–89.

Adamiak, Richard. 1970. "The 'Withering Away' of the State: A Reconsideration." *Journal of Politics* 32 (1): 3–18.

Adkins, Julie, Laurie Occhipinti, and Tara Hefferan, eds. 2010. *Not by Faith Alone: Social Services, Social Justice, and Faith-Based Organizations in the United States*. Lanham, MD: Lexington.

Adkins, Lisa. 2005. "The New Economy, Property and Personhood." *Theory, Culture and Society* 22 (1): 111–30.

Agamben, Giorgio. 1998. *Homo Sacer: Sovereign Power and Bare Life*, trans. Daniel Heller-Roazen. Stanford, CA: Stanford University Press.

Agamben, Giorgio. 2005. *State of Exception*, trans. Kevin Attell. Chicago: University of Chicago Press.

Agathangelou, Anna M., M. Daniel Bassichis, and Tamara L. Spira. 2008. "Intimate Investments: Homonormativity, Global Lockdown, and the Seductions of Empire." *Radical History Review* 100 (2008): 120–43.

Ahdar, Rex. 2016. "Companies as Religious Liberty Claimants." *Oxford Journal of Law and Religion* 5 (1): 1–27.

Ahmed, Sara. 2004. *Cultural Politics of Emotion*. Edinburgh: Edinburgh University Press.

Ahmed, Sara. 2006. *Queer Phenomenology: Orientations, Objects, Others*. Durham, NC: Duke University Press.

Ahmed, Sara. 2012. *On Being Included: Racism and Diversity in Institutional Life*. Durham, NC: Duke University Press.

Albert, Mathias. 2014. "World State: Brunkhorst's 'Cosmopolitan State' and Varieties of Differentiation." *Social and Legal Studies* 23 (4): 517–31.

Albrow, Martin. 1992. "Sine Ira et Studio—Or Do Organizations Have Feelings?" *Organization Studies* 13 (3): 313–29.

Aldecoa, Francisco, and Michael Keating. 1999. *Paradiplomacy in Action: The Foreign Relations of Subnational Governments.* London: Routledge.

Aldridge, Theresa, and Alan Patterson. 2002. "LETS Get Real: Constraints on the Development of Local Exchange Trading Schemes." *Area* 34 (4): 370–81.

Allen, John. 2011. "Powerful Assemblages?" *Area* 43 (2): 154–57.

Allen, John, and Allan Cochrane. 2010. "Assemblages of State Power: Topological Shifts in the Organization of Government and Politics." *Antipode* 42 (5): 1071–89.

Allen, Judith. 1990. "Does Feminism Need a Theory of the State?" In *Playing the State: Australian Feminist Interventions,* ed. Sophie Watson, 21–37. London: Verso.

Alvarez, Sonia E., Jeffrey W. Rubin, Millie Thayer, Gianpaolo Baiocchi, and Agustín Laó-Montes, eds. 2017. *Beyond Civil Society: Activism, Participation, and Protest in Latin America.* Durham, NC: Duke University Press.

Anderson, Rosie. 2014. "Playing the Fool: Activists' Performances of Emotion in Policy Making Spaces." *Emotion, Space and Society* 13: 16–23.

Anderson, Warwick. 2010. "Crap on the Map, or Postcolonial Waste." *Postcolonial Studies* 13 (2): 169–78.

Andersson, Johan, Robert M. Vanderbeck, Gill Valentine, Kevin Ward, and Joanna Sadgrove. 2011. "New York Encounters: Religion, Sexuality, and the City." *Environment and Planning A: Economy and Space* 43 (3): 618–33.

Angel, James. 2017. "Towards an Energy Politics in-against-and-beyond the State: Berlin's Struggle for Energy Democracy." *Antipode* 49 (3): 557–76.

Angel, James, and Alex Loftus. 2017. "With-against-and-beyond the Human Right to Water." *Geoforum.* http://dx.doi.org/10.1016/j.geoforum.2017.05.002.

Aretxaga, Begoña. 2000. "Playing Terrorist: Ghastly Plots and the Ghostly State." *Journal of Spanish Cultural Studies* 1 (1): 43–58.

Aretxaga, Begoña. 2001. "The Sexual Games of the Body Politic: Fantasy and State Violence in Northern Ireland." *Culture, Medicine and Psychiatry* 25 (1): 1–27.

Aretxaga, Begoña. 2003. "Maddening States." *Annual Review of Anthropology* 32 (1): 393–410.

Asad, Talal. 1983. "Anthropological Conceptions of Religion: Reflections on Geertz." *Man* 18 (2): 237–59.

Ashcraft, Karen Lee. 2000. "Empowering 'Professional' Relationships: Organizational Communication Meets Feminist Practice." *Management Communication Quarterly* 13 (3): 347–92.

Ashcraft, Karen Lee. 2001. "Organized Dissonance: Feminist Bureaucracy as Hybrid Form." *Academy of Management Journal* 44 (6): 1301–22.

Ashcraft, Karen Lee. 2006. "Feminist-Bureaucratic Control and Other Adversarial Allies: Extending Organized Dissonance to the Practice of 'New' Forms." *Communication Monographs* 73 (1): 55–86.

Atkinson, Michael. 2009. "Parkour, Anarcho-Environmentalism, and Poiesis." *Journal of Sport and Social Issues* 33 (2): 169–94.

Baiocchi, Gianpaolo, and Ernesto Ganuza. 2017. *Popular Democracy: The Paradox of Participation.* Stanford, CA: Stanford University Press.

Bakhtin, Mikhail. 1968. *Rabelais and His World.* Cambridge, MA: MIT Press.

Bakonyi, Jutta. 2013. "Authority and Administration beyond the State: Local Governance in Southern Somalia, 1995–2006." *Journal of Eastern African Studies* 7 (2): 272–90.

Bal, Mieke. 2002. *Travelling Concepts in the Humanities: A Rough Guide*. Toronto: University of Toronto Press.

Balug, Katarzyna, and Maria Vidart-Delgado. 2015. "Imagine! You Have Nothing to Lose: Collaboration and Play in Urban Development." *Critical Sociology* 41 (7–8): 1027–44.

Barad, Karen. 2003. "Posthumanist Performativity: Toward an Understanding of how Matter Comes to Matter." *Signs* 28 (3): 801–31.

Baron, Jane B., and Julia Epstein. 1997. "Is Law Narrative?" *Buffalo Law Review* 45 (1): 141–88.

Barrett, Susan. 2004. "Implementation Studies: Time for a Revival? Personal Reflections on 20 Years of Implementation Studies." *Public Administration* 82 (2): 249–62.

Barsoux, Jean-Louis. 1996. "Why Organisations Need Humour." *European Management Journal* 14 (5): 500–8.

Baskerville, Stephen. 2011. "The Sexual Agenda and Religious Freedom-Challenges in the Western World." *International Journal for Religious Freedom* 4 (2): 91–105.

Bateman, Thomas M. J. 2015. "Trinity Western University's Law School and the Associational Dimension of Religious Freedom: Toward Comprehensive Liberalism." *University of New Brunswick Law Journal* 66: 78–116.

Bateson, Gregory. 1987. *Steps to an Ecology of Mind: Collected Essays in Anthropology, Psychiatry, Evolution, and Epistemology*. Northvale, NJ: Jason Aronson.

Bavinton, Nathaniel. 2007. "From Obstacle to Opportunity: Parkour, Leisure, and the Reinterpretation of Constraints." *Annals of Leisure Research* 10 (3–4): 391–412.

Beasley, Chris, and Carol Bacchi. 2012. "Making Politics Fleshly: The Ethic of Social Flesh." In *Engaging with Carol Bacchi: Strategic Interventions and Exchanges*, ed. Chris Beasley and Angelique Bletsas, 99–121. Adelaide: University of Adelaide Press.

Beckett, Katherine, and Steve Herbert. 2010. "Penal Boundaries: Banishment and the Expansion of Punishment." *Law and Social Inquiry* 35 (1): 1–38.

Benkler, Yochai. 2013. "Practical Anarchism: Peer Mutualism, Market Power, and the Fallible State." *Politics and Society* 41 (2): 213–51.

Bennett, David. 2010. "Libidinal Economy, Prostitution and Consumer Culture." *Textual Practice* 24 (1): 93–121.

Bennett, David. 2016. *Currency of Desire: Libidinal Economy, Psychoanalysis and Sexual Revolution*. London: Lawrence and Wishart.

Bennett, Jane. 2009. *Vibrant Matter: A Political Ecology of Things*. Durham, NC: Duke University Press.

Berman, Paul Schiff. 2007. "Global Legal Pluralism." *Southern California Law Review* 80 (6): 1155–1237.

Benson, Iain T. 2007. "The Freedom of Conscience and Religion in Canada: Challenges and Opportunities." *Emory International Law Review* 21: 111–65.

Bevir, Mark, and Rod Rhodes. 2006. *Governance Stories*. London: Routledge.

Bhandar, Brenna. 2009. "Constituting Practices and Things: The Concept of the Network and Studies in Law, Gender and Sexuality." *Feminist Legal Studies* 17 (3): 325–32.

Bhandar, Brenna, and Davina Bhandar. 2016. "Cultures of Dispossession: Critical Reflections on Rights, Status and Identities." *Darkmatter Journal* 14. http://www.darkmatter101.org/site/2016/05/16/cultures-of-dispossession.

Bielo, James S. 2012. "Belief, Deconversion, and Authenticity among U.S. Emerging Evangelicals." *Ethos* 40 (3): 258–76.

Black, Julia. 2001. "Decentring Regulation: Understanding the Role of Regulation and Self-Regulation in a 'Post-Regulatory' World." *Current Legal Problems* 54 (1): 103–46.

Blatter, Joachim K. 2001. "Debordering the World of States: Towards a Multi-Level System in Europe and a Multi-Polity System in North America? Insights from Border Regions." *European Journal of International Relations* 7 (2): 175–209.

Bloom, Solomon F. 1946. "The 'Withering Away' of the State." *Journal of the History of Ideas* 7 (1): 113–21.

Boal, Augusto. (1974) 2000. *Theater of the Oppressed*. London: Pluto.

Boal, Augusto. 2005. *Legislative Theatre: Using Performance to Make Politics*. London: Routledge.

Boggs, Carl. 1977. "Marxism, Prefigurative Communism, and the Problem of Workers' Control." *Radical America* 11 (6): 99–122.

Borowiak, Craig. 2008. "The World Tribunal on Iraq: Citizens' Tribunals and the Struggle for Accountability." *New Political Science* 30 (2): 161–86.

Boucher, Daniel. 2010. *A Little Bit against Discrimination? Reflection on the Opportunities and Challenges Presented by the Equality Bill 2009–2010*. London: Christian Action Research and Education.

Boyle, Mark, and Audrey Kobayashi. 2015. "In the Face of Epistemic Injustices? On the Meaning of People-Led War Crimes Tribunals." *Environment and Planning D: Society and Space* 33 (4): 697–713.

Bracey, Glenn E. 2015. "Toward a Critical Race Theory of State." *Critical Sociology* 41 (3): 553–72.

Braun, Virginia, and Sue Wilkinson. 2001. "Socio-Cultural Representations of the Vagina." *Journal of Reproductive and Infant Psychology* 19 (1): 17–32.

Breakey, Hugh. 2014. "Parsing Macpherson: The Last Rites of Locke the Possessive Individualist." *Theoria* 80 (1): 62–83.

Bresnihan, Patrick, and Michael Byrne. 2015. "Escape into the City: Everyday Practices of Commoning and the Production of Urban Space in Dublin." *Antipode* 47 (1): 36–54.

Browne, Kath, and Leela Bakshi. 2013. "Insider Activists: The Fraught Possibilities of LGBT Activisms from Within." *Geoforum* 49: 253–62.

Browne, Katherine, and Catherine J. Nash. 2014. "Resisting LGBT Rights where "We have Won": Canada and Great Britain." *Journal of Human Rights* 13 (3): 322–36.

Bruner, M. Lane. 2005. "Carnivalesque Protest and the Humorless State." *Text and Performance Quarterly* 25 (2): 136–55.

Brunkhorst, Hauke. 2012. "The Co-Evolution of Cosmopolitan and National Statehood—Preliminary Theoretical Considerations on the Historical Evolution of Constitutionalism." *Cooperation and Conflict* 47 (2): 176–99.

Buss, Doris, and Didi Herman. 2003. *Globalizing Family Values*. Minneapolis: University of Minnesota Press.

Bumiller, Kristin. 1992. *The Civil Rights Society: The Social Construction of Victims*. Baltimore: Johns Hopkins University Press.

Butler, Judith. 1997. *The Psychic Life of Power: Theories in Subjection*. Palo Alto, CA: Stanford University Press.

Butler, Judith. 2008. "Sexual Politics, Torture, and Secular Time." *British Journal of Sociology* 59 (1): 1–23.

Butler, Judith, and Athena Athanasiou. 2013. *Dispossession: The Performative in the Political*. Cambridge, MA: Polity.

Buzard, James M. 1990. "The Fiction of a Finished World: Utopia and Ideology in Morris's *News from Nowhere*." *Minnesota Review* 34 (1): 81–98.

Byrnes, Andrew, and Gabrielle Simm, eds. 2018. *Peoples' Tribunals and International Law*. Cambridge: Cambridge University Press.

Caporaso, James A. 1996. "The European Union and Forms of State: Westphalian, Regulatory or Post-Modern?" *Journal of Common Market Studies* 34 (1): 29–52.

Carens, Joseph H. 1993. *Democracy and Possessive Individualism: The Intellectual Legacy of C. B. Macpherson*. Albany: State University of New York Press.

Carroll, Patrick. 2009. "Articulating Theories of States and State Formation." *Journal of Historical Sociology* 22 (4): 553–603.

Catto, Kyle D. 2017. "The S&M Man Can? Thinking about Submission and the Submissive Soldier—A Response to Jesse Paul Crane-Seeber (2016)." *Critical Military Studies*. doi: 10.1080/23337486.2017.1417959.

Chambers, Samuel A. 2011. "Jacques Rancière and the Problem of Pure Politics." *European Journal of Political Theory* 10 (3): 303–26.

Cheah, Pheng. 2013. "Hospitality and Alienation." In *The Conditions of Hospitality: Ethics, Politics, and Aesthetics on the Threshhold of the Possible*, ed. Thomas Claviez, 57–80. New York: Fordham University Press.

Chesler, Susan M., and Karen J. Sneddon. 2017. "Tales from a Form Book: Stock Stories and Transactional Documents." *Montana Law Review* 78 (2): art. 3. https://scholarship.law.umt.edu/mlr/vol78/iss2/3.

Christian Institute. 2009. *Marginalising Christians: Instances of Christians Being Sidelined in Modern Britain*. Newcastle upon Tyne, UK: Christian Institute.

Clapham, Christopher. 1998. "Degrees of Statehood." *Review of International Studies* 24 (2): 143–57.

Clark, Timothy, and Iain Mangham. 2004. "From Dramaturgy to Theatre as Technology: The Case of Corporate Theatre." *Journal of Management Studies* 41 (1): 37–59.

Clarke, John. 2019. "Harmful Thoughts: Re-Imagining the Coercive State?" In *Reimagining the State*, ed. Davina Cooper, Nikita Dhawan and Janet Newman, 213–30. Abingdon, UK: Routledge.

Clucas, Rob. 2012. "Religion, Sexual Orientation and the Equality Act 2010: Gay Bishops in the Church of England Negotiating Rights Against Discrimination." *Sociology* 46 (5): 936–50.

Colgan, Fiona, and Tessa Wright. 2011. "Lesbian, Gay and Bisexual Equality in a Modernizing Public Sector 1997–2010: Opportunities and Threats." *Gender, Work and Organization* 18 (5): 548–70.

Collier, David, Fernando Daniel Hidalgo, and Andra Olivia Maciuceanu. 2006. "Essentially Contested Concepts: Debates and Applications." *Journal of Political Ideologies* 11 (3): 211–46.

Commission on Religion and Belief in British Public Life. 2015. *Living with Difference*. Cambridge: Woolf Institute.

Coombe, Rosemary J. 1998. *The Cultural Life of Intellectual Properties: Authorship, Appropriation, and the Law*. Durham, NC: Duke University Press.

Cooper, Davina. 1994. *Sexing the City: Lesbian and Gay Politics within the Activist State*. London: Rivers Oram.

Cooper, Davina. 1995. *Power in Struggle: Feminism, Sexuality and the State*. New York: New York University Press.

Cooper, Davina. 1996. "Institutional Illegality and Disobedience: Local Government Narratives." *Oxford Journal of Legal Studies* 16 (2): 255–74.

Cooper, Davina. 1998. *Governing Out of Order: Space, Law and the Politics of Belonging*. London: Rivers Oram.

Cooper, Davina. 1999. "Punishing Councils: Political Power, Solidarity and the Pursuit of Freedom." In *Feminist Perspectives on Public Law*, ed. Susan Milns and Noel Whitty, 245–69. London: Cavendish.

Cooper, Davina. 2002. "Far beyond 'The Early Morning Crowing of a Farmyard Cock': Revisiting the Place of Nuisance within Legal and Political Discourse." *Social and Legal Studies* 11 (1): 5–35.

Cooper, Davina. 2006. "Active Citizenship and the Governmentality of Local Lesbian and Gay Politics." *Political Geography* 25 (8): 921–43.

Cooper, Davina. 2013. "Public Bodies: Conceptualising Active Citizenship and the Embodied State." In *Beyond Citizenship? Feminism and the Transformation of Belonging*, ed. Sasha Roseneil, 112–37. London: Palgrave Macmillan.

Cooper, Davina. 2014. *Everyday Utopias: The Conceptual Life of Promising Spaces*. Durham, NC: Duke University Press.

Cooper, Davina. 2015. "Bringing the State Up Conceptually: Forging a Body Politics through Anti-Gay Christian Refusal." *Feminist Theory* 16 (1): 87–107.

Cooper, Davina. 2016a. "Transformative State Publics." *New Political Science* 38 (3): 315–34.

Cooper, Davina. 2016b. "Enacting Counter-States through Play." *Contemporary Political Theory* 15 (4): 453–61.

Cooper, Davina. 2016c. "Retrieving the State for Radical Politics—A Conceptual and Playful Challenge." *Journal of Social Policy Studies* 14 (3): 409–22.

Cooper, Davina. 2017. "Prefiguring the State." *Antipode* 49 (2): 335–56.

Cooper, Davina. 2019. "A Very Binary Drama: The Conceptual Struggle for Gender's Future." *feminists@law* 9(1). http://journals.kent.ac.uk/index.php/feministsatlaw/article/view/655.

Cooper, Davina, and Didi Herman. 2013. "Up against the Property Logic of Equality Law: Conservative Christian Accommodation Claims and Gay Rights." *Feminist Legal Studies* 21 (1): 61–80.

Cooper, Davina, and Didi Herman. 2019. "Revisiting Municipal Activism: Boycotts, Israel/ Palestine and Progressive Local Government." *Environment and Planning C: Politics and Space* (forthcoming).

Cooper, Davina, and Flora Renz. 2016. "If the State Decertified Gender, What Might Happen to Its Meaning and Value?" *Journal of Law and Society* 43 (4): 483–505.

Cooper, Robert, and John Law. 1995. "Organisation: Distal and Proximal Views." In *Research in the Sociology of Organisations*, ed. Samuel B. Bachrach, Pasquale Gadliardi, and Bryan Mundell, 237–74. Greenwich, CT: JAI.

Corbridge, Stuart, Glyn Williams, Manoj Srivastava, and Réne Véron. 2005. *Seeing the State: Governance and Governmentality in India.* Cambridge: Cambridge University Press.

Costea, Bogdan, Norman Crump, and John Holm. 2007. "The Spectre of Dionysus: Play, Work, and Managerialism." *Society and Business Review* 2 (2): 153–65.

Crane-Seeber, Jesse Paul. 2016. "Sexy Warriors: The Politics and Pleasures of Submission to the State." *Critical Military Studies* 2 (1–2): 41–55.

Crawford, Adam. 2006. "Networked Governance and the Post-Regulatory State? Steering, Rowing and Anchoring the Provision of Policing and Security." *Theoretical Criminology* 10 (4): 449–79.

Creed, Barbara. 1993. *The Monstrous-Feminine: Film, Feminism, Psychoanalysis.* London; New York: Routledge.

Cruz, David B. 1994. "Piety and Prejudice: Free Exercise Exemption from Laws Prohibiting Sexual Orientation Discrimination." *New York University Law Review* 69 (6): 1176–1237.

Cullinan, Cormac. 2003. *Wild Law: A Manifesto for Earth Justice.* Totnes, UK: Green Books.

Cumbers, Andrew. 2015. "Constructing a Global Commons in, against and beyond the State." *Space and Polity* 19 (1): 62–75.

Cumbers, Andrew, Ross Beveridge, Matthias Naumann, Lazaros Karaliotas, and Angela Last. 2016. "Public Ownership and Alternative Political Imaginations." *Soundings* 64: 83–104.

Darden, Keith. 2008. "The Integrity of Corrupt States: Graft as an Informal State Institution." *Politics and Society* 36 (1): 35–59.

Das, Veena, and Deborah Poole, eds. 2004. *Anthropology in the Margins of the State.* Santa Fe, NM: School of American Research Press.

Daskalaki, Maria, Alexandra Stara, and Miguel Imas. 2008. "The 'Parkour Organisation': Inhabitation of Corporate Spaces." *Culture and Organization* 14 (1): 49–64.

Davies, Margaret. 1999. "Queer Property, Queer Persons: Self-Ownership and Beyond." *Social and Legal Studies* 8 (3): 327–52.

Davies, Margaret. 2006. "Pluralism and Legal Philosophy." *Northern Ireland Legal Quarterly* 57 (4): 577–96.

Davies, Margaret. 2012. "The Law Becomes Us: Rediscovering Judgment." *Feminist Legal Studies* 20 (2): 167–81.

Davies, Margaret. 2017. *Law Unlimited: Materialism, Pluralism, and Legal Theory*. Abingdon, UK: Routledge.

Dawney, Leila, Samuel Kirwan, and Julian Brigstocke. 2016. "Introduction: The Promise of the Commons." In *Space, Power and the Commons: The Struggle for Alternative Futures*, ed. Samuel Kirwan, Leila Dawney, and Julian Brigstocke, 1–28. London: Routledge.

Day, Richard. 2001. "Who Is This We That Gives the Gift? Native American Political Theory and *The Western Tradition.*" *Critical Horizons* 2 (2): 173–201.

de Cesari, Chiara. 2012. "Anticipatory Representation: Building the Palestinian Nation(-State) through Artistic Performance." *Studies in Ethnicity and Nationalism* 12 (1): 82–100.

De Dreu, Carsten K. W., and Daan van Knippenberg. 2005. "The Possessive Self as a Barrier to Conflict Resolution: Effects of Mere Ownership, Process Accountability, and Self-Concept Clarity on Competitive Cognitions and Behavior." *Journal of Personality and Social Psychology* 89 (3): 345–57.

Dean, Mitchell, and Kaspar Villadsen. 2016. *State Phobia and Civil Society: The Political Legacy of Michel Foucault*. Stanford, CA: Stanford University Press.

Dean, Tim. 2009. *Unlimited Intimacy: Reflections on the Subculture of Barebacking*. Chicago: University of Chicago Press.

Deleuze, Gilles, and Félix Guattari. 1994. *What Is Philosophy?* London: Verso.

Design Council. 2004. *Touching the State: What Does It Mean to Be a Citizen in the 21st Century?* London: Design Council.

Dhawan, Nikita. 2016. "Homonationalism and State-Phobia: The Postcolonial Predicament of Queering Modernities." In *Queering Paradigms V: Queering Narratives of Modernity*, ed. María Amelia Viteri and Manuela Lavinas Picq, 51–68. Oxford: Peter Lang.

Dhawan, Nikita. 2019. "State as *Pharmakon.*" In *Reimagining the State*, ed. Davina Cooper, Nikita Dhawan, and Janet Newman, 57–76. Abingdon, UK: Routledge.

Dickens, Sarah, Martin Mitchell, and Chris Creegan. 2009. *Management Handling of Sexual Orientation, Religion and Belief in the Workplace*. Research Paper no. 01/09. London: Advisory, Conciliation and Arbitration Service.

Dinham, Adam, and Vivien Lowndes. 2008. "Religion, Resources, and Representation: Three Narratives of Faith Engagement in British Urban Governance." *Urban Affairs Review* 43 (6): 817–45.

Dittmer, Jason. 2013. "Humour at the Model United Nations: The Role of Laughter in Constituting Geopolitical Assemblages." *Geopolitics* 18 (3): 493–513.

Dittmer, Jason. 2014. "Geopolitical Assemblages and Complexity." *Progress in Human Geography* 38 (3): 385–401.

Douglas, Heather, Francesca Bartlett, Trish Luker, and Rosemary Hunter, eds. 2014. *Australian Feminist Judgments: Righting and Rewriting Law*. London: Bloomsbury.

Driskill, Qwo-Li. 2004. "Stolen from Our Bodies: First Nations Two-Spirits/Queers and the Journey to a Sovereign Erotic." *Studies in American Indian Literatures* 16 (2): 50–64.

Druckman, Daniel, and Noam Ebner. 2008. "Onstage or Behind the Scenes? Relative Learning Benefits of Simulation Role-Play and Design." *Simulation and Gaming* 39 (4): 465–97.

Dryzek, John S. 2016. "Can There Be a Human Right to an Essentially Contested Concept? The Case of Democracy." *Journal of Politics* 78 (2): 357–67.

Duggan, Lisa. 2002. "The New Homonormativity: The Sexual Politics of Neoliberalism." In *Materializing Democracy: Toward a Revitalized Cultural Politics*, ed. Dana D. Nelson and Russ Castronovo, 175–94. Durham, NC: Duke University Press.

Dumm, Thomas. 1998. "Leaky Sovereignty: Clinton's Impeachment and the Crisis of Infantile Republicanism." *Theory and Event* 2 (4). http://muse.jhu.edu/article/32525.

Dunn, Elizabeth. 2007. "Escherichia Coli, Corporate Discipline and the Failure of the Sewer State." *Space and Polity* 11 (1): 35–53.

Eaton, Mary. 1995. "Homosexual Unmodified: Speculations on Law's Discourse, Race, and the Construction of Sexual Identity." In *Legal Inversions: Lesbians, Gay Men, and the Politics of Law*, ed. Didi Herman and Carl Stychin, 46–73. Philadelphia: Temple University Press.

Edwards, Jason. 2013. "Play and Democracy: Huizinga and the Limits of Agonism." *Political Theory* 41 (1): 90–115.

Eisgruber, Christopher L., and Lawrence G. Sager. 1994. "The Vulnerability of Conscience: The Constitutional Basis for Protecting Religious Conduct." *University of Chicago Law Review* 61 (4): 1245–1315.

Engels, Frederick. (1878) 1934. *Anti-Dühring*, trans. Emile Burns. London: Lawrence and Wishart.

Enright, Máiréad, Julie McCandless, and Aoife O'Donoghue, eds. 2017. *Northern/Irish Feminist Judgments: Judges' Troubles and the Gendered Politics of Identity*. Oxford: Hart.

Etxabe, Julen. 2018. "Jacques Rancière and the Dramaturgy of Law." In *Rancière and Law*, ed. Monica Lopez Lerma and Julen Etxabe, 17–43. London: Routledge.

Evans, Michael S. 2009. "Zelizer's Theory of Money and the Case of Local Currencies." *Environment and Planning A: Economy and Space* 41 (5): 1026–41.

Ewen, Shane, and Michael Hebbert. 2007. "European Cities in a Networked World in the Long Twentieth Century." *Environment and Planning C: Government and Policy* 25 (3): 327–40.

Ewick, Patricia, and Susan S. Silbey. 1995. "Subversive Stories and Hegemonic Tales: Toward a Sociology of Narrative." *Law and Society Review* 29 (2): 197–226.

Farah, Randa. 2009. "Refugee Camps in the Palestinian and Sahrawi National Liberation Movements: A Comparative Perspective." *Journal of Palestine Studies* 38 (2): 76–93.

Farías, Ignacio, and Patricio Flores. 2017. "A Different State of Exception: Governing Urban Reconstruction in Post-27F Chile." *Urban Studies* 54 (5): 1108–25.

Federici, Silvia. 2012. *Revolution at Point Zero: Housework, Reproduction and Feminist Struggle*. Oakland, CA: PM Press.

Feinstein, Pippa, and Sarah E. Hamill. 2018. "The Silencing of Queer Voices in the Litigation over Trinity Western University's Proposed Law School." *Windsor Year Book of Access to Justice* 34 (2): 156–85.

Feldman, Allen. 2006. "Violence and Vision: The Prosthetics and Aesthetics of Terror." In *States of Violence*, ed. Fernando Coronil and Julie Skurski, 425–68. Ann Arbor: University of Michigan Press.

Felski, Rita. 2015. *The Limits of Critique*. Chicago: University of Chicago Press.

Ferguson, James G. 2011. "Toward a Left Art of Government: From 'Foucauldian Critique' to Foucauldian Politics." *History of the Human Sciences* 24 (4): 61–68.

Ferrell, Jeff. 2001. *Tearing Down the Streets: Adventures in Urban Anarchy*. New York: Palgrave.

Fetner, Tina. 2008. *How the Religious Right Shaped Lesbian and Gay Activism*. Minneapolis: University of Minnesota Press.

Fisher, Daniel. 2013. "Becoming the State in Northern Australia: Urbanisation, Intra-Indigenous Relatedness, and the State Effect." *Oceania* 83 (3): 238–58.

Fleming, Peter, and Andrew Sturdy. 2009. "'Just Be Yourself!': Towards Neonormative Control in Organizations?" *Employee Relations* 31 (6): 569–83.

Forman, David M. 2012. "A Room for Adam and Steve at Mrs. Murphy's Bed and Breakfast: Avoiding the Sin of Inhospitality in Places of Public Accommodation." *Columbia Journal of Gender and Law* 23: 326–94.

Foucault, Michel. 2008. *The Birth of Biopolitics: Lectures at the Collège de France, 1978–1979*, ed. Michel Senellart, trans. Graham Burchell. London: Palgrave Macmillan.

Fournier, Valérie. 2013. "Commoning: On the Social Organisation of the Commons." *M@n@gement* 16 (4): 433–53.

Franke, Katherine M. 2012. "Dating the State: The Moral Hazards of Winning Gay Rights." *Columbia Human Rights Law Review* 44 (1): 1–46.

Fraser, Nancy. 1990. "Rethinking the Public Sphere: A Contribution to the Critique of Actually Existing Democracy." *Social Text* 25–26: 56–80.

Frenzel, Fabian. 2014. "Exit the System? Anarchist Organization in the British Climate Camps." 14 (4): 901–21.

Fuglerud, Oivind. 2004. "Constructing Exclusion. The Micro-Sociology of an Immigration Department." *Social Anthropology* 12 (1): 25–40.

Fung, Archon, and Erik Olin Wright. 2003. *Deepening Democracy: Institutional Innovations in Empowered Participatory Governance*. London: Verso.

Fudge, Judy, and Harry Glasbeek. 1992. "The Politics of Rights: A Politics with Little Class." *Social and Legal Studies* 1 (1): 45–70.

Gallie, Walter Bryce. 1955. "Essentially Contested Concepts." *Proceedings of the Aristotelian Society* 56: 167–98.

Garmany, Jeff. 2009. "The Embodied State: Governmentality in a Brazilian Favela." *Social and Cultural Geography* 10 (7): 721–39.

Gatens, Moira, and Genevieve Lloyd. 1999. *Collective Imaginings: Spinoza, Past and Present*. London: Routledge.

Gear, Rachel. 2001. "All those Nasty Womanly Things: Women Artists, Technology and the Monstrous-Feminine." *Women's Studies International Forum* 24 (3–4): 321–33.

Geels, Frank W., and Wim A. Smit. 2000. "Failed Technology Futures: Pitfalls and Lessons from a Historical Survey." *Futures* 32 (9): 867–85.

Ghachem, Malick W. 2003. "The Slave's Two Bodies: The Life of an American Legal Fiction." *William and Mary Quarterly* 60 (4): 809–42.

Gibson-Graham, J. K. 1996. *The End of Capitalism (as We Knew It): A Feminist Critique of Political Economy*. Malden, MA: Wiley-Blackwell.

Gibson-Graham, J. K., Jenny Cameron, and Stephen Healy. 2016. "Commoning as a Postcapitalist Politics." In *Releasing the Commons: Rethinking the Futures of the Commons*, ed. Ash Amin and Philip Howell, 192–212. Routledge: London.

Gill, Nick. 2010. "Tracing Imaginations of the State: The Spatial Consequences of Different State Concepts among Asylum Activist Organisations." *Antipode* 42 (5): 1048–70.

Gill, Nick. 2019. "Border Abolition and How to Achieve it." In *Reimagining the State*, ed. Davina Cooper, Nikita Dhawan and Janet Newman, 231–50. Abingdon, UK: Routledge.

Goh, Bee Chen, and Tom Round. 2017. "Wild Negligence: *Donoghue v. Stevenson*." In *Law as if Earth Really Mattered: The Wild Law Judgment Project*, ed. Nicole Rogers and Michelle Maloney, 91–106. London: Routledge.

Goldberg-Hiller, Jonathan. 2002. *The Limits to Union: Same-Sex Marriage and the Politics of Civil Rights* Ann Arbor: University of Michigan Press.

Goldberg-Hiller, Jonathan, Renisa Mawani, Didi Herman, Denise Ferreira da Silva, and Eve Darian-Smith. 2011. "Roundtable on Eve Darian-Smith, Religion, Race, Rights: Landmarks in the History of Modern Anglo-American Law." *Feminist Legal Studies* 19 (3): 265–88.

Goldberg-Hiller, Jonathan, and Neal Milner. 2003. "Rights as Excess: Understanding the Politics of Special Rights." *Law and Social Inquiry* 28 (4): 1075–1118.

Gordon, Avery. 1997. *Ghostly Matters: Haunting and the Sociological Imagination*. Minneapolis: University of Minnesota Press.

Gordon, Eric, Jason Haas, and Becky Michelson. 2017. "Civic Creativity: Role-Playing Games in Deliberative Process." *International Journal of Communication* 11: 3789–3807.

Goss, Sue. 2001. *Making Local Governance Work: Networks, Relationships, and the Management of Change*. Basingstoke, UK: Palgrave Macmillan.

Grabham, Emily. 2009. "'Flagging' the Skin: Corporeal Nationalism and the Properties of Belonging." *Body and Society* 15 (1): 63–82.

Grabham, Emily. 2017. *Brewing Legal Times: Things, Form, and the Enactment of Law*. Toronto: University of Toronto Press.

Grace, André P., and Kristopher Wells. 2005. "The Marc Hall Prom Predicament: Queer Individual Rights versus Institutional Church Rights in Canadian Public Education." *Canadian Journal of Education/Revue Canadienne de l'Éducation* 28 (3): 237–70.

Graff, Agnieszka. 2010. "Looking at Pictures of Gay Men: Political Uses of Homophobia in Contemporary Poland." *Public Culture* 22 (3): 583–603.

Gray, Chris Hables. 2000. *Cyborg Citizen: Politics in the Posthuman Age*. New York: Routledge.

Gray, Neil, and Libby Porter. 2015. "By Any Means Necessary: Urban Regeneration and the 'State of Exception' in Glasgow's Commonwealth Games 2014." *Antipode* 47 (2): 380–400.

Griffiths, John. 1986. "What Is Legal Pluralism?" *Journal of Legal Pluralism and Unofficial Law* 18 (24): 1–55.

Gross, Aeyal. 2014. "The Politics of LGBT Rights in Israel and Beyond: Nationality, Normativity, and Queer Politics." *Columbia Human Rights Law Review* 46 (2): 81–152.

Grosz, Elizabeth A. 1995. "Animal Sex: Libido as Desire and Death." In *Sexy Bodies: The Strange Carnalities of Feminism*, ed. Elizabeth A. Grosz and Elspeth Probyn, 278–99. London: Routledge.

Grundy-Warr, Carl, and Elaine Wong Siew Yin. 2002. "Geographies of Displacement: The Karenni and the Shan across the Myanmar-Thailand Border." *Singapore Journal of Tropical Geography* 23 (1): 93–122.

Gupta, Akhil. 2012. *Red Tape: Bureaucracy, Structural Violence, and Poverty in India*. Durham, NC: Duke University Press.

Haiven, Max, and Alex Khasnabish. 2014. *The Radical Imagination: Social Movement Research in the Age of Austerity*. London: Zed.

Hajer, Maarten A. 2005. "Setting the Stage: A Dramaturgy of Policy Deliberation." *Administration and Society* 36 (6): 624–47.

Hallward, Peter. 2006. "Staging Equality: Rancière's Theatrocracy." *New Left Review* (37): 109–29.

Hamber, Brandon. 2009. *Transforming Societies after Political Violence: Truth, Reconciliation, and Mental Health*. London: Springer Science and Business Media.

Hamlin, Alan, and Zofia Stemplowska. 2012. "Theory, Ideal Theory and the Theory of Ideals." *Political Studies Review* 10 (1): 48–62.

Hancox, Dan. 2013. *The Village against the World*. London: Verso.

Haraway, Donna. 1991. *Simians, Cyborgs and Women: The Reinvention of Nature*. London: Free Association.

Harold, Christine. 2004. "Pranking Rhetoric: 'Culture Jamming' as Media Activism." *Critical Studies in Media Communication* 21 (3): 189–211.

Harris, Cheryl I. 1993. "Whiteness as Property." *Harvard Law Review* 106 (8): 1707–91.

Haugaard, Mark. 2010. "Power: A 'Family Resemblance' Concept." *European Journal of Cultural Studies* 13 (4): 419–38.

Hawley, Thomas M. 2005. *The Remains of War: Bodies, Politics, and the Search for American Soldiers Unaccounted for in Southeast Asia*. Durham, NC: Duke University Press.

Hay, Colin. 2014. "Neither Real nor Fictitious but 'as if Real'? A Political Ontology of the State." *British Journal of Sociology* 65 (3): 459–80.

Hayles, N. Katherine. 1999. *How We Became Posthuman: Virtual Bodies in Cybernetics, Literature, and Informatics*. Chicago: University of Chicago Press.

Herman, Didi. 1993. "Beyond the Rights Debate." *Social and Legal Studies* 2 (1): 25–43.

Herman, Didi. 1994. *Rights of Passage: Struggles for Lesbian and Gay Legal Equality*. Toronto: University of Toronto Press.

Herman, Didi. 1997. *The Antigay Agenda: Orthodox Vision and the Christian Right*. Chicago: University of Chicago Press.

Herman, Didi. 2011. *An Unfortunate Coincidence: Jews, Jewishness, and English Law*. Oxford: Oxford University Press.

Hetherington, Kevin. 2003. "Spatial Textures: Place, Touch, and Praesentia." *Environment and Planning A: Economy and Space* 35 (11): 1933–44.

Hinthorne, Lauren Leigh, and Katy Schneider. 2012. "Playing with Purpose: Using Serious Play to Enhance Participatory Development Communication." *International Journal of Communication* 6: 2801–24.

Hirst, Paul. 1997. *From Statism to Pluralism: Democracy, Civil Society, and Global Politics.* London: UCL Press.

Hoag, Colin. 2010. "The Magic of the Populace: An Ethnography of Illegibility in the South African Immigration Bureaucracy." *Political and Legal Anthropology Review* 33 (1): 6–25.

Hobbs, Heidi H. 1994. *City Hall Goes Abroad: The Foreign Policy of Local Politics.* Thousand Oaks, CA: Sage.

Hocking, Brian. 1986. "Regional Governments and International Affairs: Foreign Policy Problem or Deviant Behaviour?" *International Journal* 41(3): 477–506.

Hodge, David R. 2002. "Does Social Work Oppress Evangelical Christians? A 'New Class' Analysis of Society and Social Work." *Social Work* 47 (4): 401–14.

Hoehne, Markus V. 2009. "Mimesis and Mimicry in Dynamics of State and Identity Formation in Northern Somalia." *Africa* 79 (2): 252–81.

Hollis-Brusky, Amanda, and Joshua C. Wilson. 2017. "Playing for the Rules: How and Why New Christian Right Public Interest Law Firms Invest in Secular Litigation." *Law and Policy* 39 (2): 121–41.

Honig, Bonnie. 1997. "Ruth, the Model Emigrée: Mourning and the Symbolic Politics of Immigration." *Political Theory* 25 (1): 112–36.

Honig, Bonnie. 2009. *Emergency Politics: Paradox, Law, Democracy.* Princeton, NJ: Princeton University Press.

Honig, Bonnie. 2015. "The Laws of the Sabbath (Poetry): Arendt, Heine, and the Politics of Debt." *University of California Irvine Law Review* 5: 463–82.

Honig, Bonnie. 2017. *Public Things: Democracy in Disrepair.* Oxford: Oxford University Press.

Houdek, Matthew. 2017. "'Once an Eagle, Always an Eagle?': Symbolic Divestment, Recuperative Critique, and in-House Protests Against the Anti-Gay BSA." *Communication and Critical/Cultural Studies* 14 (1): 48–65.

Huizinga, Johan. (1949) 1970. *Homo Ludens: A Study of the Play Element in Culture.* London: Temple Smith.

Hunt, Stephen. 2014. "Christian Lobbyist Groups and the Negotiation of Sexual Rights in the UK." *Journal of Contemporary Religion* 29 (1): 121–36.

Hunter, Rosemary, Clare McGlynn, and Erika Rackley. 2010. *Feminist Judgments: From Theory to Practice.* Oxford: Hart.

Hunter, Shona. 2015. *Power, Politics and the Emotions: Impossible Governance?* London: Routledge.

Hyde, Lewis. 1979. *Imagination and the Erotic Life of Property.* New York: Vintage.

Innes, Judith E., and David E. Booher. 1999. "Consensus Building as Role Playing and Bricolage: Toward a Theory of Collaborative Planning." *Journal of the American Planning Association* 65 (1): 9–26.

Jackson, Thomas. 2018. "Paradiplomacy and Political Geography: The Geopolitics of Substate Regional Diplomacy." *Geography Compass.* doi: 10.1111/gec3.12357.

Jameson, Fredric. 1982. "Progress versus Utopia; or, Can We Imagine the Future?" *Science Fiction Studies* 9 (2): 147–58.

Jeffrey, Alex. 2012. *The Improvised State: Sovereignty, Performance and Agency in Dayton Bosnia*. Chichester, UK: Wiley-Blackwell.

Jessop, Bob. 1990. *State Theory*. Cambridge: Polity.

Jessop, Bob. 2002. *The Future of the Capitalist State*. Cambridge: Polity.

Jessop, Bob. 2010. "The 'Return' of the National State in the Current Crisis of the World Market." *Capital and Class* 34 (1): 38–43.

Jessop, Bob. 2016. *The State: Past, Present, Future*. Cambridge: Polity.

Jupp, Eleanor, Jessica Pykett, and Fiona M. Smith. 2017. *Emotional States: Sites and Spaces of Affective Governance*. Oxford; New York: Routledge.

Joronen, Mikko. 2017. "Spaces of Waiting: Politics of Precarious Recognition in the Occupied West Bank." *Environment and Planning D: Society and Space* 35 (6): 994–1011.

Kalb, Don. 2017. "Afterword: After the Commons-Commoning!" *Focaal* 79: 67–73.

Kallio, Kirsi Pauliina, and Jouni Häkli. 2011. "Tracing Children's Politics." *Political Geography* 30 (2): 99–109.

Kamoche, Ken, and João Vieira da Cunha. 2003. "Towards a Theory of Organizational Improvisation: Looking Beyond the Jazz Metaphor." *Journal of Management Studies* 40 (8): 2023–51.

Kane, Pat. 2005. *The Play Ethic: A Manifesto for a Different Way of Living*. London: Pan.

Kantola, Johanna. 2006. *Feminists Theorize the State*. Houndmills, UK: Palgrave Macmillan.

Kantorowicz, Ernst H. (1957) 1997. *The King's Two Bodies*. Princeton, NJ: Princeton University Press.

Kaplan, Louis. 2013. "Mapping Ararat: Augmented Reality, Virtual Tourism, and Grand Island's Jewish Ghosts." *CR: New Centennial Review* 13 (2): 239–64.

Kautzer, Chad. 2015. "Good Guys with Guns: From Popular Sovereignty to Self-Defensive Subjectivity." *Law and Critique* 26 (2): 173–87.

Keenan, Sarah. 2010. "Subversive Property: Reshaping Malleable Spaces of Belonging." *Social and Legal Studies* 19 (4): 423–39.

Keenan, Sarah. 2015. *Subversive Property: Law and the Production of Spaces of Belonging*. London: Routledge.

Keeshig-Tobias, Lenore. 1997. "Stop Stealing Native Stories." In *Borrowed Power: Essays on Cultural Appropriation*, ed. Bruce Ziff and Pratima Rao, 71–73. New Brunswick, NJ: Rutgers University Press.

Kelly, Tobias. 2018. "A Divided Conscience: The Lost Convictions of Human Rights." *Public Culture* 30 (3): 367–92.

Kerr, Orin S. 2008. "Criminal Law in Virtual Worlds." *University of Chicago Legal Forum* 2008 (1, article 11): 415–29.

Kettell, Steven. 2017. "The Collective Action Framing of Conservative Christian Groups in Britain." *Politics and Religion* 10 (2): 286–310.

Kinkade, Kathleen. 1974. *A Walden Two Experiment: The First Five Years of Twin Oaks Community*. New York: William Morrow.

Kinna, Ruth. 2019. "Using the Master's Tools: Rights and Radical Politics." In *Reimagining the State*, ed. Davina Cooper, Nikita Dhawan, and Janet Newman, 133–50. Abingdon, UK: Routledge.

Kinsman, Gary. 1996. "'Responsibility' as a Strategy of Governance: Regulating People Living with AIDS and Lesbians and Gay Men in Ontario." *Economy and Society* 25 (3): 393–409.

Klausen, Jimmy Casas, and James Martel. 2011. *How Not to Be Governed: Readings and Interpretations from a Critical Anarchist Left*. Lanham, MD: Lexington.

Klausen, Maja. 2014. "Re-Enchanting the City: Hybrid Space, Affect and Playful Performance in Geocaching, a Location-Based Mobile Game." *Journal of Urban Cultural Studies* 1 (2): 193–213.

Koppelman, Andrew. 2016. "A Free Speech Response to the Gay Rights/Religious Liberty Conflict." *Northwestern University Law Review* 110 (5): 1125–67.

Kristeva, Julia. 1993. *Nations without Nationalism*. New York: Columbia University Press.

Laderman, Gary. 1997. "The Body Politic and the Politics of Two Bodies: Abraham and Mary Todd Lincoln in Death." *Prospects* 22: 109–32.

Lake, Robert W. 2002 "Bring Back Big Government." *International Journal of Urban and Regional Research* 26 (4): 815–22.

Lammer, Christina. 2007. "Bodywork: Social Somatic Interventions in the Operating Theatres of Invasive Radiology." In *Visual Interventions: Applied Visual Anthropology*, ed. Sarah Pink, 91–118. Oxford: Berghahn.

Landemore, Hélène. 2015. "Inclusive Constitution-Making: The Icelandic Experiment." *Journal of Political Philosophy* 23 (2): 166–91.

Laski, Harold J. 1919. "The Pluralistic State." *Philosophical Review* 28 (6): 562–75.

Latour, Bruno. 2005. *Reassembling the Social: An Introduction to Actor-Network Theory*. Oxford: Oxford University Press.

Law, John, and John Urry. 2004. "Enacting the Social." *Economy and Society* 33 (3): 390–410.

Lea, Tess. 2012. "When Looking for Anarchy, Look to the State: Fantasies of Regulation in Forcing Disorder within the Australian Indigenous Estate." *Critique of Anthropology* 32 (2): 109–24.

Lee, Roger, Andrew Leyshon, Theresa Aldridge, Jane Tooke, Colin Williams, and Nigel Thrift. 2004. "Making Geographies and Histories? Constructing Local Circuits of Value." *Environment and Planning D: Society and Space* 22 (4): 595–617.

Lefebvre, Henri. 2009. *State, Space, World: Selected Essays*, ed. N. Brenner and S. Elden. Minneapolis: University of Minnesota Press.

Lenin, Vladimir I. [with Todd Chretien]. (1917) 2014. *State and Revolution*. Chicago: Haymarket.

Lerner, Josh. 2014. *Making Democracy Fun: How Game Design Can Empower Citizens and Transform Politics*. Cambridge, MA: MIT Press.

Levine, Norman. 1985. "Lenin's Utopianism." *Studies in East European Thought* 30 (2): 95–107.

Levitas, Ruth. 2000. "For Utopia: The (Limits of the) Utopian Function in Late Capitalist Society." *Critical Review of International Social and Political Philosophy* 3 (2–3): 25–43.

Levitas, Ruth. 2013. *Utopia as Method: The Imaginary Reconstitution of Society*. London: Palgrave Macmillan.

Lewis, Andrew R. 2017. *The Rights Turn in Conservative Christian Politics: How Abortion Transformed the Culture Wars*. Cambridge: Cambridge University Press.

Lind, Amy, and Christine Keating. 2013. "Navigating the Left Turn: Sexual Justice and the Citizen Revolution in Ecuador." *International Feminist Journal of Politics* 15 (4): 515–33.

Linke, Uli. 2006. "Contact Zones: Rethinking the Sensual Life of the State." *Anthropological Theory* 6 (2): 205–25.

Linstead, Stephen, and Torkild Thanem. 2007. "Multiplicity, Virtuality, and Organization: The Contribution of Gilles Deleuze." *Organization Studies* 28 (10): 1483–1501.

Loyola-Hernández, Laura. 2018. "The Porous State: Female Mayors Performing the State in Yucatecan Maya Municipalities." *Political Geography* 62: 48–57.

Lund, Christian. 2006. "Twilight Institutions: Public Authority and Local Politics in Africa." *Development and Change* 37 (4): 685–705.

Lyng, Stephen. 2005a. "Edgework and the Risk-Taking Experience." In *Edgework: The Sociology of Risk-Taking*, ed. Stephen Lyng, 3–16. New York: Routledge.

Lyng, Stephen. 2005b. "Sociology at the Edge: Social Theory and Voluntary Risk Taking." In *Edgework: The Sociology of Risk-Taking*, ed. Stephen Lyng, 17–50. New York: Routledge.

MacDougall, Bruce, and Donn Short. 2010. "Religion-Based Claims for Impinging on Queer Citizenship." *Dalhousie Law Journal* 33 (2): 133–60.

Macpherson, Crawford B. 1962. *The Political Philosophy of Possessive Individualism: Hobbes to Locke*. Oxford: Clarendon.

Maeckelbergh, Marianne. 2011. "Doing Is Believing: Prefiguration as Strategic Practice in the Alterglobalization Movement." *Social Movement Studies* 10 (1): 1–20.

Mahnič, Nika. 2014. "Gamification of Politics: Start a New Game!" *Teorija in Praksa* 51 (1): 143–61.

Major, Blair A. 2017. "Trinity Western University Law: The Boundary and Ethos of the Legal Community." *Alberta Law Review* 55 (1): 167–98.

Majury, Diana. 2006. "Introducing the Women's Court of Canada." *Canadian Journal of Women and the Law* 18 (1): 1–25.

Malabou, Catherine, and Judith Butler. 2011. "You Be My Body for Me: Body, Shape, and Plasticity in Hegel's Phenomenology of Spirit." In *A Companion to Hegel*, ed. Stephen Houlgate and Michael Bauer, 611–40. Oxford: Wiley-Blackwell.

Malik, Maleiha. 2011. "Religious Freedom, Free Speech and Equality: Conflict or Cohesion?" *Res Publica* 17 (1): 21–40.

Malloy, Jonathan. 2017. "Political Opportunity Structures, Evangelical Christians and Morality Politics in Canada, Australia and New Zealand." *Australian Journal of Political Science* 52 (3): 402–18.

Maloney, Michelle. 2016. "Building an Alternative Jurisprudence for the Earth: The International Rights of Nature Tribunal." *Vermont Law Review* 41 (1): 129–42.

Mann, Dale. 1996. "Serious Play." *Teachers College Record* 97 (3): 446–69.

Mantouvalou, Virginia. 2008. "Human Rights and Unfair Dismissal: Private Acts in Public Spaces." *Modern Law Review* 71 (6): 912–39.

Martin, Deborah G., and Joseph Pierce. 2013. "Reconceptualizing Resistance: Residuals of the State and Democratic Radical Pluralism." *Antipode* 45 (1): 61–79.

Martin, Lauren L. 2010. "Bombs, Bodies, and Biopolitics: Securitizing the Subject at the Airport Security Checkpoint." *Social and Cultural Geography* 11 (1): 17–34.

Massaro, Toni M. 2010. "*Christian Legal Society v. Martinez*: Six Frames." *Hastings Constitutional Law Quarterly* 38 (3): 569–630.

Massey, Doreen. 2006. *For Space.* London: Sage.

Maurutto, Paula. 2003. *Governing Charities: Church and State in Toronto's Catholic Archdiocese, 1850–1950.* Montreal: McGill-Queen's University Press.

Mauss, Marcel. 1967. *The Gift: Forms and Functions of Exchange in Archaic Societies,* trans. Ian Cunnison. New York: W. W. Norton.

Mayer-Schoenberger, Viktor, and John Crowley. 2006. "Napster's Second Life: The Regulatory Challenges of Virtual Worlds." *Northwestern University Law Review* 100 (4): 1775–1826.

Maynard-Moody, Steven, and Michael Musheno. 2000. "State Agent or Citizen Agent: Two Narratives of Discretion." *Journal of Public Administration Research and Theory* 10 (2): 329–58.

Maynard-Moody, Steven, and Michael Musheno. 2012. "Social Equities and Inequities in Practice: Street-Level Workers as Agents and Pragmatists." *Public Administration Review* 72 (1): 16–23.

Mbembe, Achille. 1992. "The Banality of Power and the Aesthetics of Vulgarity in the Postcolony." *Public Culture* 4 (2): 1–30.

Mbembe, Achille. 2006. "On Politics as a Form of Expenditure." In *Law and Disorder in the Postcolony,* ed. Jean Comaroff and John L. Comaroff, 299–335. Chicago: University of Chicago Press.

McClain, Linda C. 2010. "Religious and Politician Virtues and Values in Congruence or Conflict: On Smith, Bob Jones University, and Christian Legal Society." *Cardozo Law Review* 32 (5): 1959–2008.

McConnell, Fiona. 2016. *Rehearsing the State: The Political Practices of the Tibetan Government-in-Exile.* Chichester, UK: John Wiley and Sons.

McConnell, Fiona, Terri Moreau, and Jason Dittmer. 2012. "Mimicking State Diplomacy: The Legitimizing Strategies of Unofficial Diplomacies." *Geoforum* 43 (4): 804–14.

McDermont, Morag. 2019. "Regulating with Social Justice in Mind: An Experiment in Reimagining the State." In *Reimagining the State,* ed. Davina Cooper, Nikita Dhawan, and Janet Newman, 191–209. Abingdon, UK: Routledge.

McGranahan, Carole. 2016. "Refusal and the Gift of Citizenship." *Cultural Anthropology* 31 (3): 334–41.

McIvor, Méadhbh. 2018. "Human Rights and Broken Cisterns: Counterpublic Christianity and Rights-Based Discourse in Contemporary England." *Ethnos*. doi: 10.1080/00141844.2017.1420671.

McNay, Lois. 2009. "Self as Enterprise." *Theory, Culture and Society* 26 (6): 55–77.

McNeilly, Kathryn. 2018. *Human Rights and Radical Social Transformation: Futurity, Alterity, Power*. Abingdon, UK: Routledge.

Meadowcroft, James. 1995. *Conceptualizing the State: Innovation and Dispute in British Political Thought 1880–1914*. Oxford: Oxford University Press.

Meagher, Kate. 2012. "The Strength of Weak States? Non-State Security Forces and Hybrid Governance in Africa." *Development and Change* 43 (5): 1073–1101.

Medby, Ingrid A. 2018. "Articulating State Identity: 'Peopling' the Arctic State." *Political Geography* 62: 116–25.

Meisiek, Stefan. 2002. "Situation Drama in Change Management: Types and Effects of a New Managerial Tool." *International Journal of Arts Management* 4 (3): 48–55.

Melissaris, Emmanuel. 2004. "The More the Merrier? A New Take on Legal Pluralism." *Social and Legal Studies* 13 (1): 57–79.

Merry, Sally Engle. 1988. "Legal Pluralism." *Law and Society Review* 22 (5): 869–96.

Meyer, Camille, and Marek Hudon. 2017. "Alternative Organizations in Finance: Commoning in Complementary Currencies." *Organization* 24 (5): 629–47.

Misztal, Bronislaw. 1992. "Between the State and Solidarity: One Movement, Two Interpretations: The Orange Alternative Movement in Poland." *British Journal of Sociology* 43 (1): 55–78.

Mitchell, Timothy. 1991. "The Limits of the State: Beyond Statist Approaches and Their Critics." *American Political Science Review* 85 (1): 77–96.

Miyazaki, Hirokazu. 2004. *The Method of Hope: Anthropology, Philosophy, and Fijian Knowledge*. Stanford, CA: Stanford University Press.

Miyazaki, Hirokazu. 2016. "The Economy of Hope: An Introduction." In *The Economy of Hope*, ed. Hirokazu Miyazaki and Richard Swedberg, 1–36. Philadelphia: University of Pennsylvania Press.

Mizielińska, Joanna. 2011. "Travelling Ideas, Travelling Times: On the Temporalities of LGBT and Queer Politics in Poland and the 'West.'" In *De-Centring Western Sexualities: Central and Eastern European Perspectives*, ed. Robert Kulpa and Joanna Mizielińska, 85–106. Farnham, UK: Ashgate.

Mizielińska, Joanna, and Robert Kulpa. 2011. "'Contemporary Peripheries': Queer Studies, Circulation of Knowledge and East/West Divide." In *De-Centring Western Sexualities: Central and Eastern European Perspectives*, ed. Robert Kulpa and Joanna Mizielińska, 11–26. Farnham, UK: Ashgate.

Montemaggi, Francesca E. S. 2017. "Belief, Trust, and Relationality: A Simmelian Approach for the Study of Faith." *Religion* 47 (2): 147–60.

Morefield, Jeanne. 2005. "States Are Not People: Harold Laski on Unsettling Sovereignty, Rediscovering Democracy." *Political Research Quarterly* 58 (4): 659–69.

Morris, Debra, Anne Morris, and Jennifer Sigafoos. 2016. "Adopting (In)equality in the U.K.: The Equality Act 2010 and Its Impact on Charities." *Journal of Social Welfare and Family Law* 38 (1): 14–35.

Morris, William. (1890) 2003. *News from Nowhere and Other Writings.* Oxford: Oxford University Press.

Mould, Oli. 2009. "Parkour, the City, the Event." *Environment and Planning D: Society and Space* 27 (4): 738–50.

Mountz, Alison. 2004. "Embodying the Nation-State: Canada's Response to Human Smuggling." *Political Geography* 23 (3): 323–45.

Moylan, Tom. 1986. *Demand the Impossible: Science Fiction and the Utopian Imagination.* New York: Methuen.

Müller, Martin. 2012. "Opening the Black Box of the Organization: Socio-Material Practices of Geopolitical Ordering." *Political Geography* 31 (6): 379–88.

Müller, Martin. 2015. "Assemblages and Actor-Networks: Rethinking Socio-Material Power, Politics and Space." *Geography Compass* 9 (1): 27–41.

Müller, Martin, and Carolin Schurr. 2016. "Assemblage Thinking and Actor-Network Theory: Conjunctions, Disjunctions, Cross-Fertilisations." *Transactions of the Institute of British Geographers* 41 (3): 217–29.

Mundy, Jacob A. 2007. "Performing the Nation, Pre-Figuring the State: The Western Saharan Refugees, Thirty Years Later." *Journal of Modern African Studies* 45 (2): 275–97.

Nachmanovitch, Stephen. 2009. "This Is Play." *New Literary History* 40 (1): 1–24.

Nadel, Sean. 2016. "Closely Held Conscience: Corporate Personhood in the Post–Hobby Lobby World." *Colum. JL & Soc. Probs.* 50 (3): 417–48.

Naffine, Ngaire. 1998. "The Legal Structure of Self-Ownership: Or the Self-Possessed Man and the Woman Possessed." *Journal of Law and Society* 25 (2): 193–212.

Nairn, Tom. 1998. "Sovereignty Scapes after the Election." *New Left Review* 224: 3–18.

Navaro-Yashin, Yael. 2002. *Faces of the State: Secularism and Public Life in Turkey.* Princeton, NJ: Princeton University Press.

Navaro-Yashin, Yael. 2012. *The Make-Believe Space.* Durham, NC: Duke University Press.

Nayar, Jayan. 2001. "A People's Tribunal against the Crime of Silence? The Politics of Judgement and an Agenda for People's Law." *Law, Social Justice and Global Development* 2001 (2). http://www2.warwick.ac.uk/fac/soc/law/elj/lgd/2001_2/nayar.

Nayar, Jayan. 2007. "Peoples' Law: Decolonising Legal Imagination." *Law, Social Justice and Global Development* (2007) 1. https://warwick.ac.uk/fac/soc/law/elj/lgd/2007_1/nayar.

Nehushtan, Yossi. 2016. *Intolerant Religion in a Tolerant-Liberal Democracy.* Oxford: Hart.

Neilson, Brett. 2014. "Zones: Beyond the Logic of Exception?" *Concentric: Literary and Cultural Studies* 40 (2): 11–28.

NeJaime, Douglas, and Reva B. Siegel. 2014. "Conscience Wars: Complicity-Based Conscience Claims in Religion and Politics." *Yale Law Journal* 124 (7): 2516–91.

Neocleous, Mark. 2003. *Imagining the State.* Maidenhead, UK: Open University Press.

Neocleous, Mark. 2005. "Long Live Death! Fascism, Resurrection, Immortality." *Journal of Political Ideologies* 10 (1): 31–49.

Newmahr, Staci. 2011. *Playing on the Edge: Sadomasochism, Risk, and Intimacy.* Bloomington: Indiana University Press.

Newman, Janet. 2012a. *Working the Spaces of Power: Activism, Neoliberalism and Gendered Labour.* London: Bloomsbury Academic.

Newman, Janet. 2012b. "Beyond the Deliberative Subject? Problems of Theory, Method and Critique in the Turn to Emotion and Affect." *Critical Policy Studies* 6 (4): 465–79.

Newman, Janet. 2014. "Governing the Present: Activism, Neoliberalism, and the Problem of Power and Consent." *Critical Policy Studies* 8 (2): 133–47.

Newman, Janet, and John Clarke. 2014. "States of Imagination." *Soundings* 57 (1): 153–69.

Newman, Saul. 2001. "War on the State: Stirner's and Deleuze's Anarchism." *Anarchist Studies* 9 (2): 147–64.

North, Peter. 2007. *Money and Liberation: The Micropolitics of Alternative Currency Movements*. Minneapolis: University of Minnesota Press.

North, Peter. 2014. "Ten Square Miles Surrounded by Reality? Materialising Alternative Economies Using Local Currencies." *Antipode* 46 (1): 246–65.

Norton, Anne. 2011. "Pentecost: Democratic Sovereignty in Carl Schmitt." *Constellations* 18 (3): 389–402.

Noxolo, Pat, Parvati Raghuram, and Clare Madge. 2012. "Unsettling Responsibility: Postcolonial Interventions." *Transactions of the Institute of British Geographers* 37 (3): 418–29.

Nugent, David. 2010. "States, Secrecy, Subversives: APRA and Political Fantasy in mid-20th-Century Peru." *American Ethnologist* 37 (4): 681–702.

O'Grady, Alice. 2012. "Tracing the City—Parkour Training, Play and the Practice of Collaborative Learning." *Theatre, Dance and Performance Training* 3 (2): 145–62.

Ong, Aihwa. 2007. *Neoliberalism as Exception: Mutations in Citizenship and Sovereignty*. Durham, NC: Duke University Press.

Otto, Dianne. 2007. "'Taking a Break' from 'Normal': Thinking Queer in the Context of International Law." *Proceedings of the Annual Meeting (American Society of International Law)* 101: 119–22.

Painter, Joe. 2006. "Prosaic Geographies of Stateness." *Political Geography* 25 (7): 752–74.

Panagia, Davide. 2009. *The Political Life of Sensation*. Durham, NC: Duke University Press.

Panagia, Davide. 2018. *Rancière's Sentiments*. Durham, NC: Duke University Press.

Parker, Noel, and Rebecca Adler-Nissen. 2012. "Picking and Choosing the 'Sovereign' Border: A Theory of Changing State Bordering Practices." *Geopolitics* 17 (4): 773–96.

Parkinson, Patrick. 2011. "Accommodating Religious Beliefs in a Secular Age: The Issue of Conscientious Objection in the Workplace." *University of New South Wales Law Journal* 34 (1): 281–99.

Passoth, Jan-Hendrik, and Nicholas J. Rowland. 2010. "Actor-Network State: Integrating Actor-Network Theory and State Theory." *International Sociology* 25 (6): 818–41.

Pateman, Carole. 1988. "The Patriarchal Welfare State." In *Democracy and the Welfare State*, ed. Amy Gutmann, 231–61. Princeton, NJ: Princeton University Press.

Pateman, Carole. 2002. "Self-Ownership and Property in the Person: Democratization and a Tale of Two Concepts." *Journal of Political Philosophy* 10 (1): 20–53.

Patton, Paul. 2010. *Deleuzian Concepts: Philosophy, Colonization, Politics*. Stanford, CA: Stanford University Press.

Perry, Ruth. 1990. "Mary Astell and the Feminist Critique of Possessive Individualism." *Eighteenth-Century Studies* 23 (4): 444–57.

Purser, Gretchen, and Brian Hennigan. 2017. ""Work as unto the Lord": Enhancing Employability in an Evangelical Job-Readiness Program." *Qualitative Sociology* 40 (1): 111–33.

Petchesky, Rosalind Pollack. 1995. "The Body as Property: A Feminist Re-Vision." In *Conceiving the New World Order: The Global Politics of Reproduction*, ed. Faye D Ginsburg, 387–406. London: University of California Press.

Pickerill, Jenny. 2016. "Building the Commons in Eco-Communities." In *Space, Power and the Commons: The Struggle for Alternative Futures*, ed. Samuel Kirwan, Leila Dawney, and Julian Brigstocke, 31–54. London: Routledge.

Pickerill, Jenny, and Paul Chatterton. 2006. "Notes towards Autonomous Geographies: Creation, Resistance and Self-Management as Survival Tactics." *Progress in Human Geography* 30 (6): 730–46.

Pink, Sarah, Jennie Morgan, and Andrew Dainty. 2014. "The Safe Hand: Gels, Water, Gloves and the Materiality of Tactile Knowing." *Journal of Material Culture* 19 (4): 425–42.

Pogge, Thomas W. 1992. "Cosmopolitanism and Sovereignty." *Ethics* 103 (1): 48–75.

Pors, Justine Grønbaek. 2016. "'It Sends a Cold Shiver down My Spine': Ghostly Interruptions to Strategy Implementation." *Organization Studies* 37 (11): 1641–59.

Poulantzas, Nicos. 1980. *State, Power, Socialism*. London: Verso.

Povinelli, Elizabeth A. 1994. "Sexual Savages/Sexual Sovereignty: Australian Colonial Texts and the Postcolonial Politics of Nationalism." *Diacritics* 24 (2–3): 122–50.

Puar, Jasbir K. 2004. "Abu Ghraib: Arguing against Exceptionalism." *Feminist Studies* 30 (2): 522–34.

Puar, Jasbir K. 2006. "Mapping U.S. Homonormativities." *Gender, Place and Culture* 13 (1): 67–88.

Puar, Jasbir K. 2011 "Citation and Censorship: The Politics of Talking about the Sexual Politics of Israel." *Feminist Legal Studies* 19 (2): 133–42.

Puwar, Nirmal. 2001. "The Racialised Somatic Norm and the Senior Civil Service." *Sociology* 35 (3): 651–70.

Rackley, Erika. 2012. "Why Feminist Legal Scholars Should Write Judgments: Reflections on the Feminist Judgments Project in England and Wales." *Canadian Journal of Women and the Law* 24 (2): 389–413.

Raeymaekers, Timothy. 2012. "Reshaping the State in Its Margins: The State, the Market and the Subaltern on a Central African Frontier." *Critique of Anthropology* 32 (3): 334–50.

Raghuram, Parvati, Clare Madge, and Pat Noxolo. 2009. "Rethinking Responsibility and Care for a Postcolonial World." *Geoforum* 40 (1): 5–13.

Rai, Shirin M. 2015. "Political Performance: A Framework for Analysing Democratic Politics." *Political Studies* 63 (5): 1179–97.

Raitt, Jill. 1980. "The 'Vagina Dentata' and the 'Immaculatus Uterus Divini Fontis.'" *Journal of the American Academy of Religion:* 48 (3): 415–31.

Ramshaw, Sara. 2013. *Justice as Improvisation: The Law of the Extempore*. Oxford: Routledge.

Rancière, Jacques. 1999. *Disagreement: Politics and Philosophy*, trans. Julie Rose. Minneapolis: University of Minnesota Press.

Rancière, Jacques. 2009. "A Few Remarks on the Method of Jacques Rancière." *Parallax* 15 (3): 114–23.

Rancière, Jacques. 2010. *Dissensus: On Politics and Aesthetics*, trans. Steven Corcoran. London: Continuum International.

Rasmussen, Claire, and Michael Brown. 2005. "The Body Politic as Spatial Metaphor." *Citizenship Studies* 9 (5): 469–84.

Ratcliffe, Matthew. 2012. "What Is Touch?" *Australasian Journal of Philosophy* 90 (3): 413–32.

Renee Baptiste, Nicole. 2009. "Fun and Well-Being: Insights from Senior Managers in a Local Authority." *Employee Relations* 31 (6): 600–12.

Reuveni, Erez. 2006. "On Boy Scouts and Anti-Discrimination Law: The Associational Rights of Quasi-Religious Organizations." *Boston University Law Review* 86 (1): 109–72.

Reyes, Allison. 1995. "Freedom of Expression and Public School Teachers." *Dalhousie Journal of Legal Studies* 4: 35–72.

Reynolds, Nicola. 2015. "Discourses of Love, Compassion, and Belonging: Reframing Christianity for a Secular Audience." *Journal of Contemporary Religion* 30 (1): 39–54.

Reyntjens, Filip. 2014. "Regulation, Taxation and Violence: The State, Quasi-State Governance and Cross-Border Dynamics in the Great Lakes Region." *Review of African Political Economy* 41 (142): 530–44.

Reyntjens, Filip. 2016. "Legal Pluralism and Hybrid Governance: Bridging Two Research Lines." *Development and Change* 47 (2): 346–66.

Richardson, Diane. 2004. "Locating Sexualities: From Here to Normality." *Sexualities* 7 (4): 391–411.

Richardson, Diane, and Surya Monro. 2012. *Sexuality, Equality and Diversity*. Basingstoke, UK: Palgrave Macmillan.

Richter-Montpetit, Melanie. 2007. "Empire, Desire and Violence: A Queer Transnational Feminist Reading of the Prisoner 'Abuse' in Abu Ghraib and the Question of 'Gender Equality'." *International Feminist Journal of Politics* 9 (1): 38–59.

Rifkin, Mark. 2012. *The Erotics of Sovereignty: Queer Native Writing in the Era of Self-Determination*. Minneapolis: University of Minnesota Press.

Rivers, Julian. 2007. "Law, Religion and Gender Equality." *Ecclesiastical Law Journal* 9 (1): 24–52.

Rogers, Nicole. 2008. "The Play of Law: Comparing Performances in Law and Theatre." *Queensland University of Technology Law and Justice Journal* 8 (2): 429–43.

Rogers, Nicole. 2017. "Performance and Pedagogy in the Wild Law Judgment Project." *Legal Education Review* 27 (1): 1–19.

Rose, Mitch. 2014. "Negative Governance: Vulnerability, Biopolitics and the Origins of Government." *Transactions of the Institute of British Geographers* 39 (2): 209–23.

Routledge, Paul. 1997. "The Imagineering of Resistance: Pollok Free State and the Practice of Postmodern Politics." *Transactions of the Institute of British Geographers* 22 (3): 359–76.

Roy, Srirupa. 2006. "Seeing a State: National Commemorations and the Public Sphere in India and Turkey." *Comparative Studies in Society and History* 48 (1): 200–232.

Ruel, Malcolm. 1982. "Christians as Believers." In *Religious Organization and Religious Experience*, ed. John Davis, 9–31. London: Academic.

Ruggie, John Gerard. 1983. "Continuity and Transformation in the World Polity: Toward a Neorealist Synthesis." *World Politics* 35 (2): 261–85.

Ruggie, John Gerard. 1993. "Territoriality and Beyond: Problematizing Modernity in International Relations." *International Organization* 47 (1): 139–74.

Runciman, David. 1997. *Pluralism and the Personality of the State*. Cambridge: Cambridge University Press.

Ruskola, Teemu. 2010. "Raping Like a State." UCLA *Law Review* 57 (5): 1477–1536.

Rutledge, Colleen Theresa. 2008. "Caught in the Crossfire: How Catholic Charities of Boston Was Victim to the Clash between Gay Rights and Religious Freedom." *Duke Journal of Gender Law and Policy* 15 (2): 297–314.

Sachs, William L. 2009. *Homosexuality and the Crisis of Anglicanism*. Cambridge: Cambridge University Press.

Salen, Katie, and Eric Zimmerman. 2004. *Rules of Play: Game Design Fundamentals*. Cambridge, MA: MIT Press.

Sarat, Austin, and Conor Clarke. 2008. "Beyond Discretion: Prosecution, the Logic of Sovereignty, and the Limits of Law." *Law and Social Inquiry* 33 (2): 387–416.

Saville, Stephen John. 2008. "Playing with Fear: Parkour and the Mobility of Emotion." *Social and Cultural Geography* 9 (8): 891–914.

Schmitt, Carl. (1934) 2005. *Political Theology: Four Chapters on the Concept of Sovereignty*, trans. George Schwab. Chicago: University of Chicago Press.

Schueth, Samuel. 2012. "Apparatus of Capture: Fiscal State Formation in the Republic of Georgia." *Political Geography* 31 (3): 133–43.

Scott, James C. 1998. *Seeing Like a State: How Certain Schemes to Improve the Human Condition Have Failed*. New Haven, CT: Yale University Press.

Scott, James C. 2009. *The Art of Not Being Governed: An Anarchist History of Upland Southeast Asia*. New Haven, CT: Yale University Press.

Secor, Anna J. 2007. "Between Longing and Despair: State, Space, and Subjectivity in Turkey." *Environment and Planning D: Society and Space* 25 (1): 33–52.

Sepper, Elizabeth. 2014a. "Doctoring Discrimination in the Same-Sex Marriage Debates." *Indiana Law Journal* 89 (2): 703–62.

Sepper, Elizabeth. 2014b. "Reports of Accommodation's Death Have Been Greatly Exaggerated." *Harvard Law Review Forum* 128: 24–30.

Seyfang, G. 2001. "Community Currencies: Small Change for a Green Economy." *Environment and Planning A: Economy and Space* 33 (6): 975–96.

Shaw, Julia. 2018. "Introducing Post-Secular Social Work: Towards a Post-Liberal Ethics of Care." *British Journal of Social Work* 48 (2): 412–29.

Shearing, Clifford, and Jennifer Wood. 2003. "Nodal Governance, Democracy, and the New 'Denizens.'" *Journal of Law and Society* 30 (3): 400–19.

Shepard, Benjamin. 2012. *Play, Creativity, and Social Movements: If I Can't Dance, It's Not My Revolution*. Oxford; New York: Routledge.

Shewly, Hosna J. 2013. "Abandoned Spaces and Bare Life in the Enclaves of the India-Bangladesh Border." *Political Geography* 32: 23–31.

Shields, Rachel. 2015. "Ludic Ontology." *American Journal of Play* 7 (3): 298–321.

Shildrick, Margrit. 2001. "Some Speculations on Matters of Touch." *Journal of Medicine and Philosophy* 26 (4): 387–404.

Shoshana, Avi. 2012. "The Self as Public Property: Made in Israel." *Symbolic Interaction* 35 (2): 185–201.

Sidaway, James D. 2003. "Sovereign Excesses? Portraying Postcolonial Sovereign-tyscapes." *Political Geography* 22 (2): 157–78.

Siltanen, Janet, Fran Klodawsky, and Caroline Andrew. 2015. "'This Is How I Want to Live My Life': An Experiment in Prefigurative Feminist Organizing for a More Equitable and Inclusive City." *Antipode* 47 (1): 260–79.

Simcik Arese, Nicholas. 2018. "Seeing like a City-State: Behavioural Planning and Governance in Egypt's First Affordable Gated Community." *International Journal of Urban and Regional Research* 42 (3): 461–82.

Simm, Gabrielle, and Andrew Byrnes. 2014. "International Peoples' Tribunals in Asia: Political Theatre, Juridical Farce, or Meaningful Intervention?" *Asian Journal of International Law* 4 (1): 103–24.

Simpson, Audra. 2014. *Mohawk Interruptus: Political Life across the Borders of Settler States*. Durham, NC: Duke University Press.

Skinner, B. F. 1948. *Walden II*. New York: Macmillan.

Skinner, Quentin. 1989. "The State." In *Political Innovation and Conceptual Change*, ed. Terence Ball, James Farr, and L. Hanson Russell, 90–131. Cambridge: Cambridge University Press.

Smith, Miriam Catherine. 1999. *Lesbian and Gay Rights in Canada: Social Movements and Equality-Seeking, 1971–1995*. Toronto: University of Toronto Press.

Smith, Miriam Catherine. 2004. "Questioning Heteronormativity: Lesbian and Gay Challenges to Education Practice in British Columbia, Canada." *Social Movement Studies* 3 (2): 131–45.

Sørensen, Bent Meier, and Sverre Spoelstra. 2012. "Play at Work: Continuation, Intervention and Usurpation." *Organization* 19 (1): 81–97.

Spraggon, Martin, and Virginia Bodolica. 2014. "Social Ludic Activities: A Polymorphous Form of Organizational Play." *Journal of Managerial Psychology* 29 (5): 524–40.

Springer, Simon. 2012. "Anarchism! What Geography Still Ought to Be." *Antipode* 44 (5): 1605–24.

Squires, Catherine. 2002. "Rethinking the Black Public Sphere: An Alternative Vocabulary for Multiple Public Spheres." *Communication Theory* 12 (4): 446–68.

Statler, Matt, Loizos Heracleous, and Claus D. Jacobs. 2011. "Serious Play as a Practice of Paradox." *The Journal of Applied Behavioral Science* 47 (2): 236–56.

Statler, Matt, Johan Roos, and Bart Victor. 2009. "Ain't Misbehavin': Taking Play Seriously in Organizations." *Journal of Change Management* 9 (1): 87–107.

Stears, Marc. 2012. "The Case for a State that Supports Relationships, Not a Relational State." In *The Relational State: How Recognising the Importance of Human Relationships Could Revolutionise the Role of the State*, ed. Graeme Cooke and Rick Muir, 35–43. London: Institute for Public Policy Research.

Stoler, Ann Laura. 2004. "Affective States." In *A Companion to the Anthropology of Politics*, ed. David Nugent and Joan Vincent, 4–20. Malden, MA: Wiley-Blackwell.

Stoup, Phillip. 2008. "The Development and Failure of Social Norms in Second Life." *Duke Law Journal* 58 (2): 311–44.

Strange, Susan. 1996. *The Retreat of the State: The Diffusion of Power in the World Economy*. Cambridge: Cambridge University Press.

Street, Alice. 2010. "Belief as Relational Action: Christianity and Cultural Change in Papua New Guinea." *Journal of the Royal Anthropological Institute* 16 (2): 260–78.

Strhan, Anna. 2015. *Aliens and Strangers? The Struggle for Coherence in the Everyday Lives of Evangelicals*. Oxford: Oxford University Press.

Stychin, Carl F. 1996. "To Take Him 'At His Word': Theorizing Law, Sexuality and the U.S. Military Exclusion Policy." *Social and Legal Studies* 5 (2): 179–200.

Stychin, Carl F. 1997. "Queer Nations: Nationalism, Sexuality and the Discourse of Rights in Quebec." *Feminist Legal Studies* 5 (1): 3–34.

Stychin, Carl F. 1998a. *A Nation by Rights: National Cultures, Sexual Identity Politics, and the Discourse of Rights*. Philadelphia: Temple University Press.

Stychin, Carl F. 1998b. "Celebration and Consolidation: National Rituals and the Legal Construction of American Identities." *Oxford Journal of Legal Studies* 18 (2): 265–91.

Stychin, Carl F. 2003. *Governing Sexuality: The Changing Politics of Citizenship and Law Reform*. Oxford: Hart.

Stychin, Carl F. 2009a. "Faith in the Future: Sexuality, Religion and the Public Sphere." *Oxford Journal of Legal Studies* 29 (4): 729–55.

Stychin, Carl F. 2009b. "'Closet Cases': Conscientious Objection to Lesbian and Gay Legal Equality." *Griffith Law Review* 18 (1): 17–38.

Swain, Dan. 2019. "Not Not but Not Yet: Present and Future in Prefigurative Politics." *Political Studies* 67 (1): 47–62.

Sykes, Karen. 2007. "Interrogating Individuals: The Theory of Possessive Individualism in the Western Pacific." *Anthropological Forum* 17 (3): 213–24.

Szymanski-Düll, Berenika. 2015. "Strategies of Protest from Wroclaw: The Orange Alternative or the Riot of the Gnomes." *Journal of Urban History* 41 (4): 665–78.

Tamanaha, Brian Z. 1993. "The Folly of the 'Social Scientific' Concept of Legal Pluralism." *Journal of Law and Society* 20 (2): 192–217.

Tamanaha, Brian Z. 2000. "A Non-Essentialist Version of Legal Pluralism." *Journal of Law and Society* 27 (2): 296–321.

Taussig, Michael T. 1993. *Mimesis and Alterity: A Particular History of the Senses*. Oxford; New York: Routledge.

Thanem, Torkild. 2004. "The Body without Organs: Nonorganizational Desire in Organizational Life." *Culture and Organization* 10 (3): 203–17.

Thiel, Sarah-Kristin, Michaela Reisinger, Kathrin Röderer, and Peter Fröhlich. 2016. "Playing (with) Democracy: A Review of Gamified Participation Approaches." *JeDEM* 8 (3): 32–60.

Thompson, Erik S. 2015. "Compromising Equality: An Analysis of the Religious Exemption in the Employment Non-Discrimination Act and Its Impact on LGBT Workers." *Boston College Journal of Law and Social Justice* 35: 285–318.

Thompson, Hunter S. 1971. *Fear and Loathing in Las Vegas*. New York: Random House.

Thompson, Kathryn. 2014. "'No One Cares, Apostolate': What Social Cheating Reveals." *Games and Culture* 9 (6): 491–502.

Toscano, Alberto. 2012. "Seeing It Whole: Staging Totality in Social Theory and Art." *Sociological Review* 60 (1): 64–83.

Trnka, Susanna, and Catherine Trundle. 2014. "Competing Responsibilities: Moving beyond Neoliberal Responsibilisation." *Anthropological Forum* 24 (2): 136–53.

Trotter, Geoffrey. 2007. "The Right to Decline Performance of Same-Sex Civil Marriages: The Duty to Accommodate Public Servants—A Response to Professor Bruce MacDougall." *Saskatchewan Law Review* 70: 365–92.

Tuck, Richard. 1999. *The Rights of War and Peace: Political Thought and the International Order from Grotius to Kant*. Oxford: Oxford University Press.

Turner, Victor. 1980. "Social Dramas and Stories about Them." *Critical Inquiry* 7 (1): 141–68.

Turner, Victor. 1982. *From Ritual to Theatre: The Human Seriousness of Play*. Baltimore: Johns Hopkins University Press.

Tutton, Richard. 2017. "Wicked Futures: Meaning, Matter and the Sociology of the Future." *Sociological Review* 65 (3): 478–92.

Ussher, Jane M. 2006. *Managing the Monstrous Feminine: Regulating the Reproductive Body*. New York: Routledge.

Valentine, Gill. 2008. "Living with Difference: Reflections on Geographies of Encounter." *Progress in Human Geography* 32 (3): 323–27.

Valentine, Gill, and Louise Waite. 2012. "Negotiating Difference through Everyday Encounters: The Case of Sexual Orientation and Religion and Belief." *Antipode* 44 (2): 474–92.

Valentini, Laura. 2012. "Ideal versus Non-ideal Theory: A Conceptual Map." *Philosophy Compass* 7 (9): 654–64.

Valiavicharska, Zhivka. 2010. "Socialist Modes of Governance and the 'Withering Away of the State': Revisiting Lenin's State and Revolution." *Theory and Event* 13 (2). doi:10.1353/tae.0.0135.

Vallier, Kevin, and Michael Weber, eds. 2018. *Religious Exemptions*. Oxford: Oxford University Press.

Valverde, Mariana. 2011. "Seeing like a City: The Dialectic of Modern and Premodern Ways of Seeing in Urban Governance." *Law and Society Review* 45 (2): 277–312.

Van den Berg, Axel. 2003. *The Immanent Utopia: From Marxism on the State to the State of Marxism*. New York: Routledge.

Vanolo, Alberto. 2018. "Cities and the Politics of Gamification." *Cities* 74: 320–26.

Velte, Kyle C. 2018. "Why the Religious Right Can't Have Its (Straight Wedding) Cake and Eat It, Too: Breaking the Preservation-through-Transformation Dynamic in *Masterpiece Cakeshop v. Colorado Civil Rights Commission*." *Law and Inequality* 36 (1): 67–94.

Vickers, Lucy. 2010. "Religious Discrimination in the Workplace: An Emerging Hierarchy?" *Ecclesiastical Law Journal* 12 (3): 280–303.

Walton, Andy, Andrea Hatcher, and Nick Spencer. 2013. *Is There a "Religious Right" Emerging in Britain?* London: Theos.

Warner, Michael. 2002. *Publics and Counter-Publics*. New York: Zone.

Weber, Cynthia. 1998. "Performative States." *Millennium* 27 (1): 77–95.

Weber, Cynthia. 2010. "Introduction: Design and Citizenship." *Citizenship Studies* 14 (1): 1–16.

Weber, Cynthia. 2016. *Queer International Relations: Sovereignty, Sexuality and the Will to Knowledge*. Oxford: Oxford University Press.

Weiss, Erica. 2014. *Conscientious Objectors in Israel: Citizenship, Sacrifice, Trials of Fealty*. Philadelphia: University of Pennsylvania Press.

Weiss, Margot. 2009. "Rumsfeld! Consensual BDSM and 'Sadomasochistic' Torture at Abu Ghraib." In *Out in Public: Reinventing Lesbian/Gay Anthropology in a Globalizing World*, ed. Ellen Lewin and William L. Leap, 180–201. Chichester, UK: Wiley-Blackwell.

Wells, H. G. (1905) 2005. *A Modern Utopia*. London: Penguin.

Wendt, Alexander. 2003. "Why a World State Is Inevitable." *European Journal of International Relations* 9 (4): 491–542.

Wessels, Shelley K. 1989. "The Collision of Religious Exercise and Governmental Non-Discrimination Policies." *Stanford Law Review* 41 (5): 1201–31.

Wheatley, Natasha. 2017. "Spectral Legal Personality in Interwar International Law: On New Ways of Not Being a State." *Law and History Review* 35 (3): 753–87.

Wilcox, Lauren. 2014. "Queer Theory and the "Proper Objects" of International Relations." *International Studies Review* 16 (4): 612–15.

Williams, Andrew, Paul Cloke, and Samuel Thomas. 2012. "Co-Constituting Neoliberalism: Faith-Based Organisations, Co-option, and Resistance in the U.K." *Environment and Planning A: Economy and Space* 44 (6): 1479–1501.

Williams, H. Howell. 2018. "From Family Values to Religious Freedom: Conservative Discourse and the Politics of Gay Rights." *New Political Science* 40 (2): 246–63.

Winnicott, Donald. 1953. "Transitional Objects and Transitional Phenomena—A Study of the First Not-Me Possession." *International Journal of Psycho-Analysis* 34: 89–97.

Wintemute, Robert. 2014. "Accommodating Religious Beliefs: Harm, Clothing or Symbols, and Refusals to Serve Others." *Modern Law Review* 77 (2): 223–53.

Woodward, Keith, and Mario Bruzzone. 2015. "Touching like a State." *Antipode* 47 (2): 539–56.

Wright, Erik Olin. 2010. *Envisioning Real Utopias*. London: Verso.

Weinryb, Bernard D. 1954. "Noah's Ararat Jewish State in Its Historical Setting." *Publications of the American Jewish Historical Society* 43 (3): 170–91.

Yates, Luke. 2015. "Rethinking Prefiguration: Alternatives, Micropolitics and Goals in Social Movements." *Social Movement Studies* 14 (1): 1–21.

Young, Iris Marion. 1997. "Asymmetrical Reciprocity: On Moral Respect, Wonder, and Enlarged Thought." *Constellations* 3 (3): 340–63.

Young, Iris Marion. 2006. "Responsibility and Global Justice: A Social Connection Model." *Social Philosophy and Policy* 23 (1): 102–30.

Young, James O., and Conrad G. Brunk. ed. 2012. *The Ethics of Cultural Appropriation*. Chichester, UK: Wiley-Blackwell.

Zacka, Bernardo. 2017. *When the State Meets the Street: Public Service and Moral Agency.* Cambridge, MA: Harvard University Press.

Zanghellini, Aleardo. 2015. *The Sexual Constitution of Political Authority: The "Trials" of Same-Sex Desire.* Abingdon, UK: Routledge.

Zengin, Asli. 2016. "Violent Intimacies: Tactile State Power, Sex/Gender Transgression, and the Politics of Touch in Contemporary Turkey." *Journal of Middle East Women's Studies* 12 (2): 225–45.

Radical imagination, 24

Rainbow Committee of Terrace v. City of Terrace, 38

Rancière, Jacques, 61, 63–64, 157, 158–59, 163, 195n36

Rasmussen, Claire, 131

Ratcliffe, Matthew, 98

Reaney v. Hereford Diocesan Board of Finance, 39, 136, 215n33, 216–17n54

Recognition: as certification, 137; counter-hegemonic, 166–67, 171; damaging, 170; equality law and, 110; of organizational identity, 96; play and, 170, 172; plural, 85; state absence, 107; of states, 96; withdrawal of, 13, 30–31, 49, 82–83

Refusal. *See* Withdrawal

Religious beliefs, 45, 53, 79, 109–10; dangerous property, 119; marketplace and, 46–47; play and, 114–15, 117–18; possessions, 108–11, 116; state parts, 63, 65. *See also* Conscientious objection

Religious Freedom Restoration laws, 185–86n24

Resistance. *See* Withdrawal

Responsibility: community-based, 14–15; employee, 33, 60; experimenting, 167–71; political, 32; refusal, 40; state, 4–5, 14–15, 69–72, 85–86, 91, 103, 167–70. *See also* State; Withdrawal

Reynolds, Nicola, 195n32

Rifkin, Mark, 135, 147, 207n26

Rights, 29, 32, 127; beliefs and, 108–11; gay, 7–8, 120–21, 123–24, 138; Christian, 8–9; property discourse and, 110–11; religious, 42–43

Rogers, Nicole, 169, 222n44

Role play. *See* Play

Rumsfeld v. Forum for Academic and Institutional Rights, Inc., 29–30, 190n77

Ruskola, Teemu, 135, 144, 151

Savage v. Gee, 187n42

Schmitt, Carl, 31

Schneider, Katy, 119

Scott, James, 83, 97

Secor, Anna, 130

Serious play. *See* Play

Sexual. *See* Erotic

Sexual orientation equality, 7–8, 60, 118–21, 138, 141, 180n21. *See also* Rights

Shepard, Benjamin, 208n34

Shewly, Hosna, 32

Shildrick, Margrit, 204n81

Short, Donn, 62, 194n25

Siegel, Reva, 38, 185n11

Silbey, Susan, 17

Siltanen, Janet, 73

Simpson, Audra, 30, 87

Skinner, B. F., 173

Skinner, Quentin, 23, 91, 202n60

Smith and Chymyshyn v. Knights of Columbus et al., 80–81, 95, 99, 199n17, 202n56

Sovereignty: erotic and, 147; indigenous, 86–87, 147; ownership and, 43–44; plural, 32, 84; political, 83; private, 46; religious, 12; withdrawing and, 30

Springer, Simon, 22

State: activist, 37, 119, 136–43, 150; affect, 63; agency, 71–72; antihegemonic projects, 61–62, 145; beliefs, 118–21; bodies, 131–32, 150; boundaries, 67, 92, 126; caretaking, 117–18; composition, 11–12, 54–57, 61; conservative Christian presence, 65; conservative depiction, 52–53; counter-hegemonic projects, 145; critique of, 18–20, 174; cuts, 134; definition, 88–91, 150, 154; enactment, 77–78; equality-promoting, 68; excess, 86; gathered, 69–70, 91, 103; heterogeneous in form, 155; imaginaries, 83–84, 92; knowledge of, 97–100; methodology, 4–5, 51, 54–55, 61, 100, 101–2, 107–8, 134–35, 154–57; overreaching, 53, 67, 138; playing, 113–14, 117–18, 120–21, 127–28; plurality, 84, 94–95, 101–2, 155; police order, 63–65; reimagining, 2–4, 16, 24–25, 72–73, 89–90, 102–3, 154–55; relations between parts, 123–27; resources, 60, 65–66; responsible, 4–5, 69–72, 117, 167–70; role playing as, 159–61, 164–67, 169–71; sexual, 133–35; significance, 20–23; standard state perspective, 54–57; touch, 15–16, 97–100, 133, 144; transitional concept, 174–75; utopian, 178n9; waste, 140, 215n33; wider presence, 66–67; withdrawal, 13–15; withering away, 174–75

Statler, Matt, 119